THE PERIODIC TABLE OF ELEMENTS

Understanding the Building Blocks of Everything

T0016750

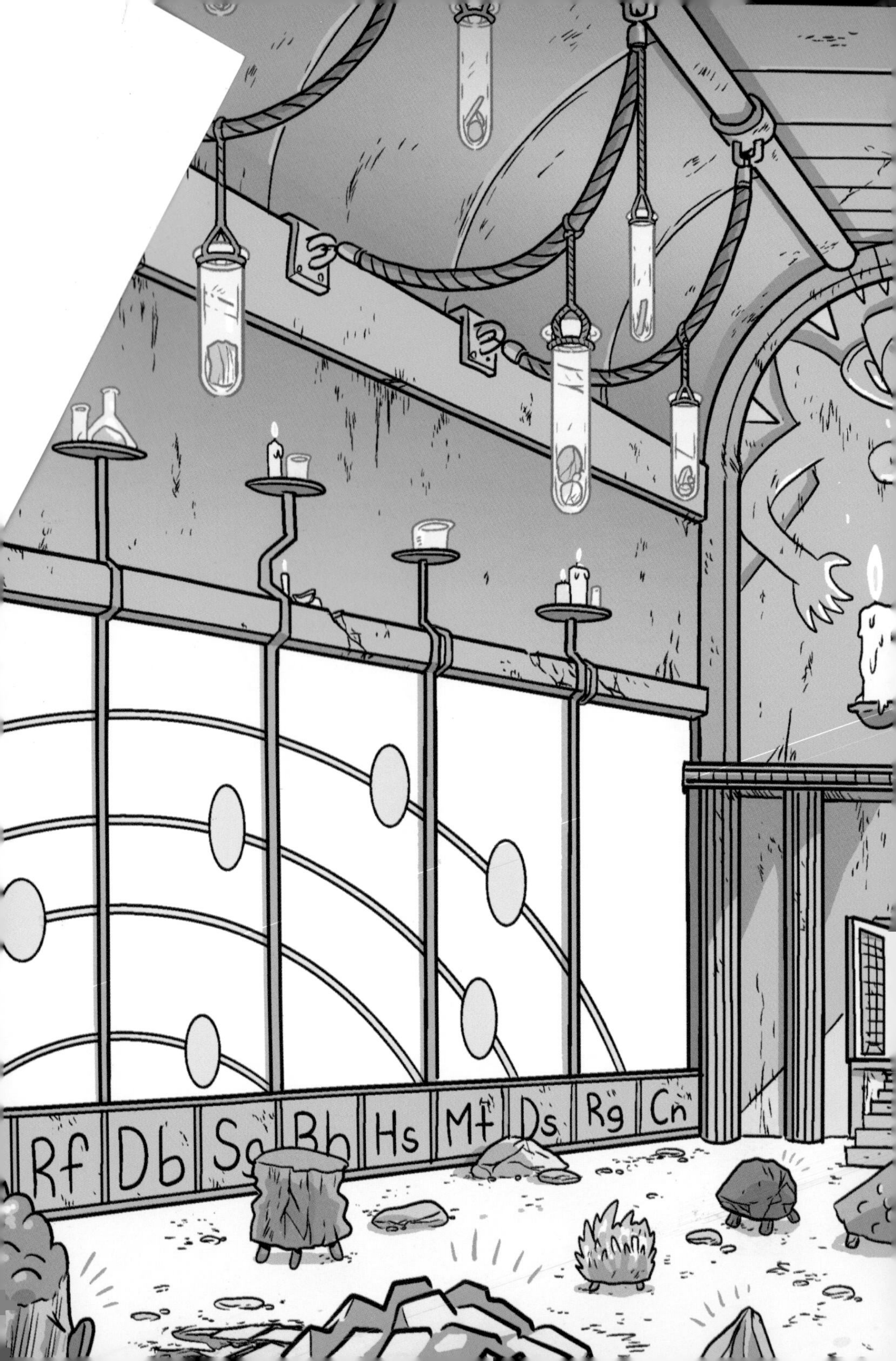
Rf
Db
Sg
Bh
Hs
Mt
Ds
Rg
Cn

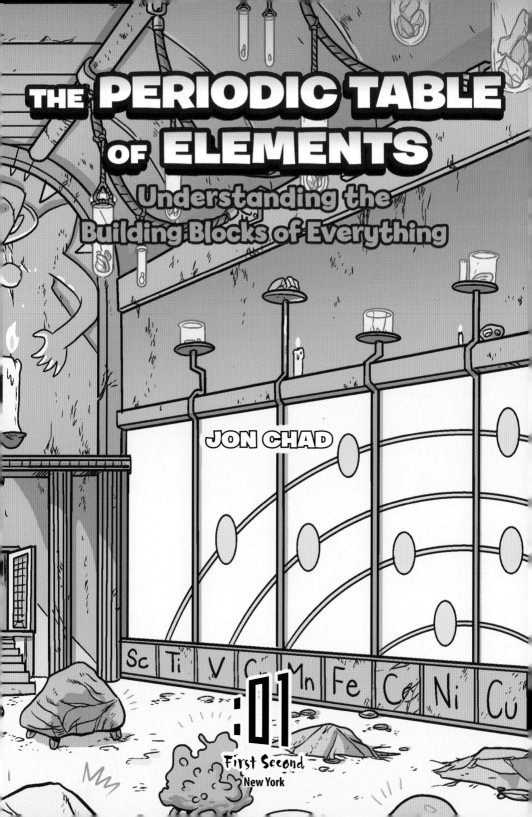

THE PERIODIC TABLE OF ELEMENTS

Understanding the Building Blocks of Everything

JON CHAD

:01
First Second
New York

First Second

Published by First Second
First Second is an imprint of Roaring Brook Press,
a division of Holtzbrinck Publishing Holdings Limited Partnership
120 Broadway, New York, NY 10271
firstsecondbooks.com
mackids.com

Library of Congress Control Number: 2022908799

Our books may be purchased in bulk for promotional, educational, or business use. Please contact your local bookseller or the Macmillan Corporate and Premium Sales Department at (800) 221-7945 ext. 5442 or by email at MacmillanSpecialMarkets@macmillan.com.

FIRST EDITION

First edition, 2023
Edited by Robyn Chapman and Tim Stout
Cover design by Sunny Lee
Interior book design by Jon Chad, Sunny Lee, and Yan L. Moy
Production editing by Avia Perez
Chemistry consultants: Scott McN. Sieburth and Ayanna Jones

Digitally penciled and inked with a Wacom One tablet and Clip Studio Paint Pro. Colored using Adobe Photoshop.

Printed in China by Toppan Leefung Printing Ltd., Dongguan City, Guangdong Province

ISBN 978-1-250-76761-5 (paperback)
10 9 8 7 6 5 4 3 2

ISBN 978-1-250-76760-8 (hardcover)
10 9 8 7 6 5 4 3 2 1

Don't miss your next favorite book from First Second! For the latest updates go to firstsecondnewsletter.com and sign up for our enewsletter.

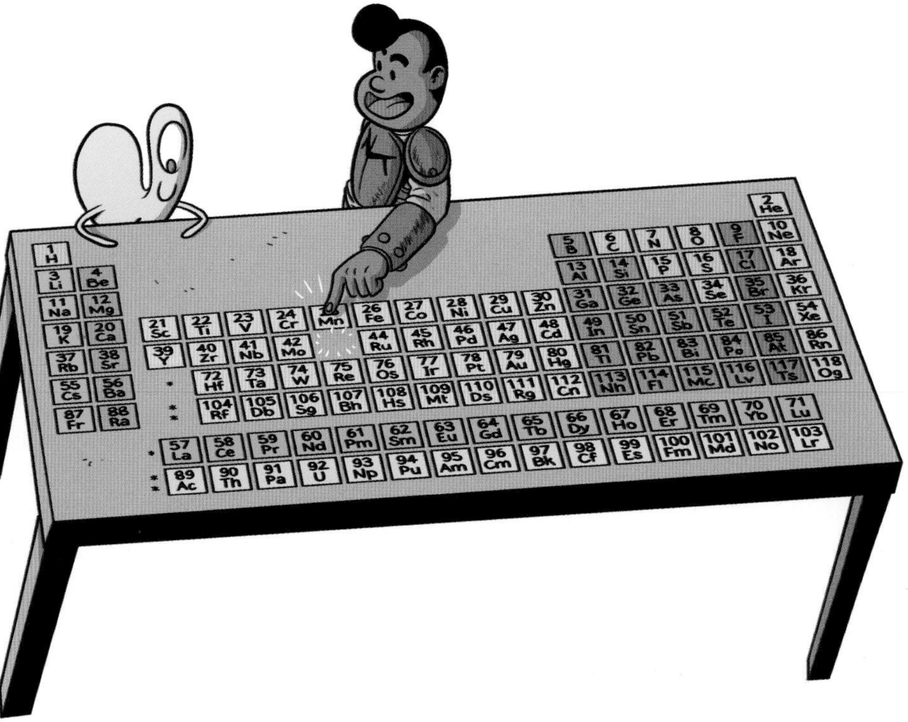
1 H
2 He
3 Li 4 Be
5 B 6 C 7 N 8 O 9 F 10 Ne
11 Na 12 Mg
13 Al 14 Si 15 P 16 S 17 Cl 18 Ar
19 K 20 Ca 21 Sc 22 Ti 23 V 24 Cr Mn 26 Fe 27 Co 28 Ni 29 Cu 30 Zn 31 Ga 32 Ge 33 As 34 Se 35 Br 36 Kr
37 Rb 38 Sr 39 Y 40 Zr 41 Nb 42 Mo 44 Ru 45 Rh 46 Pd 47 Ag 48 Cd 49 In 50 Sn 51 Sb 52 Te 53 I 54 Xe
55 Cs 56 Ba 72 Hf 73 Ta 74 W 75 Re 76 Os 77 Ir 78 Pt 79 Au 80 Hg 81 Tl 82 Pb 83 Bi 84 Po 85 At 86 Rn
87 Fr 88 Ra 104 Rf 105 Db 106 Sg 107 Bh 108 Hs 109 Mt 110 Ds 111 Rg 112 Cn 113 Nh 114 Fl 115 Mc 116 Lv 117 Ts 118 Og
57 La 58 Ce 59 Pr 60 Nd 61 Pm 62 Sm 63 Eu 64 Gd 65 Tb 66 Dy 67 Ho 68 Er 69 Tm 70 Yb 71 Lu
89 Ac 90 Th 91 Pa 92 U 93 Np 94 Pu 95 Am 96 Cm 97 Bk 98 Cf 99 Es 100 Fm 101 Md 102 No 103 Lr

If you had told me as a child that I would be working to receive a PhD in chemistry, I would have been thrilled and intrigued all at once. Also, I would not have been surprised. When I ask my parents how I was as a child, they unanimously agree that I was always curious about the world around me. As a child, I constantly questioned my surroundings and sought out answers. If I saw something that aroused my curiosity, I would wonder what it was. If I knew what it was but didn't know how it worked, I would ask how. If I knew how it worked but did not know why it worked, I would ask why. I recall treating this constant questioning and answering like a game that opened up new knowledge and new worlds to me that I had never known or considered.

This curiosity has carried me into adulthood and could even be the reason why I chose to pursue chemistry. Chemistry has always fascinated me because it truly utilizes all the natural senses, including sight, smell, taste, hearing, and touch. Chemistry also demands that we ask and answer questions about our natural world. Throughout history, we have used chemistry to discover more about who we are as people. We have also unlocked ways that chemistry can be used to understand alternative forms of life that we otherwise would not have considered. To this day, one of the best attributes that chemistry pulls out of us is our curiosity. From the discovery of the natural elements to the creation of the periodic table to the discovery of how to utilize our natural elements to create more complex elements and materials for the betterment of our lives, these ideas were sparked by someone's curiosity.

Even though we're all inherently curious, I believe that curiosity is a muscle that must be used and that can be strengthened. I also believe that it can be used to unlock new knowledge. I am continuously inspired by young scientists and chemists alike who are pushing the boundaries of science through their remarkable hunger for knowledge. I think that, as people, our curiosity is our superpower that no one can take away. It is up to us to be great stewards of our curiosity and to use this superpower to make the world a better place. No matter the circumstance, let your curiosity shine.

Stay curious!

Ayanna Jones
PhD candidate (Emory University), chemist, biogeochemist, and
cofounder of BlackInChem

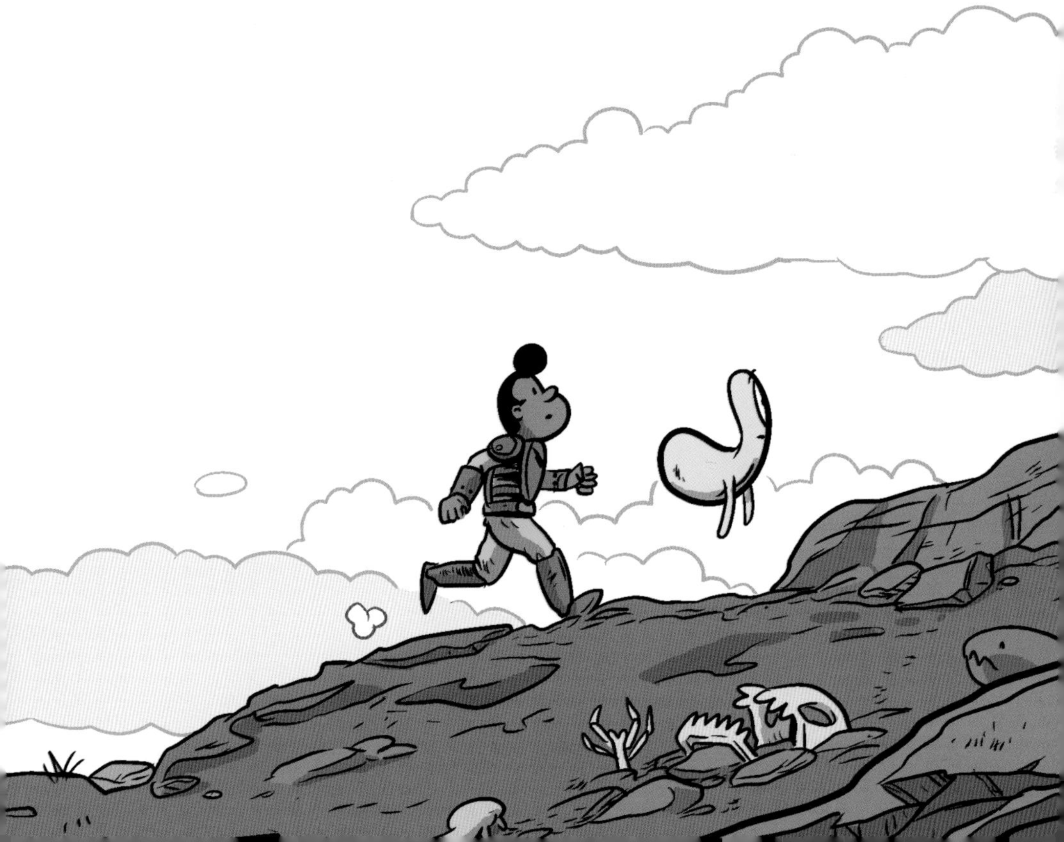

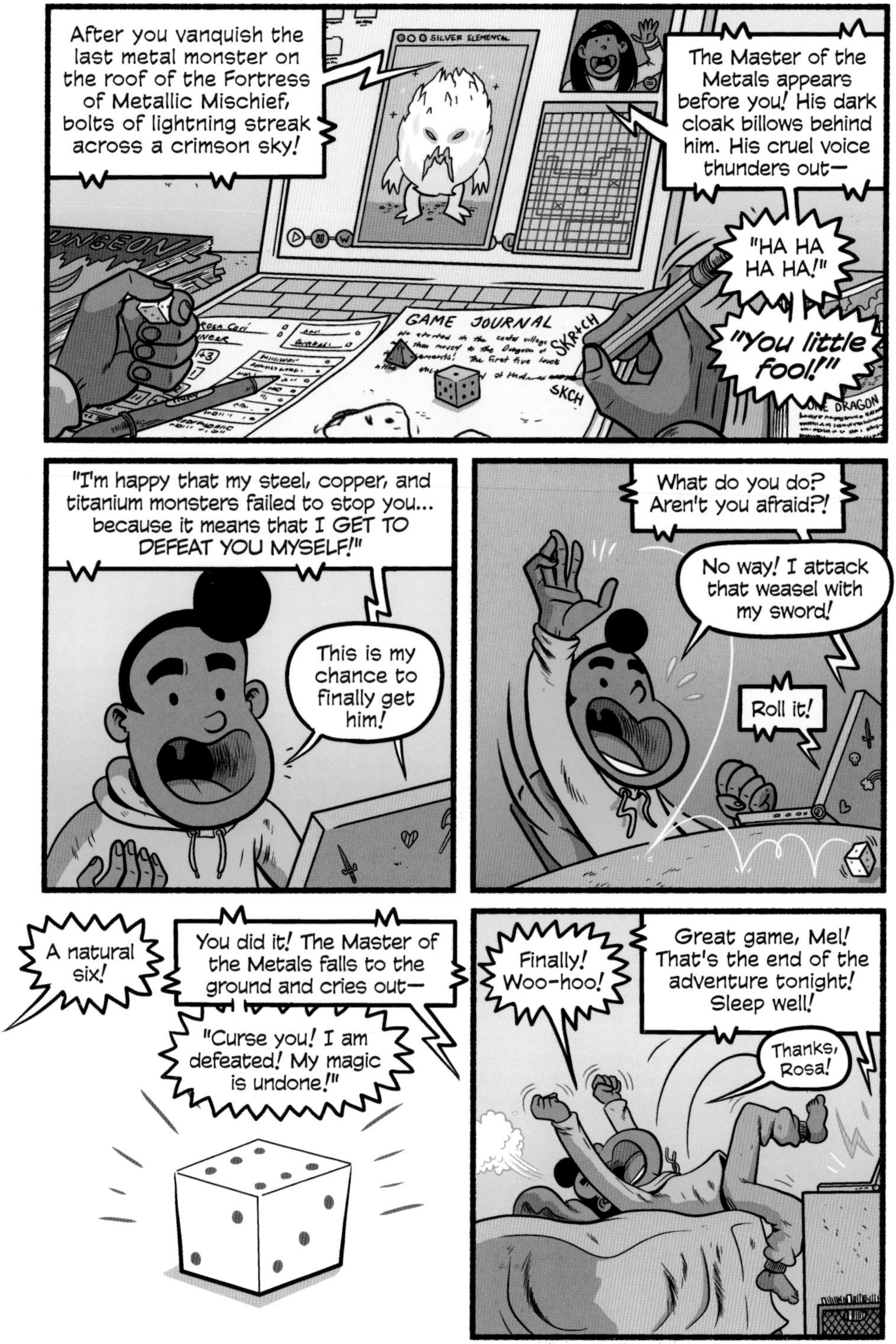

After you vanquish the last metal monster on the roof of the Fortress of Metallic Mischief, bolts of lightning streak across a crimson sky!
SILVER ELEMENTAL
The Master of the Metals appears before you! His dark cloak billows behind him. His cruel voice thunders out—
"HA HA HA HA!"
"You little fool!"
GAME JOURNAL
SKRTCH
SKCH
"I'm happy that my steel, copper, and titanium monsters failed to stop you... because it means that I GET TO DEFEAT YOU MYSELF!"
This is my chance to finally get him!
What do you do? Aren't you afraid?!
No way! I attack that weasel with my sword!
Roll it!
A natural six!
You did it! The Master of the Metals falls to the ground and cries out—
"Curse you! I am defeated! My magic is undone!"
Finally! Woo-hoo!
Great game, Mel! That's the end of the adventure tonight! Sleep well!
Thanks, Rosa!

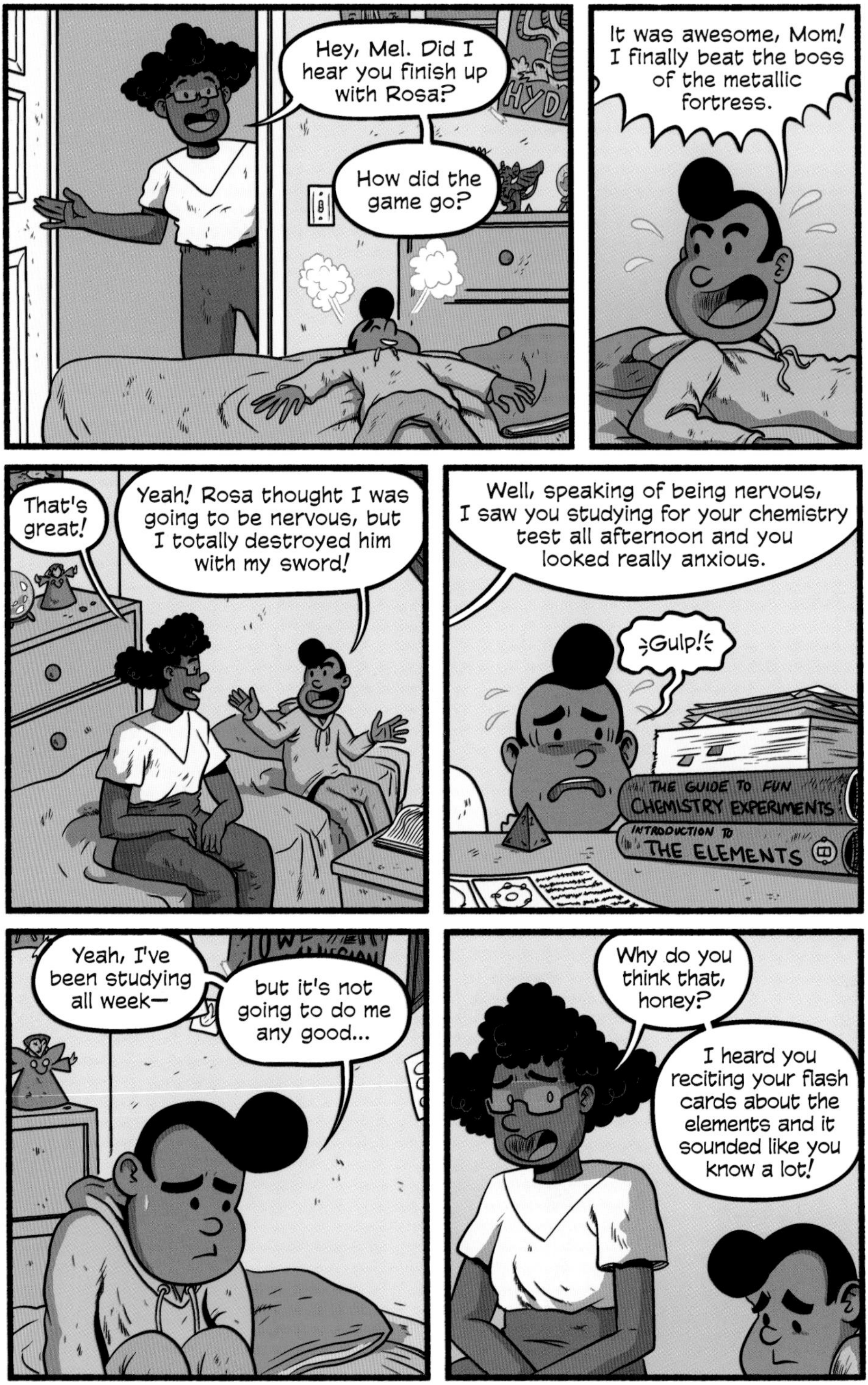
Hey, Mel. Did I hear you finish up with Rosa?
How did the game go?
It was awesome, Mom! I finally beat the boss of the metallic fortress.
That's great!
Yeah! Rosa thought I was going to be nervous, but I totally destroyed him with my sword!
Well, speaking of being nervous, I saw you studying for your chemistry test all afternoon and you looked really anxious.
Gulp!
THE GUIDE TO FUN CHEMISTRY EXPERIMENTS
INTRODUCTION TO THE ELEMENTS
Yeah, I've been studying all week—
but it's not going to do me any good...
Why do you think that, honey?
I heard you reciting your flash cards about the elements and it sounded like you know a lot!

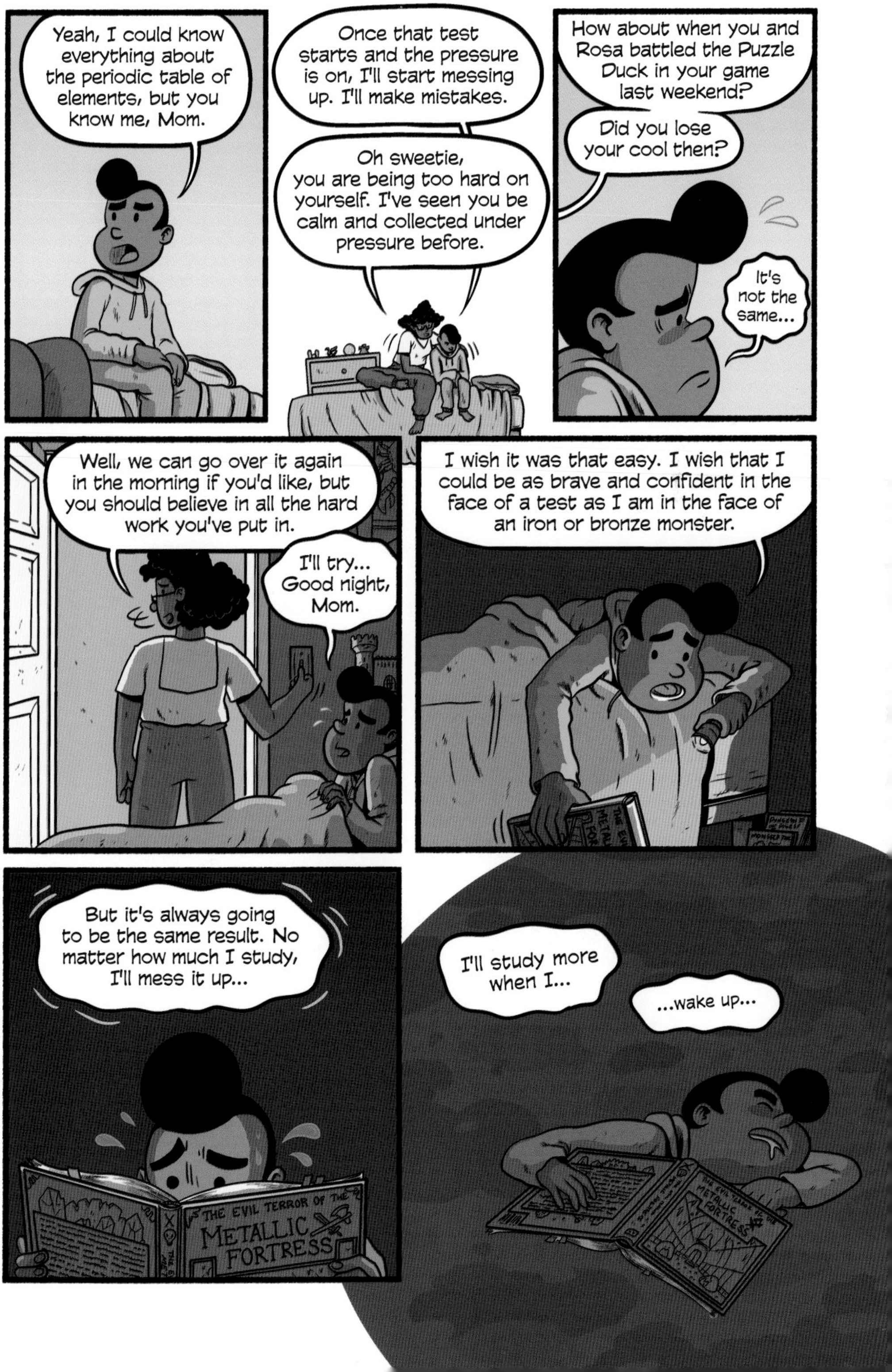
Yeah, I could know everything about the periodic table of elements, but you know me, Mom.
Once that test starts and the pressure is on, I'll start messing up. I'll make mistakes.
Oh sweetie, you are being too hard on yourself. I've seen you be calm and collected under pressure before.
How about when you and Rosa battled the Puzzle Duck in your game last weekend?
Did you lose your cool then?
It's not the same...
Well, we can go over it again in the morning if you'd like, but you should believe in all the hard work you've put in.
I'll try... Good night, Mom.
I wish it was that easy. I wish that I could be as brave and confident in the face of a test as I am in the face of an iron or bronze monster.
But it's always going to be the same result. No matter how much I study, I'll mess it up...
THE EVIL TERROR OF THE METALLIC FORTRESS
I'll study more when I...
...wake up...

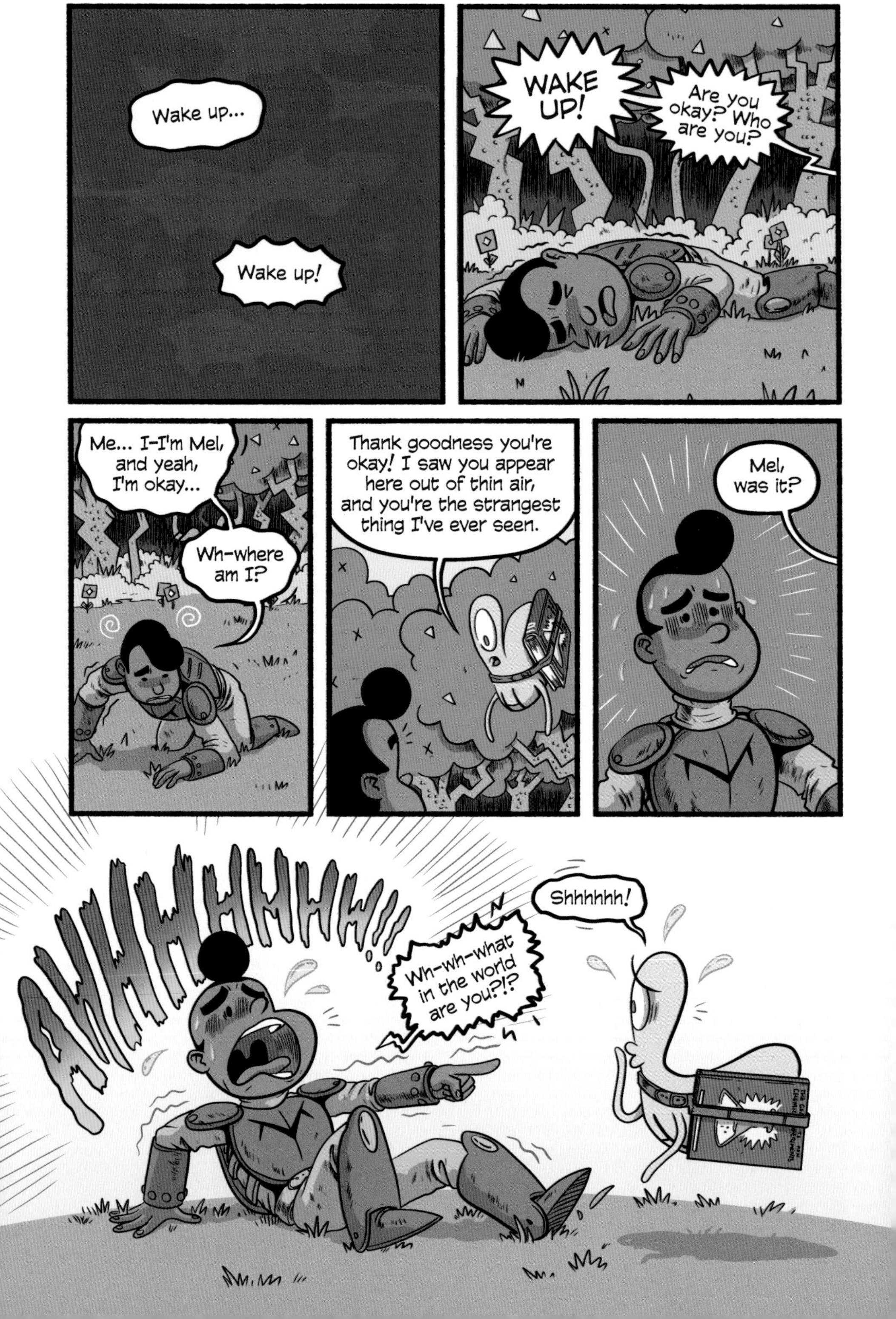

Wake up...
Wake up!
WAKE UP!
Are you okay? Who are you?
Me... I-I'm Mel, and yeah, I'm okay...
Wh-where am I?
Thank goodness you're okay! I saw you appear here out of thin air, and you're the strangest thing I've ever seen.
Mel, was it?
AHHHHHHHH!!
Wh-wh-what in the world are you?!?
Shhhhhh!

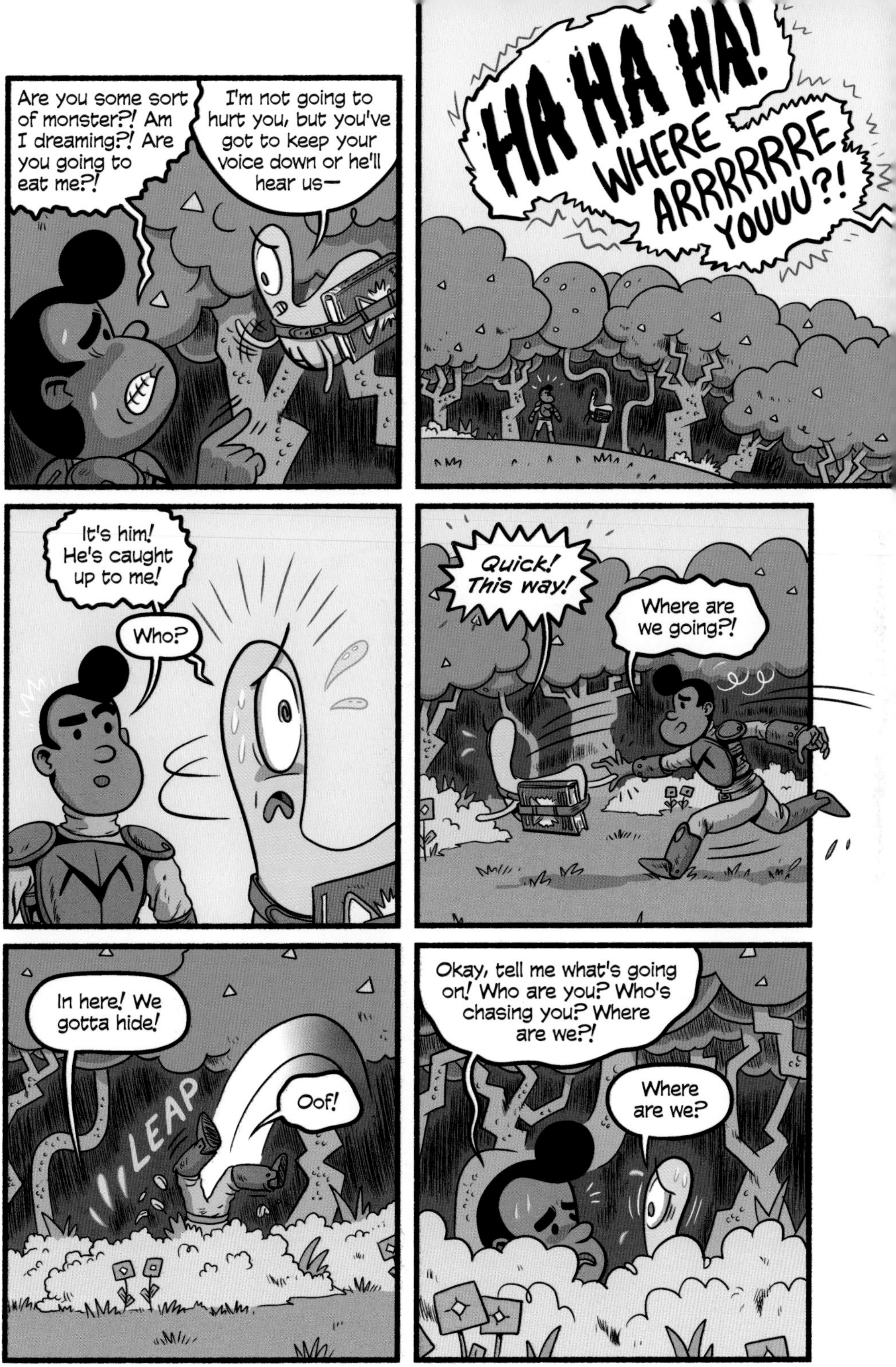
Are you some sort of monster?! Am I dreaming?! Are you going to eat me?!
I'm not going to hurt you, but you've got to keep your voice down or he'll hear us—
HA HA HA! WHERE ARRRRRRE YOUUU?!
It's him! He's caught up to me!
Who?
Quick! This way!
Where are we going?!
In here! We gotta hide!
LEAP
Oof!
Okay, tell me what's going on! Who are you? Who's chasing you? Where are we?!
Where are we?

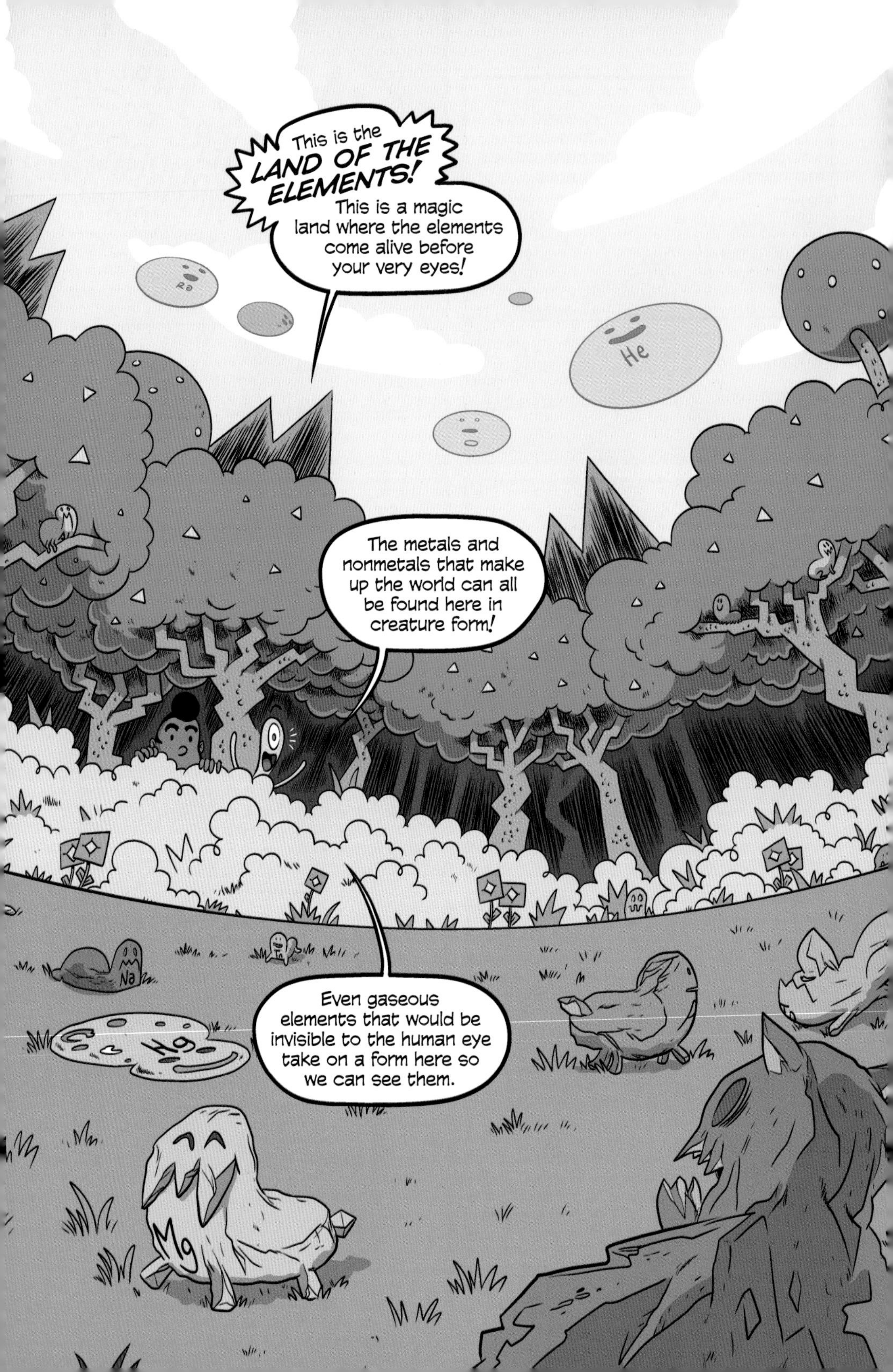
This is the LAND OF THE ELEMENTS!
This is a magic land where the elements come alive before your very eyes!
He
The metals and nonmetals that make up the world can all be found here in creature form!
Na
Hg
Even gaseous elements that would be invisible to the human eye take on a form here so we can see them.
Mg

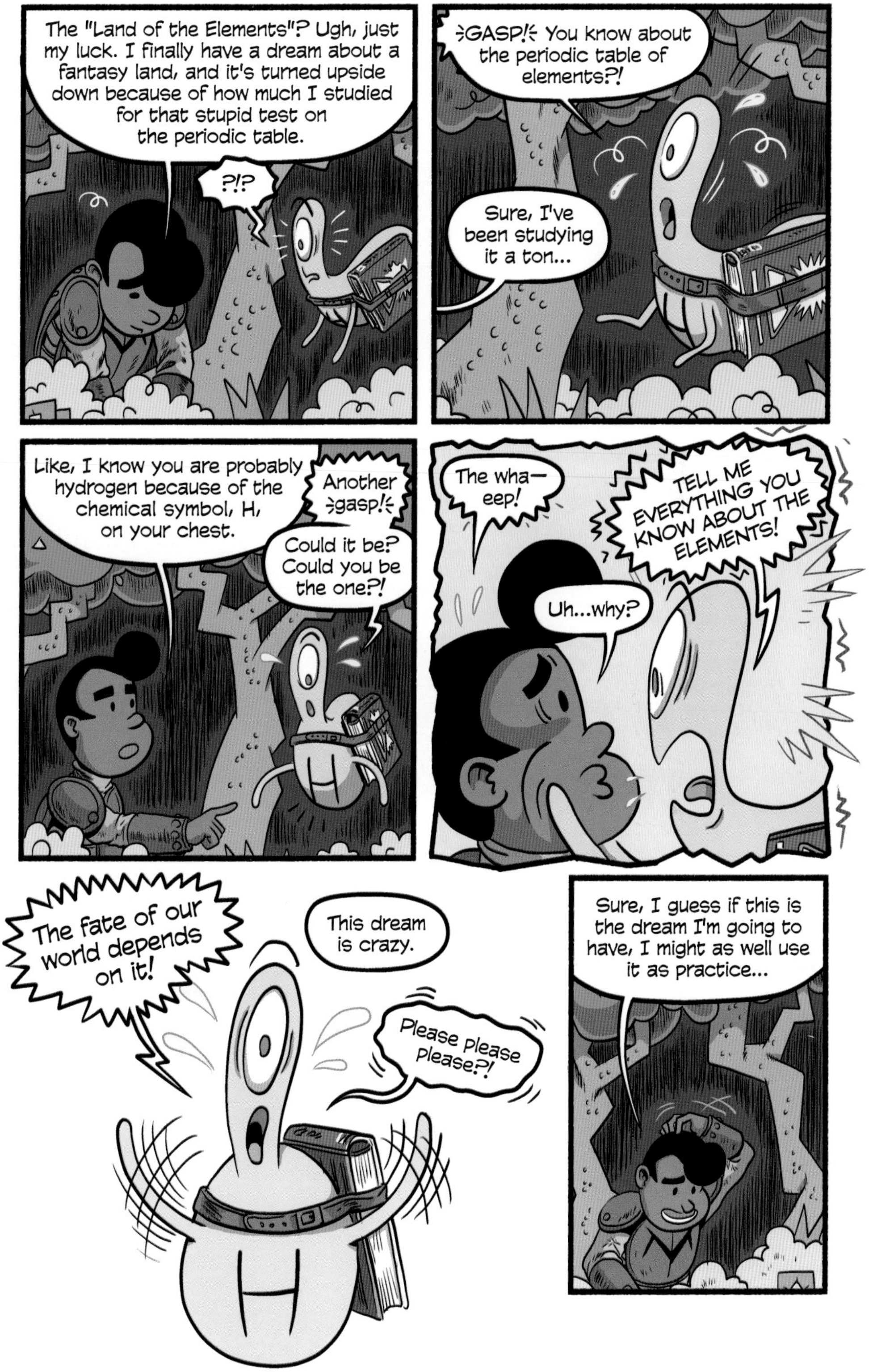

The "Land of the Elements"? Ugh, just my luck. I finally have a dream about a fantasy land, and it's turned upside down because of how much I studied for that stupid test on the periodic table.
?!?
GASP! You know about the periodic table of elements?!
Sure, I've been studying it a ton...
Like, I know you are probably hydrogen because of the chemical symbol, H, on your chest.
Another gasp!
Could it be? Could you be the one?!
The wha— eep!
TELL ME EVERYTHING YOU KNOW ABOUT THE ELEMENTS!
Uh...why?
The fate of our world depends on it!
This dream is crazy.
Please please please?!
Sure, I guess if this is the dream I'm going to have, I might as well use it as practice...

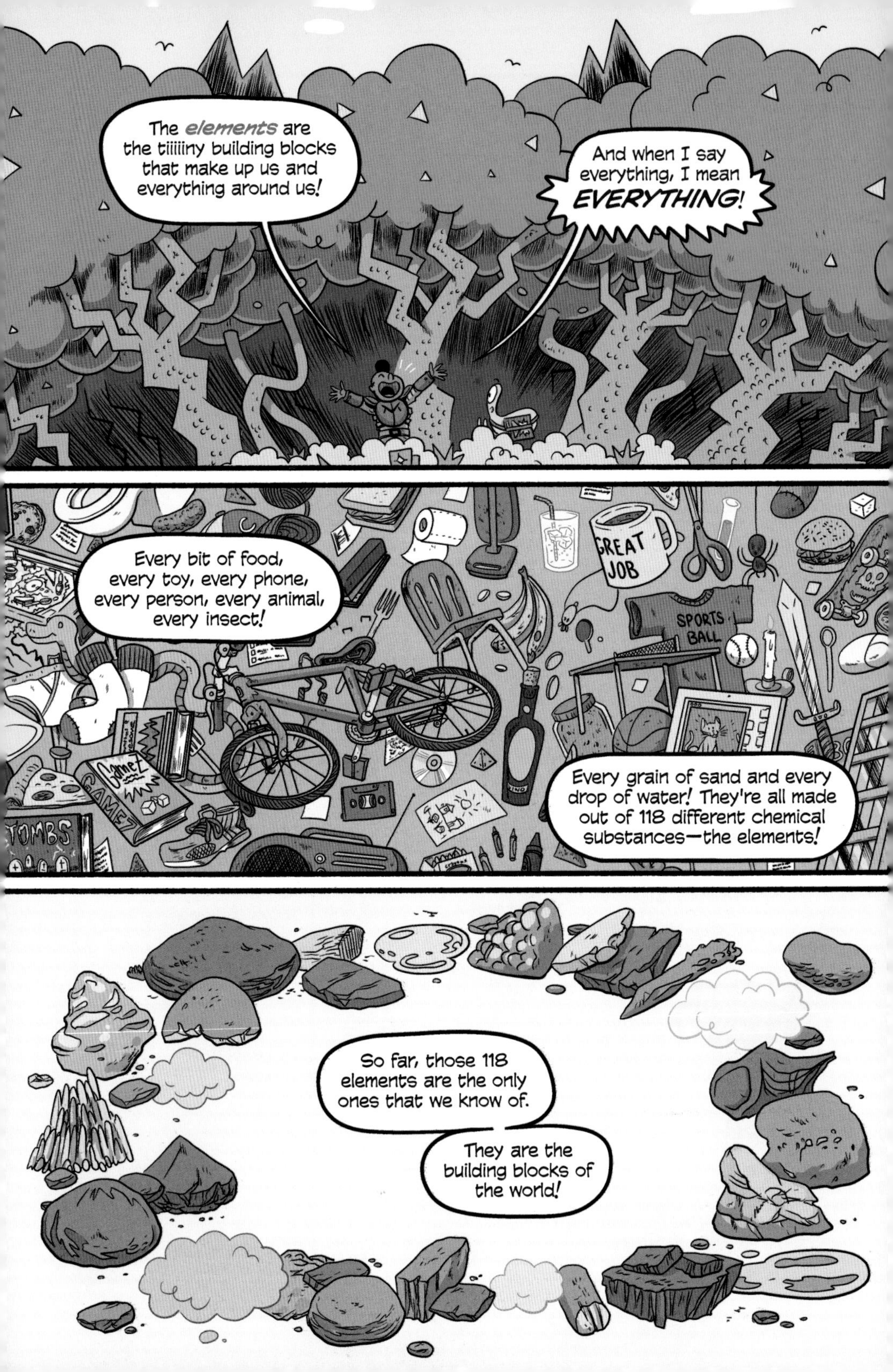

The *elements* are the tiiiiiny building blocks that make up us and everything around us!
And when I say everything, I mean **EVERYTHING!**
Every bit of food, every toy, every phone, every person, every animal, every insect!
GREAT JOB
SPORTS BALL
TOMBS
Every grain of sand and every drop of water! They're all made out of 118 different chemical substances—the elements!
So far, those 118 elements are the only ones that we know of.
They are the building blocks of the world!

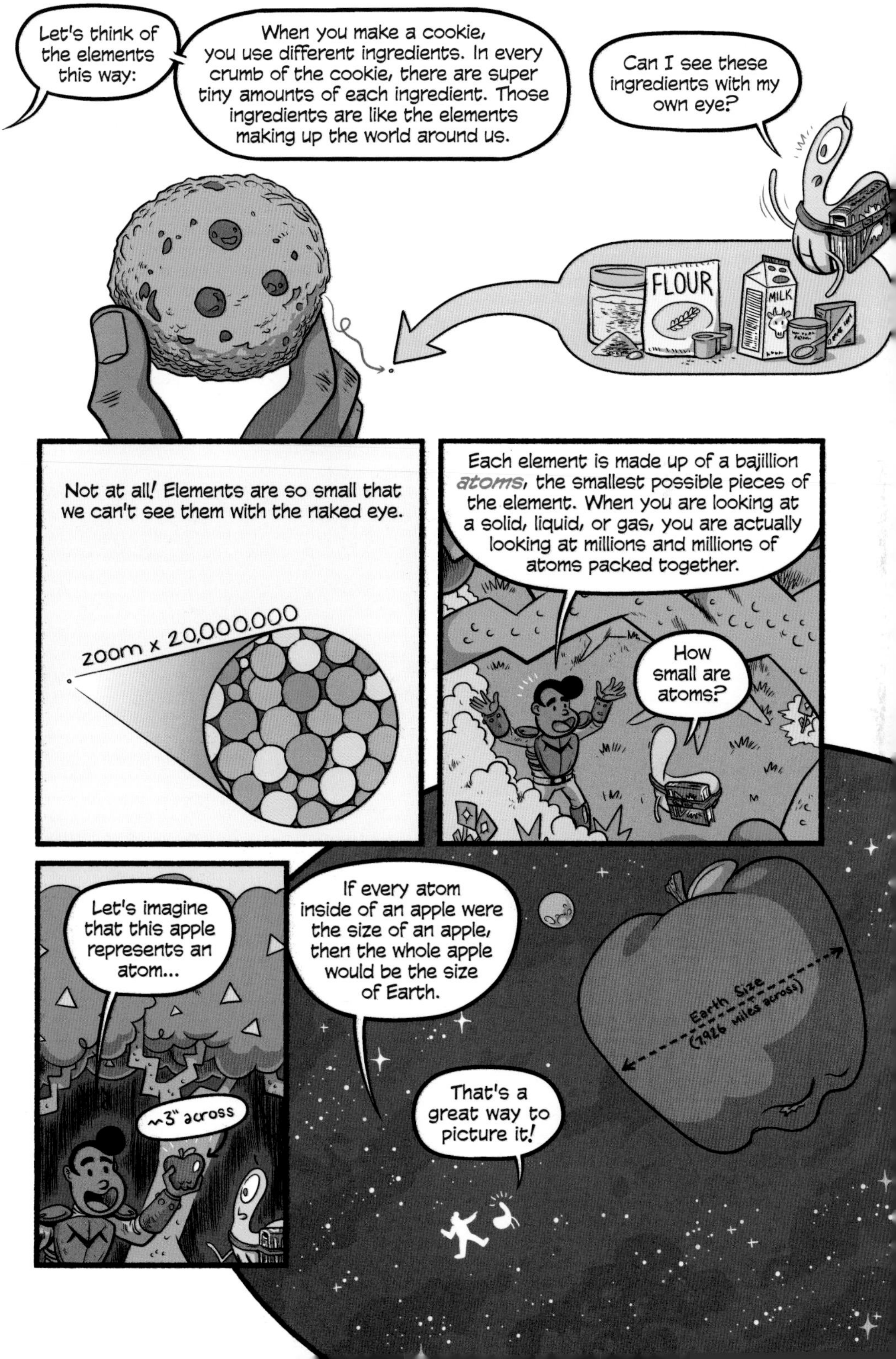
Let's think of the elements this way:
When you make a cookie, you use different ingredients. In every crumb of the cookie, there are super tiny amounts of each ingredient. Those ingredients are like the elements making up the world around us.
Can I see these ingredients with my own eye?
FLOUR
MILK
Not at all! Elements are so small that we can't see them with the naked eye.
zoom x 20,000,000
Each element is made up of a bajillion *atoms*, the smallest possible pieces of the element. When you are looking at a solid, liquid, or gas, you are actually looking at millions and millions of atoms packed together.
How small are atoms?
Let's imagine that this apple represents an atom...
~3" across
If every atom inside of an apple were the size of an apple, then the whole apple would be the size of Earth.
Earth Size (7926 miles across)
That's a great way to picture it!

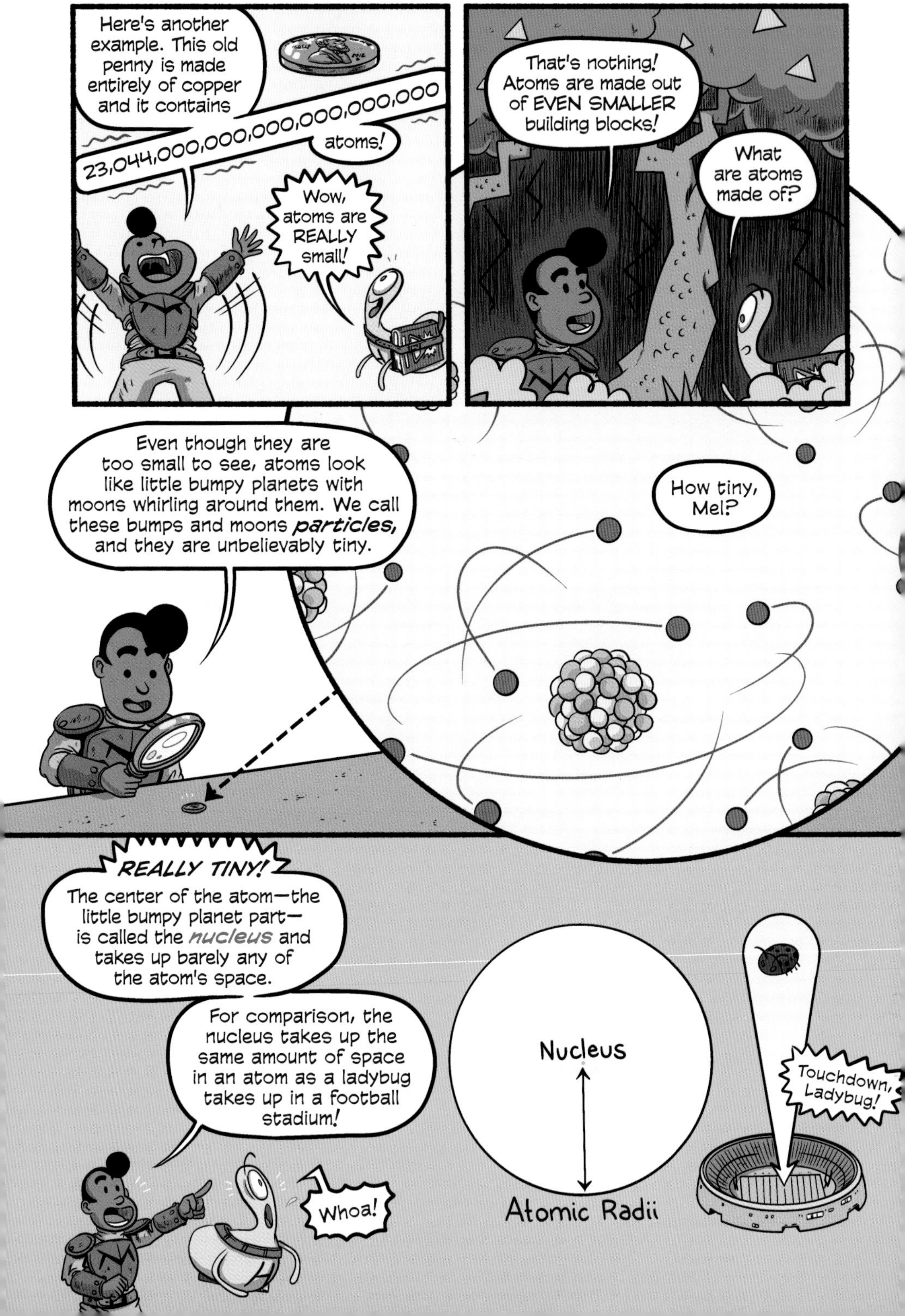
Here's another example. This old penny is made entirely of copper and it contains
23,044,000,000,000,000,000,000
atoms!
Wow, atoms are REALLY small!
That's nothing! Atoms are made out of EVEN SMALLER building blocks!
What are atoms made of?
Even though they are too small to see, atoms look like little bumpy planets with moons whirling around them. We call these bumps and moons *particles*, and they are unbelievably tiny.
How tiny, Mel?
REALLY TINY!
The center of the atom—the little bumpy planet part—is called the *nucleus* and takes up barely any of the atom's space.
For comparison, the nucleus takes up the same amount of space in an atom as a ladybug takes up in a football stadium!
Whoa!
Nucleus
Atomic Radii
Touchdown, Ladybug!

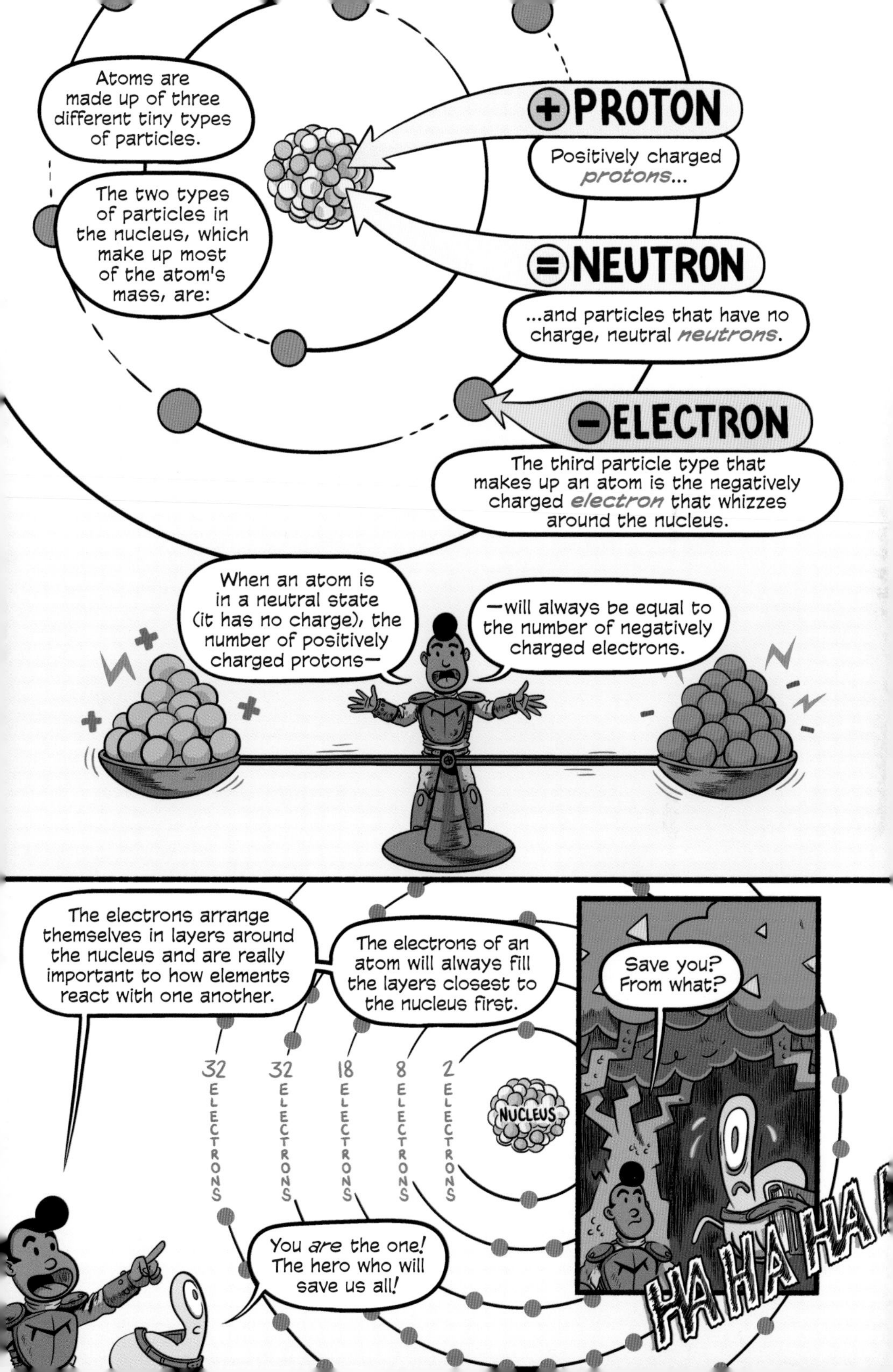

Atoms are made up of three different tiny types of particles.
The two types of particles in the nucleus, which make up most of the atom's mass, are:
PROTON
Positively charged *protons*...
NEUTRON
...and particles that have no charge, neutral *neutrons*.
ELECTRON
The third particle type that makes up an atom is the negatively charged *electron* that whizzes around the nucleus.
When an atom is in a neutral state (it has no charge), the number of positively charged protons—
—will always be equal to the number of negatively charged electrons.
The electrons arrange themselves in layers around the nucleus and are really important to how elements react with one another.
The electrons of an atom will always fill the layers closest to the nucleus first.
32 ELECTRONS
32 ELECTRONS
18 ELECTRONS
8 ELECTRONS
2 ELECTRONS
NUCLEUS
Save you? From what?
You *are* the one! The hero who will save us all!
HA HA HA

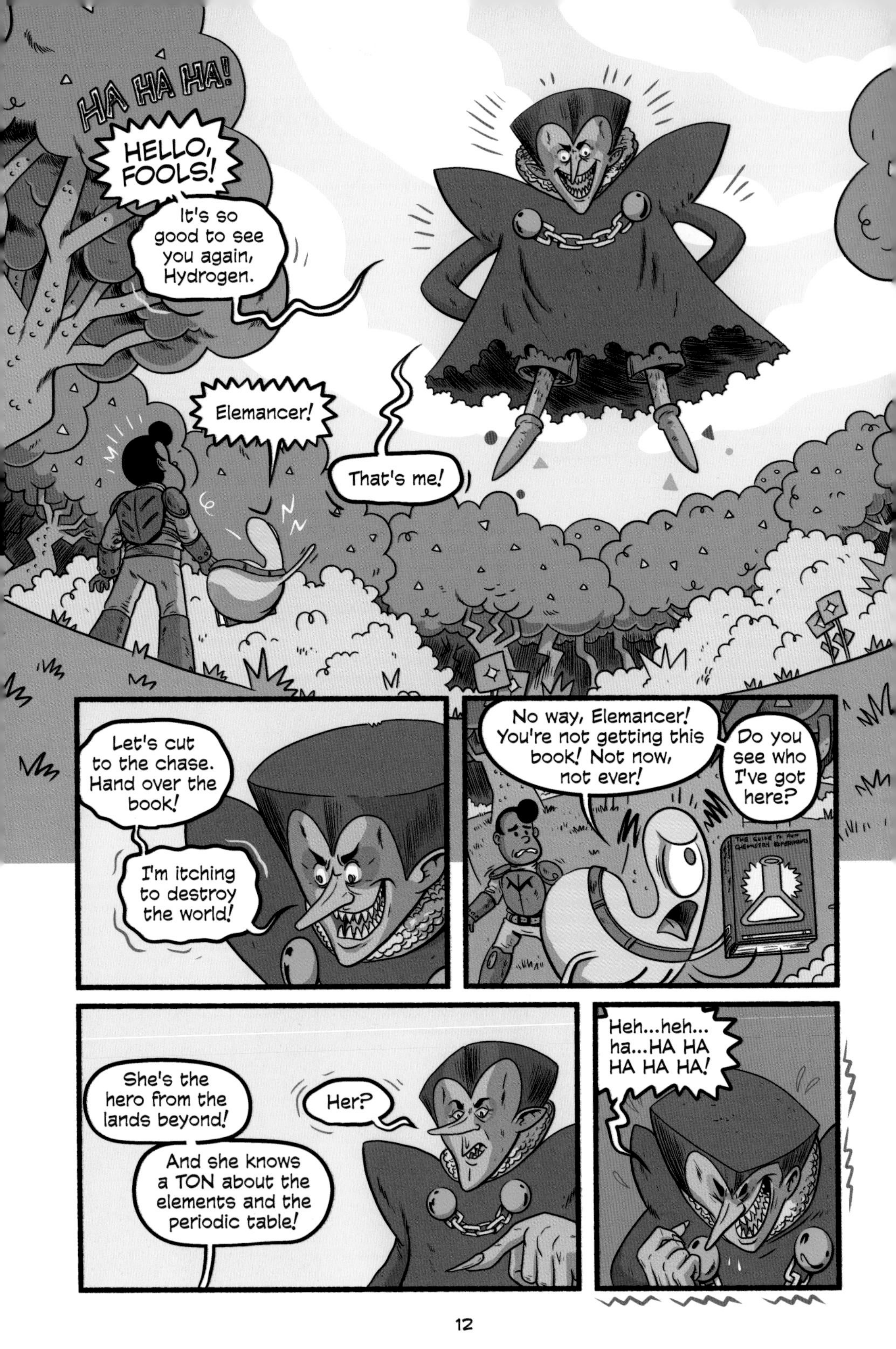
HA HA HA!
HELLO, FOOLS!
It's so good to see you again, Hydrogen.
Elemancer!
That's me!
Let's cut to the chase. Hand over the book!
I'm itching to destroy the world!
No way, Elemancer! You're not getting this book! Not now, not ever!
Do you see who I've got here?
She's the hero from the lands beyond!
And she knows a TON about the elements and the periodic table!
Her?
Heh...heh... ha...HA HA HA HA HA!

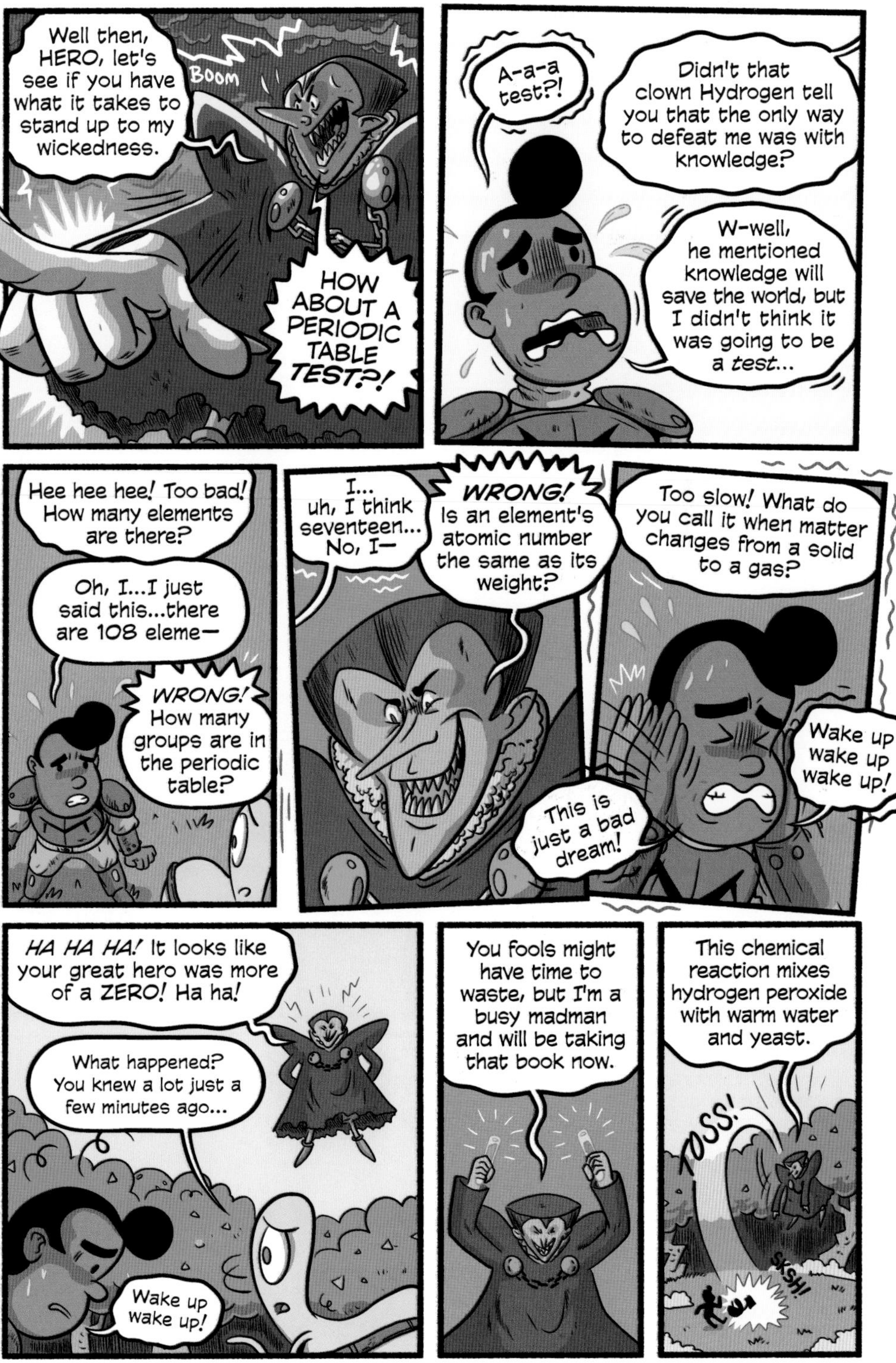

Well then, HERO, let's see if you have what it takes to stand up to my wickedness.
BOOM
HOW ABOUT A PERIODIC TABLE TEST?!
A-a-a test?!
Didn't that clown Hydrogen tell you that the only way to defeat me was with knowledge?
W-well, he mentioned knowledge will save the world, but I didn't think it was going to be a *test*...
Hee hee hee! Too bad! How many elements are there?
Oh, I...I just said this...there are 108 eleme—
WRONG! How many groups are in the periodic table?
I... uh, I think seventeen... No, I—
WRONG! Is an element's atomic number the same as its weight?
Too slow! What do you call it when matter changes from a solid to a gas?
Wake up wake up wake up!
This is just a bad dream!
HA HA HA! It looks like your great hero was more of a ZERO! Ha ha!
What happened? You knew a lot just a few minutes ago...
Wake up wake up!
You fools might have time to waste, but I'm a busy madman and will be taking that book now.
This chemical reaction mixes hydrogen peroxide with warm water and yeast.
TOSS!
SKSH!

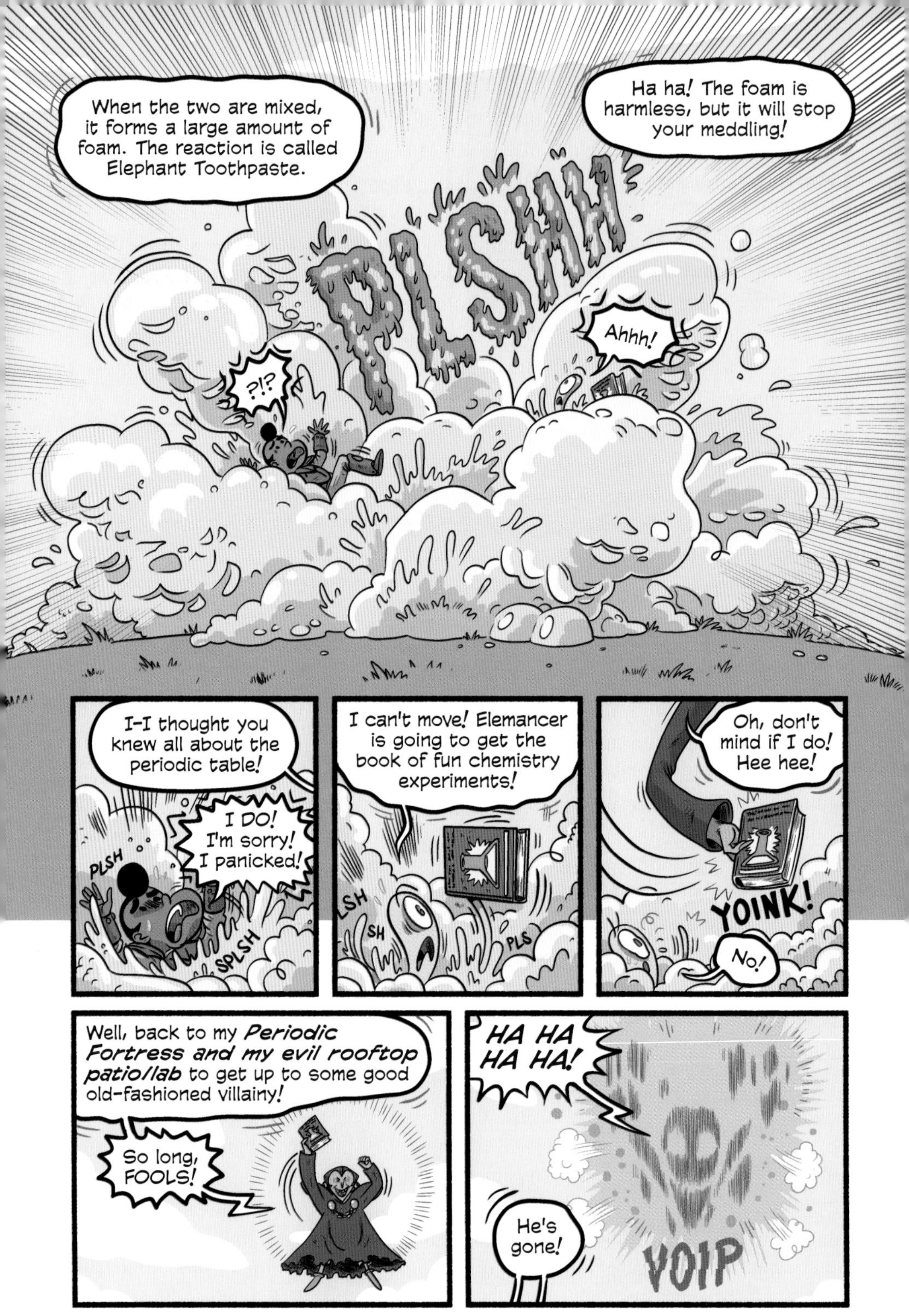
When the two are mixed, it forms a large amount of foam. The reaction is called Elephant Toothpaste.
Ha ha! The foam is harmless, but it will stop your meddling!
PLSHH
?!?
Ahhh!
I-I thought you knew all about the periodic table!
I DO! I'm sorry! I panicked!
PLSH
SPLSH
I can't move! Elemancer is going to get the book of fun chemistry experiments!
SH
PLS
Oh, don't mind if I do! Hee hee!
YOINK!
No!
Well, back to my *Periodic Fortress and my evil rooftop patio/lab* to get up to some good old-fashioned villainy!
So long, FOOLS!
HA HA HA HA!
He's gone!
VOIP

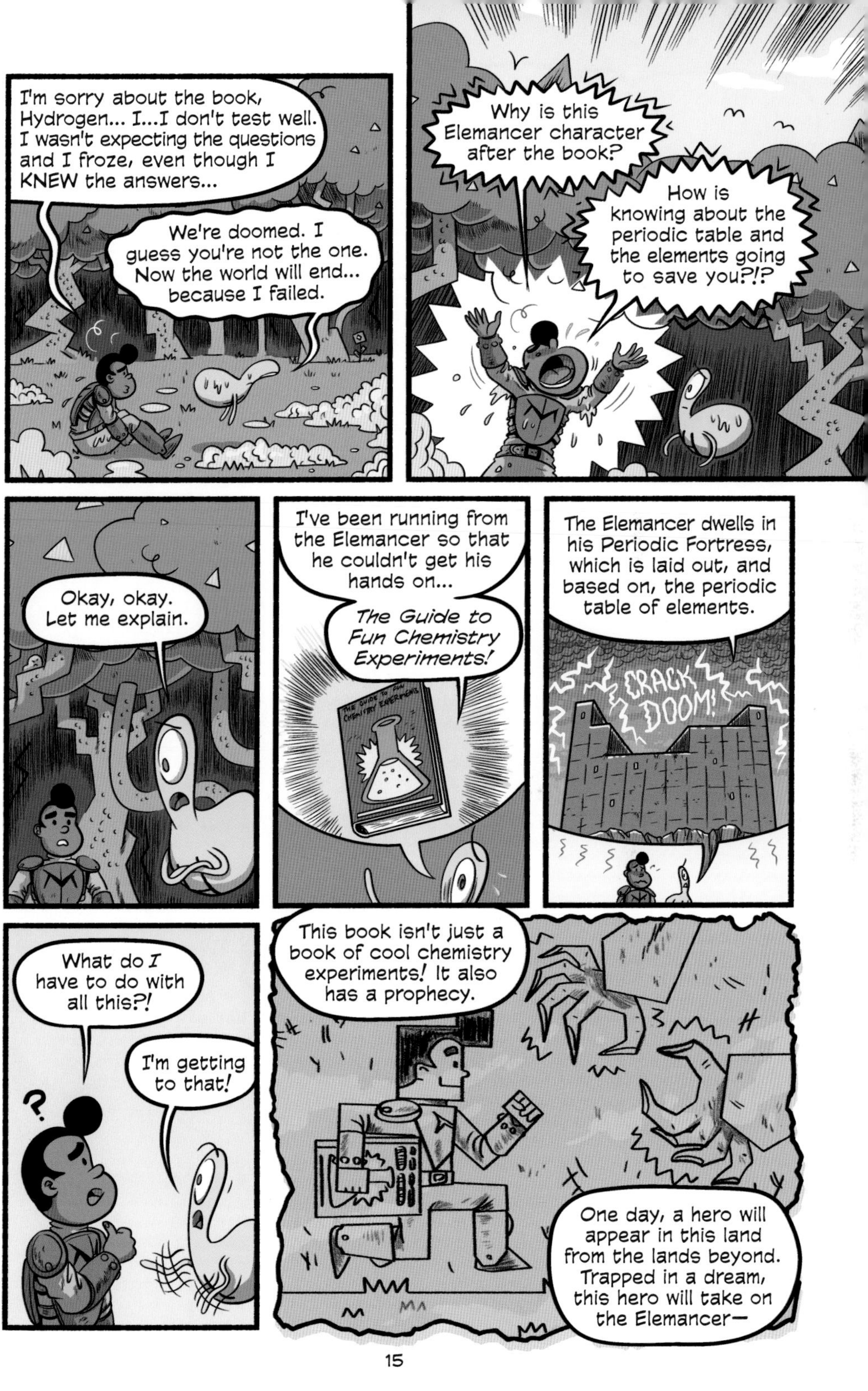
I'm sorry about the book, Hydrogen... I...I don't test well. I wasn't expecting the questions and I froze, even though I KNEW the answers...
We're doomed. I guess you're not the one. Now the world will end... because I failed.
Why is this Elemancer character after the book?
How is knowing about the periodic table and the elements going to save you?!?
Okay, okay. Let me explain.
I've been running from the Elemancer so that he couldn't get his hands on...
The Guide to Fun Chemistry Experiments!
The Elemancer dwells in his Periodic Fortress, which is laid out, and based on, the periodic table of elements.
CRACK
DOOM!
What do I have to do with all this?!
I'm getting to that!
This book isn't just a book of cool chemistry experiments! It also has a prophecy.
One day, a hero will appear in this land from the lands beyond. Trapped in a dream, this hero will take on the Elemancer—

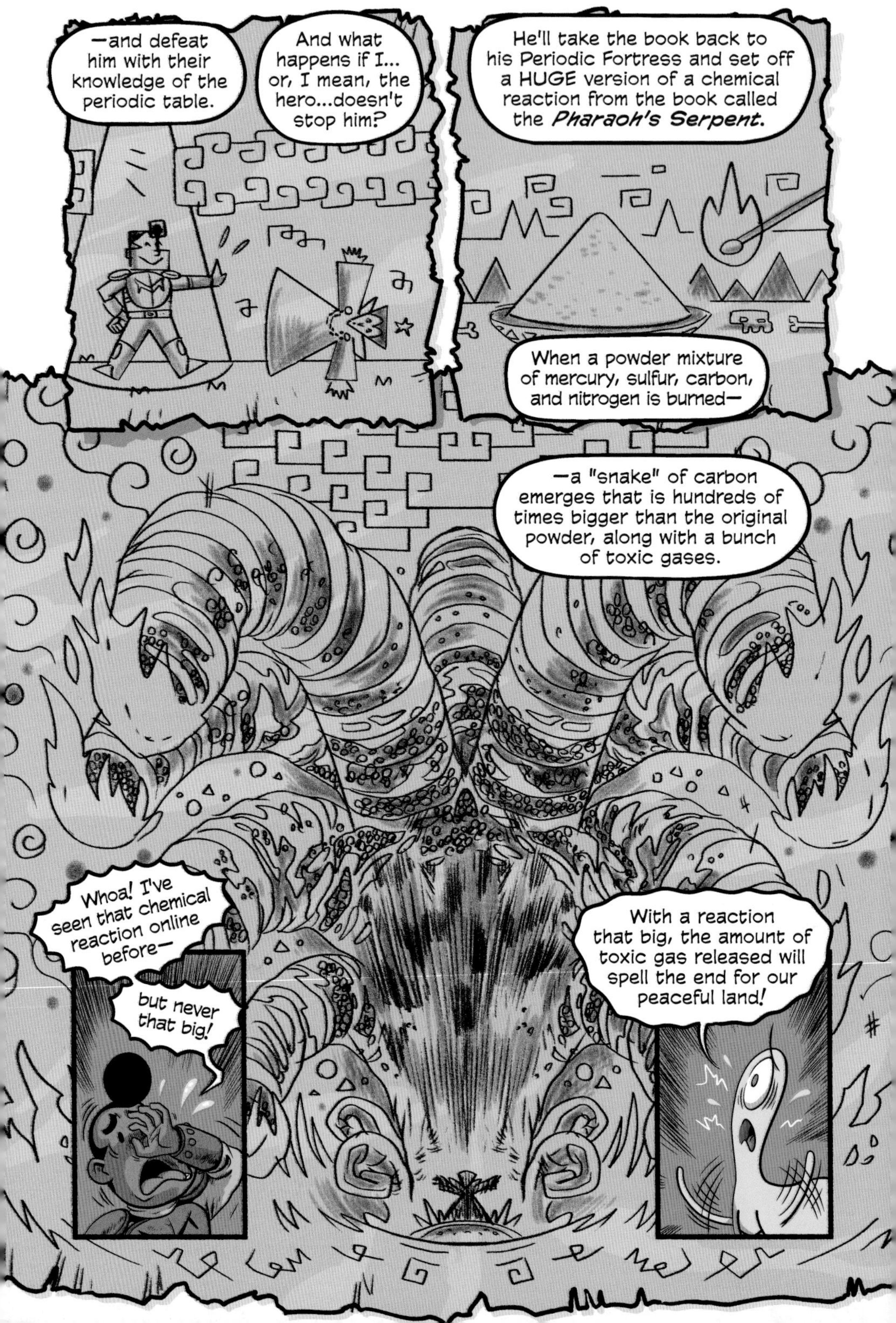
—and defeat him with their knowledge of the periodic table.
And what happens if I... or, I mean, the hero...doesn't stop him?
He'll take the book back to his Periodic Fortress and set off a HUGE version of a chemical reaction from the book called the *Pharaoh's Serpent*.
When a powder mixture of mercury, sulfur, carbon, and nitrogen is burned—
—a "snake" of carbon emerges that is hundreds of times bigger than the original powder, along with a bunch of toxic gases.
Whoa! I've seen that chemical reaction online before—
but never that big!
With a reaction that big, the amount of toxic gas released will spell the end for our peaceful land!

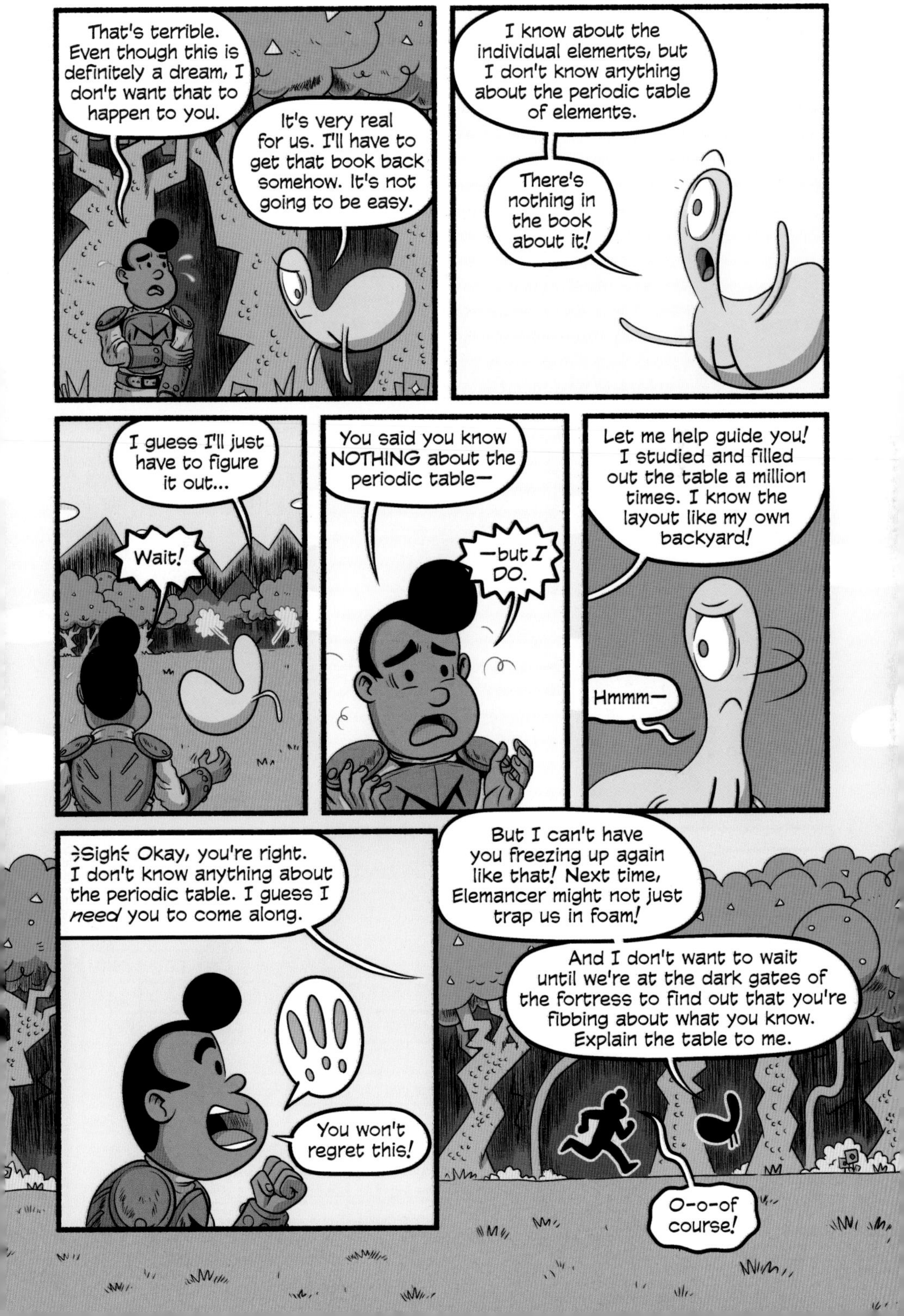

That's terrible. Even though this is definitely a dream, I don't want that to happen to you.
It's very real for us. I'll have to get that book back somehow. It's not going to be easy.
I know about the individual elements, but I don't know anything about the periodic table of elements.
There's nothing in the book about it!
I guess I'll just have to figure it out...
Wait!
You said you know NOTHING about the periodic table—
—but *I* DO.
Let me help guide you! I studied and filled out the table a million times. I know the layout like my own backyard!
Hmmm—
⟩Sigh⟨ Okay, you're right. I don't know anything about the periodic table. I guess I *need* you to come along.
You won't regret this!
But I can't have you freezing up again like that! Next time, Elemancer might not just trap us in foam!
And I don't want to wait until we're at the dark gates of the fortress to find out that you're fibbing about what you know. Explain the table to me.
O-o-of course!

This is the PERIODIC TABLE OF ELEMENTS!

The *periodic table* organizes the elements to help explain how the world around us works.

	1								9	10	11	12	13	14	15	16	17	18
1	1 H																	2 He
2	3 Li	4 Be											5 B	6 C	7 N	8 O	9 F	10 Ne
3	11 Na	12 Mg											13 Al	14 Si	15 P	16 S	17 Cl	18 Ar
4	19 K	20 Ca	21 Sc	22 Ti	23 V	24 Cr	25 Mn	26 Fe	27 Co	28 Ni	29 Cu	30 Zn	31 Ga	32 Ge	33 As	34 Se	35 Br	36 Kr
5	37 Rb	38 Sr	39 Y	40 Zr	41 Nb	42 Mo	43 Tc	44 Ru	45 Rh	46 Pd	47 Ag	48 Cd	49 In	50 Sn	51 Sb	52 Te	53 I	54 Xe
6	55 Cs	56 Ba	*	72 Hf	73 Ta	74 W	75 Re	76 Os	77 Ir	78 Pt	79 Au	80 Hg	81 Tl	82 Pb	83 Bi	84 Po	85 At	86 Rn
7	87 Fr	88 Ra	**	104 Rf	105 Db	106 Sg	107 Bh	108 Hs	109 Mt	110 Ds	111 Rg	112 Cn	113 Nh	114 Fl	115 Mc	116 Lv	117 Ts	118 Og
		*	57 La	58 Ce	59 Pr	60 Nd	61 Pm	62 Sm	63 Eu	64 Gd	65 Tb	66 Dy	67 Ho	68 Er	69 Tm	70 Yb	71 Lu	
		**	89 Ac	90 Th	91 Pa	92 U	93 Np	94 Pu	95 Am	96 Cm	97 Bk	98 Cf	99 Es	100 Fm	101 Md	102 No	103 Lr	

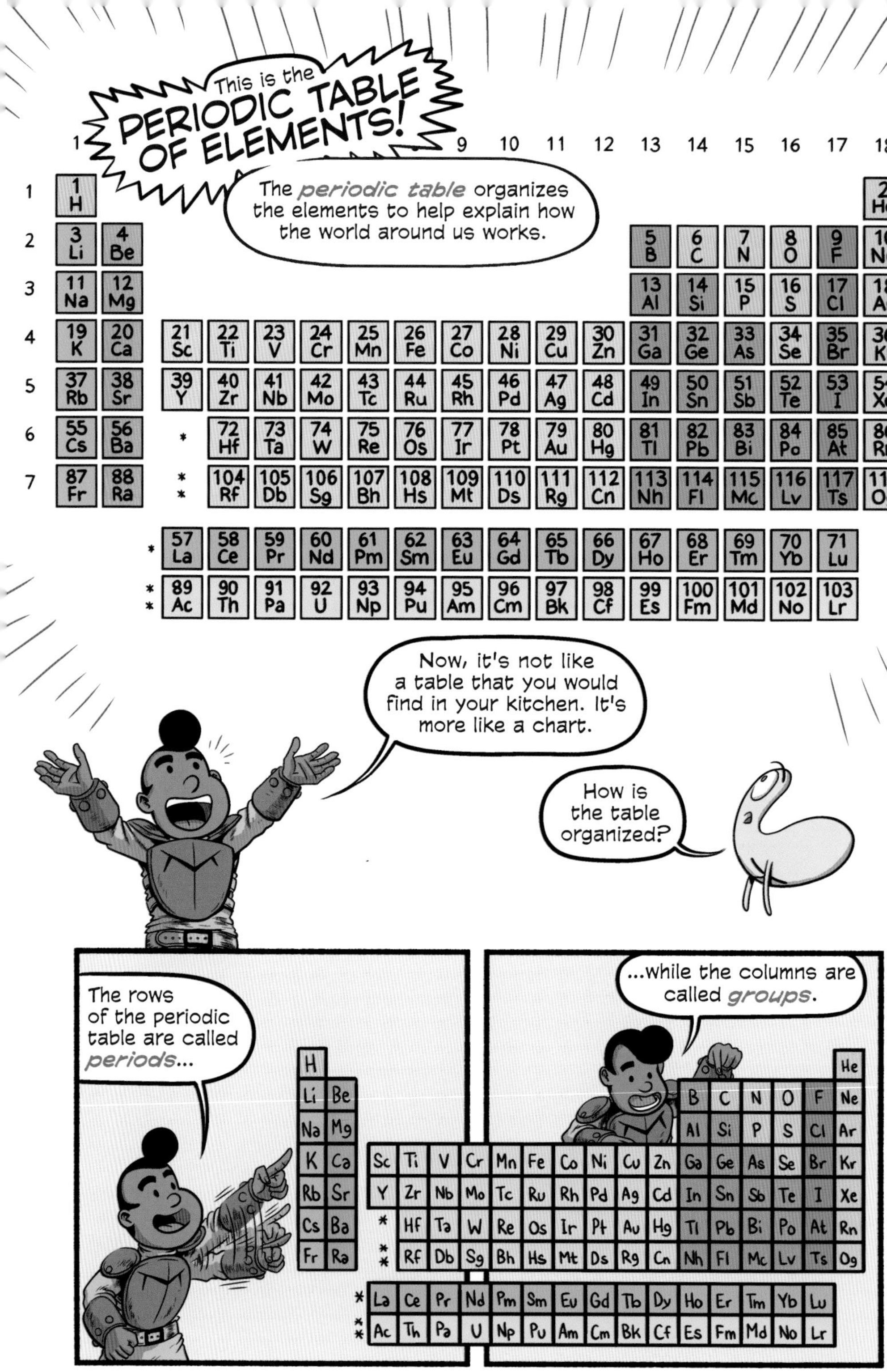
Now, it's not like a table that you would find in your kitchen. It's more like a chart.
How is the table organized?
The rows of the periodic table are called *periods*...
...while the columns are called *groups*.
H He
Li Be B C N O F Ne
Na Mg Al Si P S Cl Ar
K Ca Sc Ti V Cr Mn Fe Co Ni Cu Zn Ga Ge As Se Br Kr
Rb Sr Y Zr Nb Mo Tc Ru Rh Pd Ag Cd In Sn Sb Te I Xe
Cs Ba * Hf Ta W Re Os Ir Pt Au Hg Tl Pb Bi Po At Rn
Fr Ra ** Rf Db Sg Bh Hs Mt Ds Rg Cn Nh Fl Mc Lv Ts Og
* La Ce Pr Nd Pm Sm Eu Gd Tb Dy Ho Er Tm Yb Lu
** Ac Th Pa U Np Pu Am Cm Bk Cf Es Fm Md No Lr

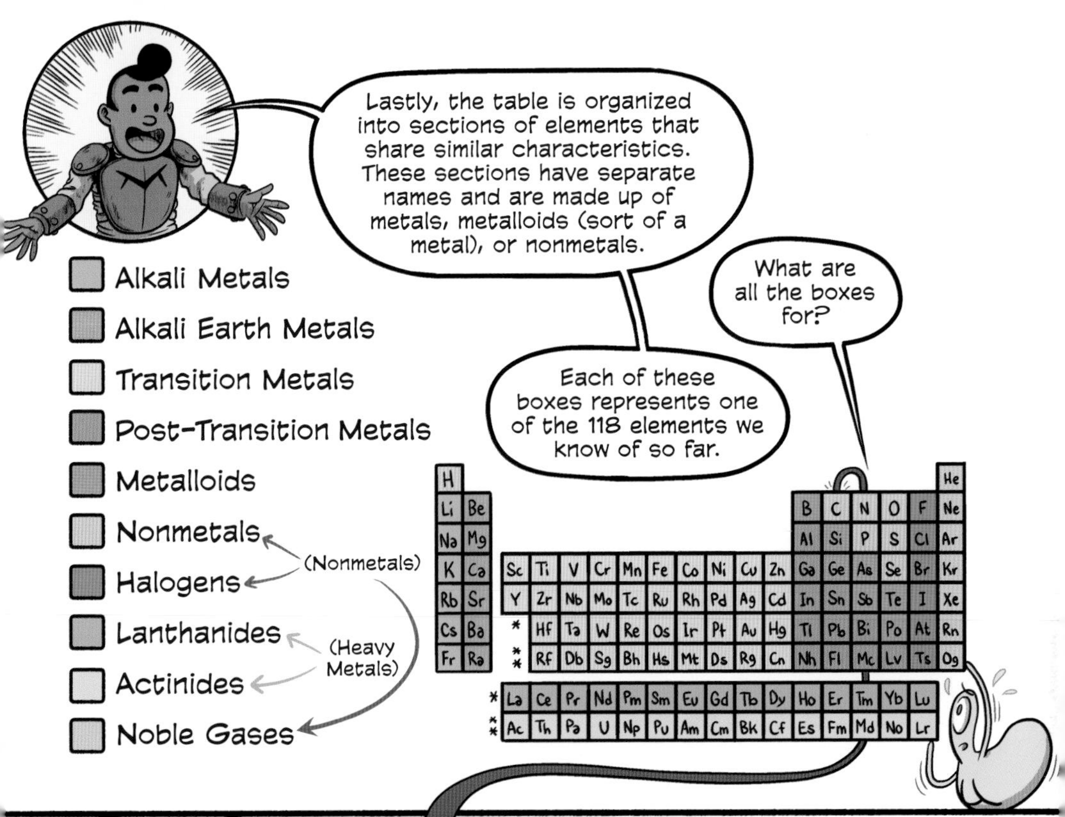
Lastly, the table is organized into sections of elements that share similar characteristics. These sections have separate names and are made up of metals, metalloids (sort of a metal), or nonmetals.
Alkali Metals
Alkali Earth Metals
Transition Metals
Post-Transition Metals
Metalloids
Nonmetals
Halogens
(Nonmetals)
Lanthanides
Actinides
(Heavy Metals)
Noble Gases
What are all the boxes for?
Each of these boxes represents one of the 118 elements we know of so far.
H He
Li Be B C N O F Ne
Na Mg Al Si P S Cl Ar
K Ca Sc Ti V Cr Mn Fe Co Ni Cu Zn Ga Ge As Se Br Kr
Rb Sr Y Zr Nb Mo Tc Ru Rh Pd Ag Cd In Sn Sb Te I Xe
Cs Ba * Hf Ta W Re Os Ir Pt Au Hg Tl Pb Bi Po At Rn
Fr Ra ** Rf Db Sg Bh Hs Mt Ds Rg Cn Nh Fl Mc Lv Ts Og
* La Ce Pr Nd Pm Sm Eu Gd Tb Dy Ho Er Tm Yb Lu
** Ac Th Pa U Np Pu Am Cm Bk Cf Es Fm Md No Lr

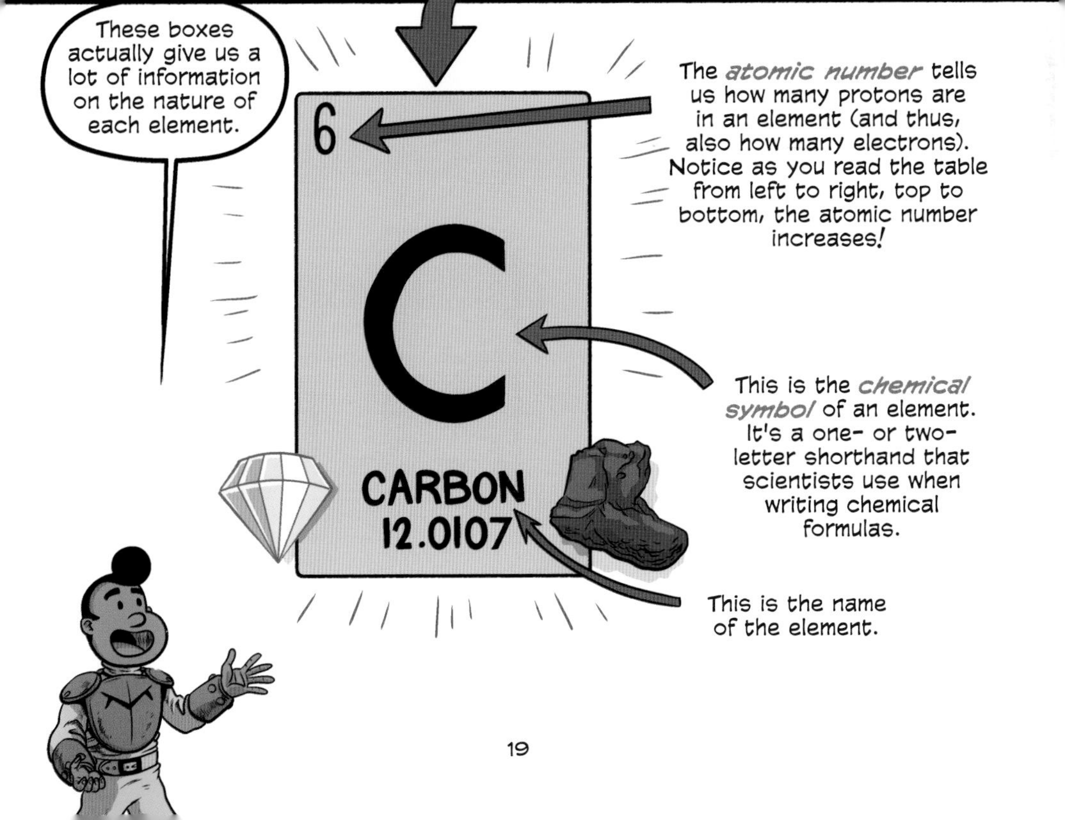
These boxes actually give us a lot of information on the nature of each element.
The *atomic number* tells us how many protons are in an element (and thus, also how many electrons). Notice as you read the table from left to right, top to bottom, the atomic number increases!
6
C
CARBON
12.0107
This is the *chemical symbol* of an element. It's a one- or two-letter shorthand that scientists use when writing chemical formulas.
This is the name of the element.

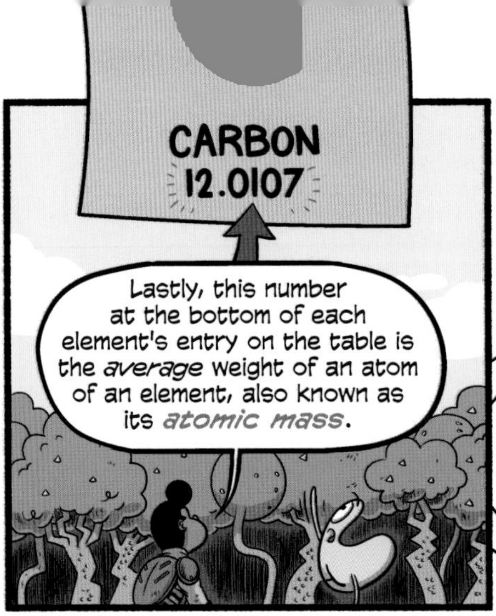
CARBON
12.0107
Lastly, this number at the bottom of each element's entry on the table is the *average* weight of an atom of an element, also known as its *atomic mass*.

Atomic mass is measured in atomic mass units (amu). Each of the three particles that makes up an atom has a slightly different mass:

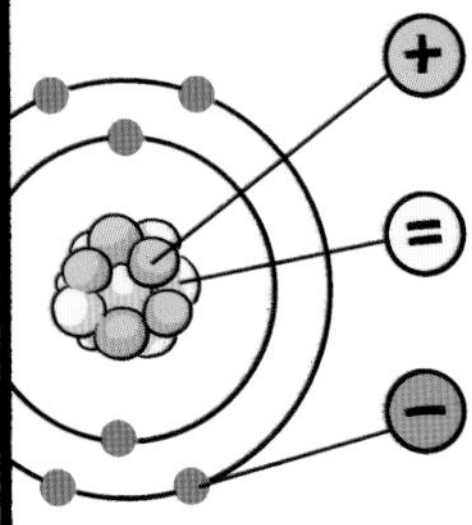

Mass of Proton = 1.007277 amu

Mass of Neutron = 1.008665 amu

Mass of Electron = 0.000549 amu

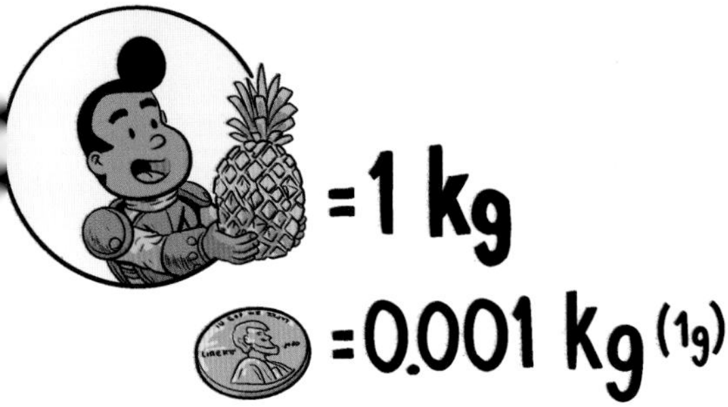
=1 kg
=0.001 kg (1g)

Atomic mass units are incredibly small.

Let's put it this way... A pineapple weighs one kilogram and a penny weighs a thousand times less (one gram). Compared to the pineapple, an atomic mass unit equals:

AMU = 0.00000000000000000000000000166054 kg

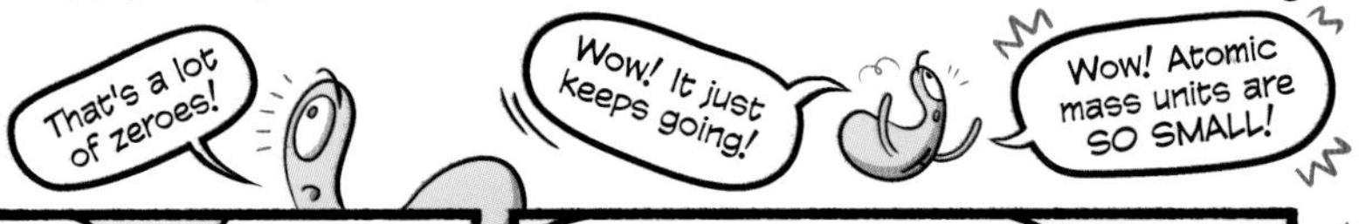
That's a lot of zeroes!
Wow! It just keeps going!
Wow! Atomic mass units are SO SMALL!

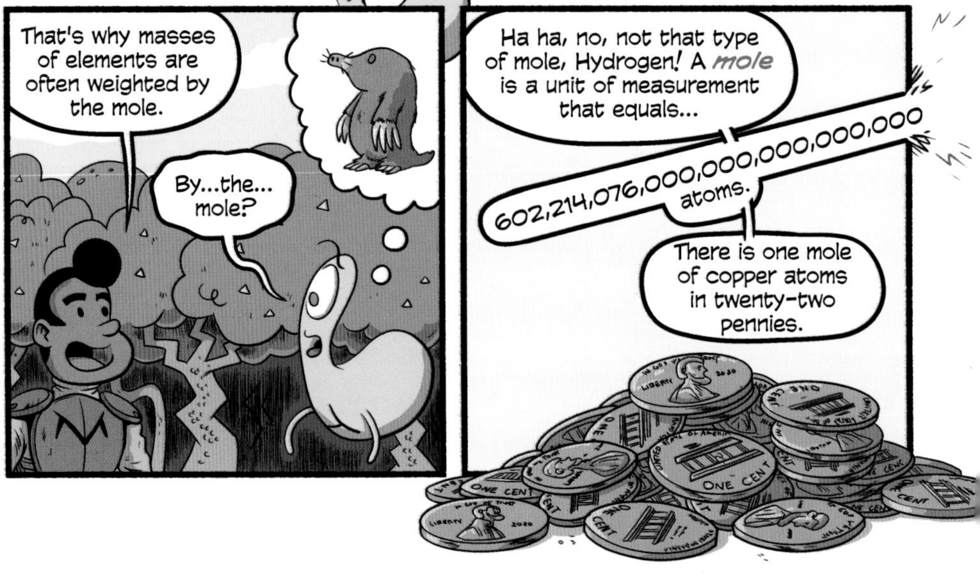
That's why masses of elements are often weighted by the mole.
By...the... mole?
Ha ha, no, not that type of mole, Hydrogen! A *mole* is a unit of measurement that equals...
602,214,076,000,000,000,000,000 atoms.
There is one mole of copper atoms in twenty-two pennies.
ONE CENT

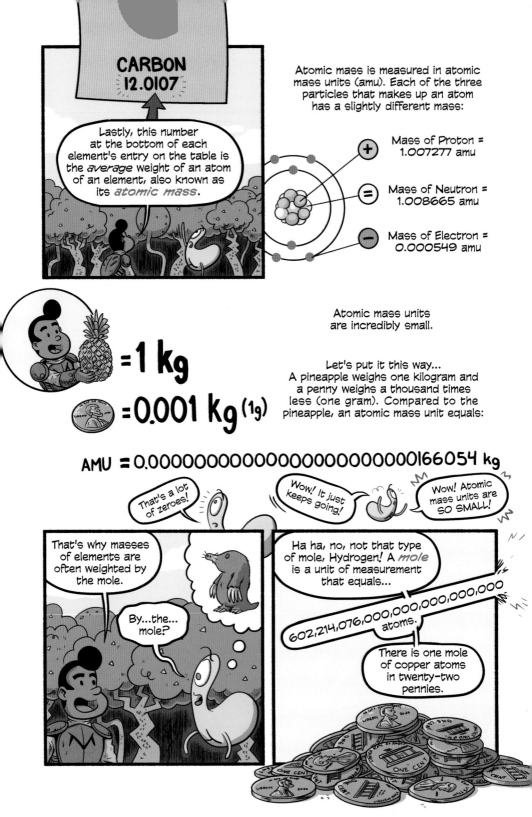

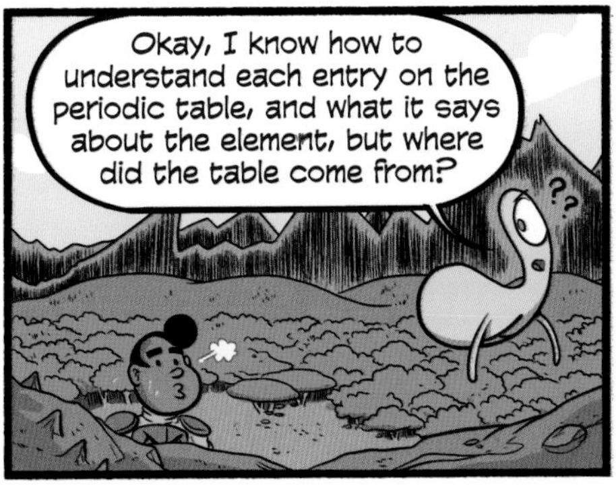
Okay, I know how to understand each entry on the periodic table, and what it says about the element, but where did the table come from?
??

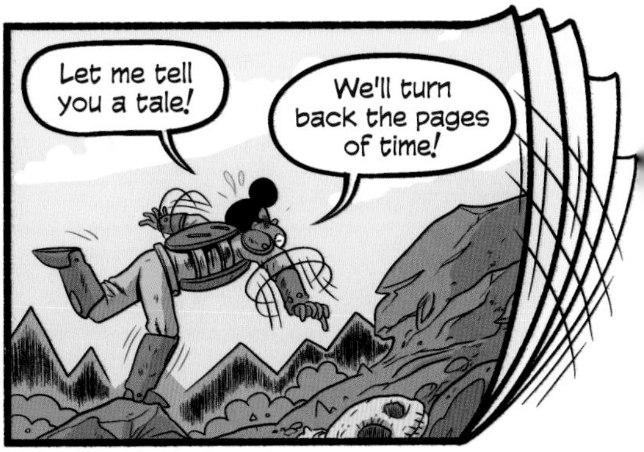
Let me tell you a tale!
We'll turn back the pages of time!

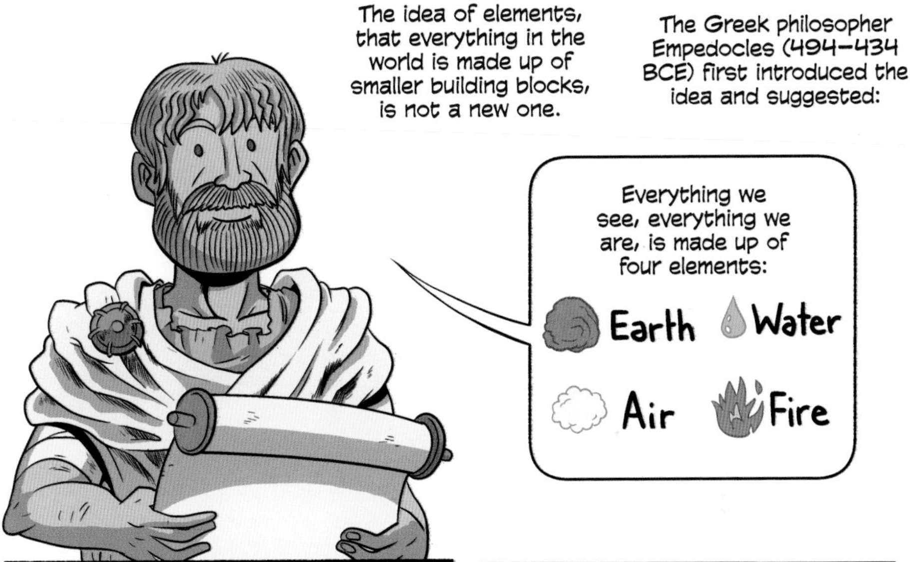
The idea of elements, that everything in the world is made up of smaller building blocks, is not a new one.
The Greek philosopher Empedocles (494–434 BCE) first introduced the idea and suggested:
Everything we see, everything we are, is made up of four elements:
Earth
Water
Air
Fire

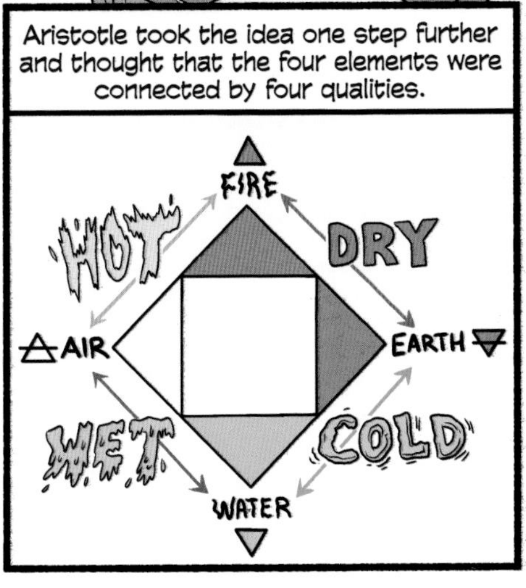
Aristotle took the idea one step further and thought that the four elements were connected by four qualities.
FIRE
HOT
DRY
AIR
EARTH
WET
COLD
WATER

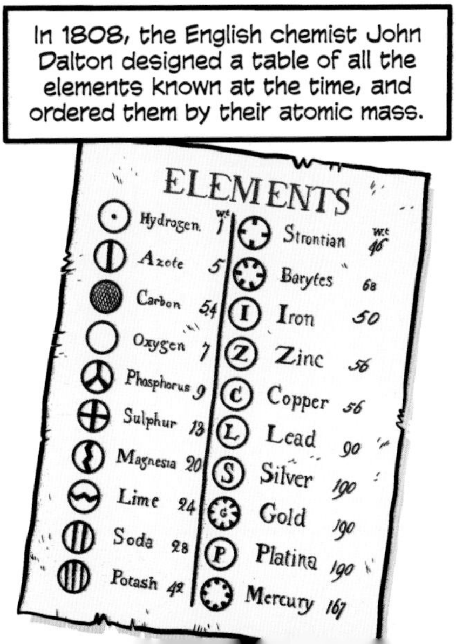
In 1808, the English chemist John Dalton designed a table of all the elements known at the time, and ordered them by their atomic mass.
ELEMENTS
wt
Hydrogen 1
Azote 5
Carbon 54
Oxygen 7
Phosphorus 9
Sulphur 13
Magnesia 20
Lime 24
Soda 28
Potash 42
wt
Strontian 46
Barytes 68
Iron 50
Zinc 56
Copper 56
Lead 90
Silver 190
Gold 190
Platina 190
Mercury 167

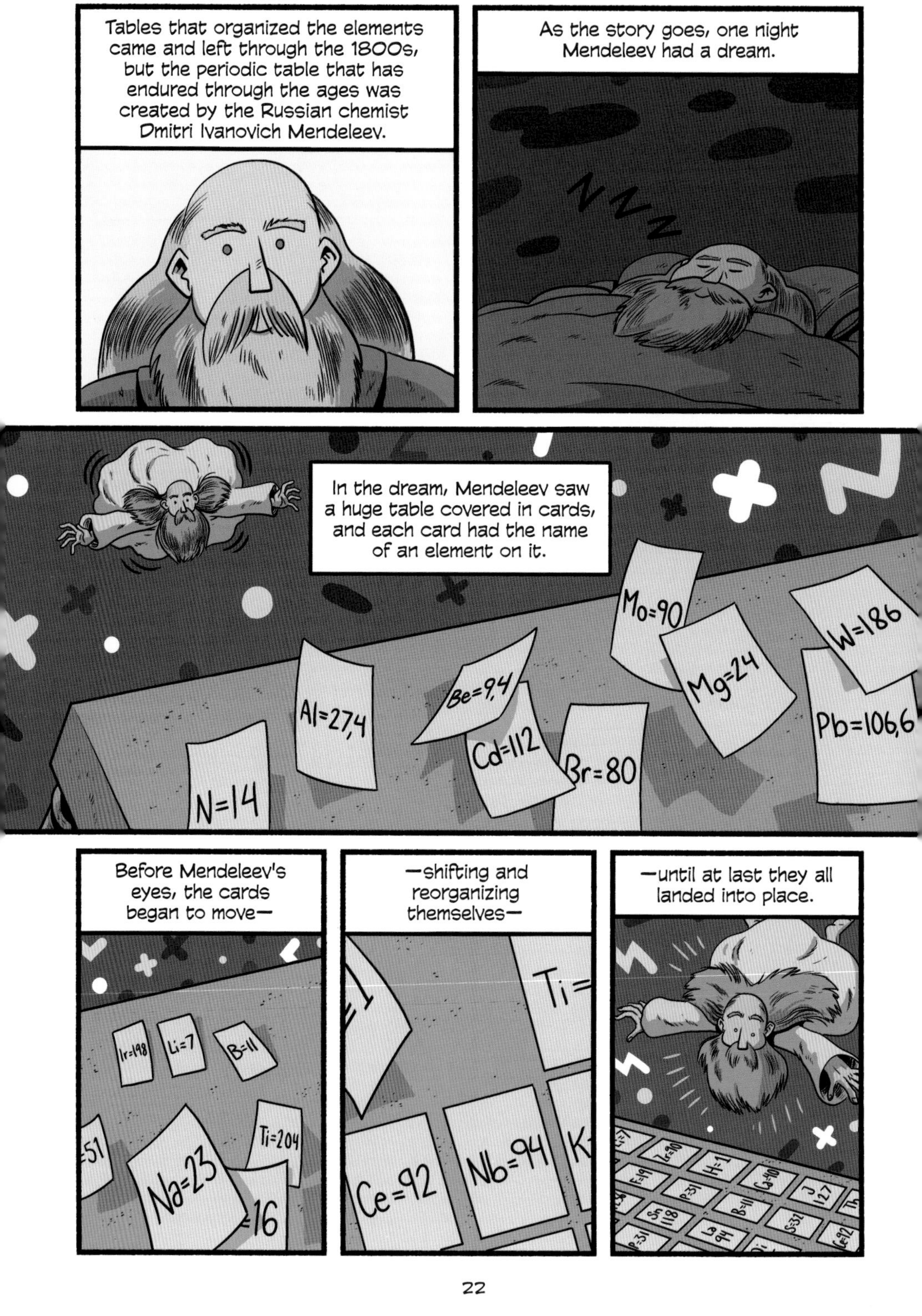
Tables that organized the elements came and left through the 1800s, but the periodic table that has endured through the ages was created by the Russian chemist Dmitri Ivanovich Mendeleev.
As the story goes, one night Mendeleev had a dream.
ZZZ
In the dream, Mendeleev saw a huge table covered in cards, and each card had the name of an element on it.
Mo=90
W=186
Mg=24
Al=27,4
Be=9,4
Cd=112
Br=80
Pb=106,6
N=14
Before Mendeleev's eyes, the cards began to move—
Ir=198
Li=7
B=11
Ti=204
Na=23
—shifting and reorganizing themselves—
Ce=92
Nb=94
—until at last they all landed into place.

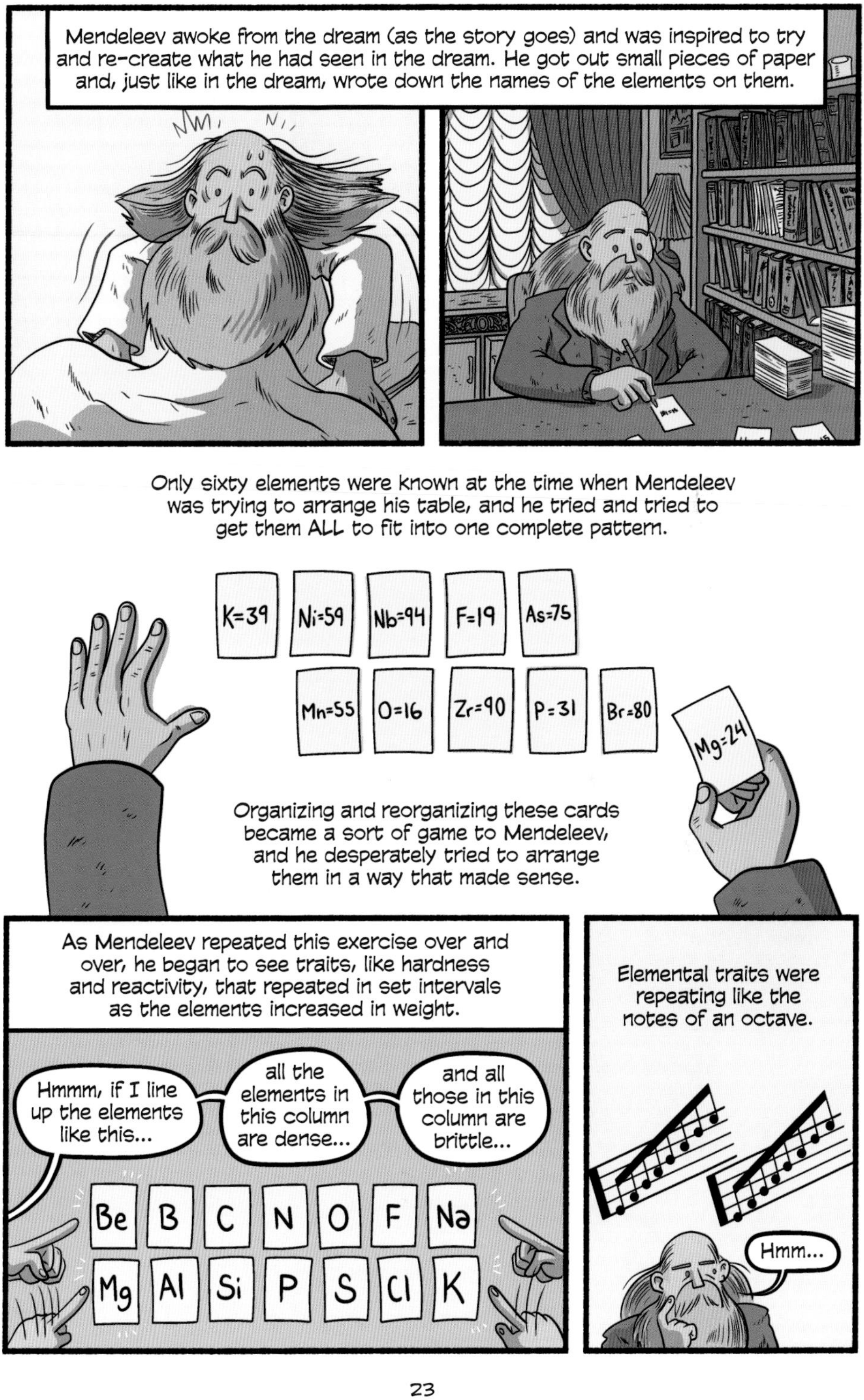
Mendeleev awoke from the dream (as the story goes) and was inspired to try and re-create what he had seen in the dream. He got out small pieces of paper and, just like in the dream, wrote down the names of the elements on them.
Only sixty elements were known at the time when Mendeleev was trying to arrange his table, and he tried and tried to get them ALL to fit into one complete pattern.
K=39
Ni=59
Nb=94
F=19
As=75
Mn=55
O=16
Zr=90
P=31
Br=80
Mg=24
Organizing and reorganizing these cards became a sort of game to Mendeleev, and he desperately tried to arrange them in a way that made sense.
As Mendeleev repeated this exercise over and over, he began to see traits, like hardness and reactivity, that repeated in set intervals as the elements increased in weight.
Hmmm, if I line up the elements like this...
all the elements in this column are dense...
and all those in this column are brittle...
Be B C N O F Na
Mg Al Si P S Cl K
Elemental traits were repeating like the notes of an octave.
Hmm...

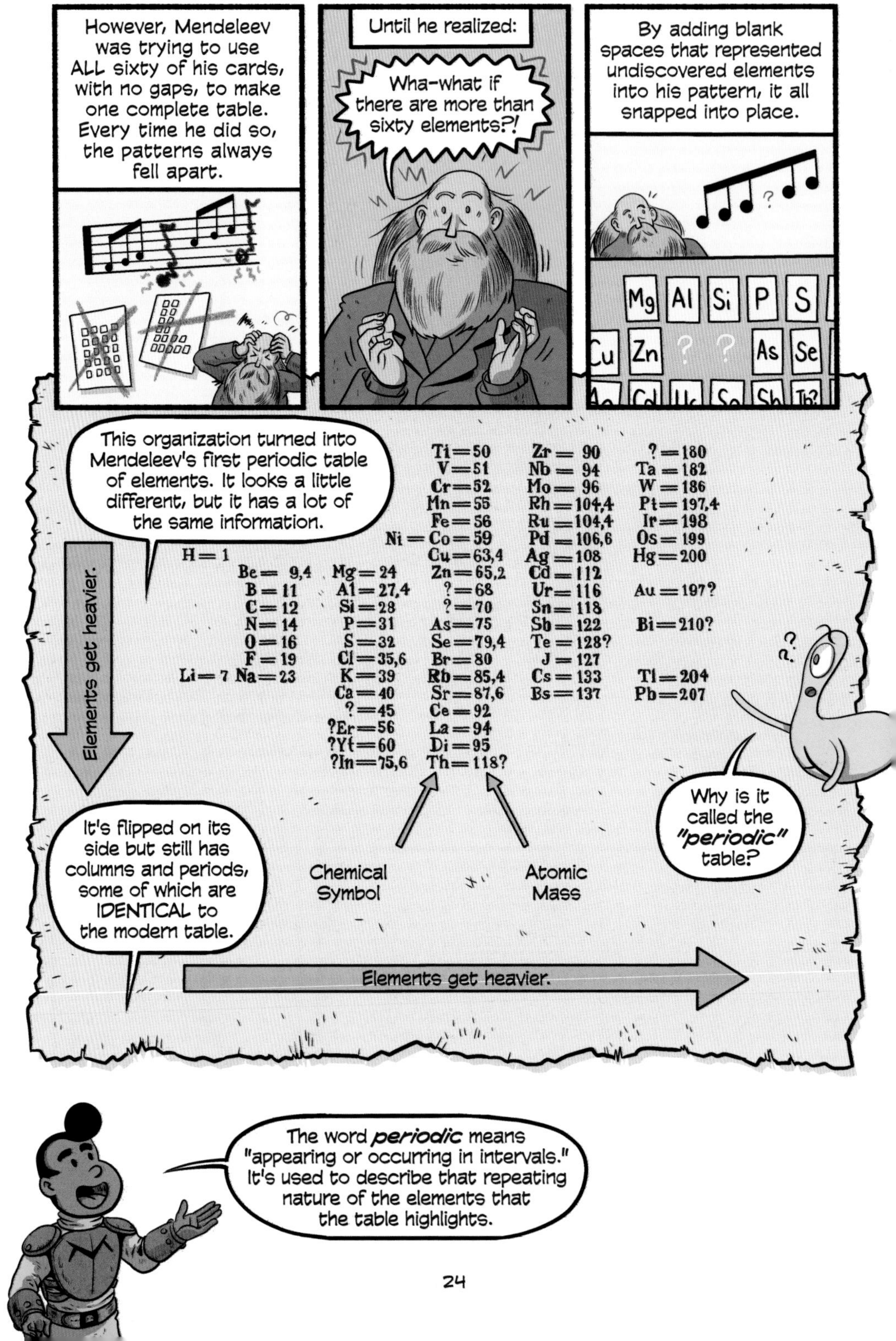
However, Mendeleev was trying to use ALL sixty of his cards, with no gaps, to make one complete table. Every time he did so, the patterns always fell apart.
Until he realized:
Wha-what if there are more than sixty elements?!
By adding blank spaces that represented undiscovered elements into his pattern, it all snapped into place.
Mg Al Si P S
Cu Zn ? ? As Se
This organization turned into Mendeleev's first periodic table of elements. It looks a little different, but it has a lot of the same information.
Ti=50 Zr=90 ?=180
V=51 Nb=94 Ta=182
Cr=52 Mo=96 W=186
Mn=55 Rh=104,4 Pt=197,4
Fe=56 Ru=104,4 Ir=198
Ni=Co=59 Pd=106,6 Os=199
H=1 Cu=63,4 Ag=108 Hg=200
Be=9,4 Mg=24 Zn=65,2 Cd=112
B=11 Al=27,4 ?=68 Ur=116 Au=197?
C=12 Si=28 ?=70 Sn=118
N=14 P=31 As=75 Sb=122 Bi=210?
O=16 S=32 Se=79,4 Te=128?
F=19 Cl=35,6 Br=80 J=127
Li=7 Na=23 K=39 Rb=85,4 Cs=133 Tl=204
Ca=40 Sr=87,6 Ba=137 Pb=207
?=45 Ce=92
?Er=56 La=94
?Yt=60 Di=95
?In=75,6 Th=118?
Elements get heavier.
Chemical Symbol
Atomic Mass
Why is it called the *"periodic"* table?
It's flipped on its side but still has columns and periods, some of which are IDENTICAL to the modern table.
Elements get heavier.
The word ***periodic*** means "appearing or occurring in intervals." It's used to describe that repeating nature of the elements that the table highlights.

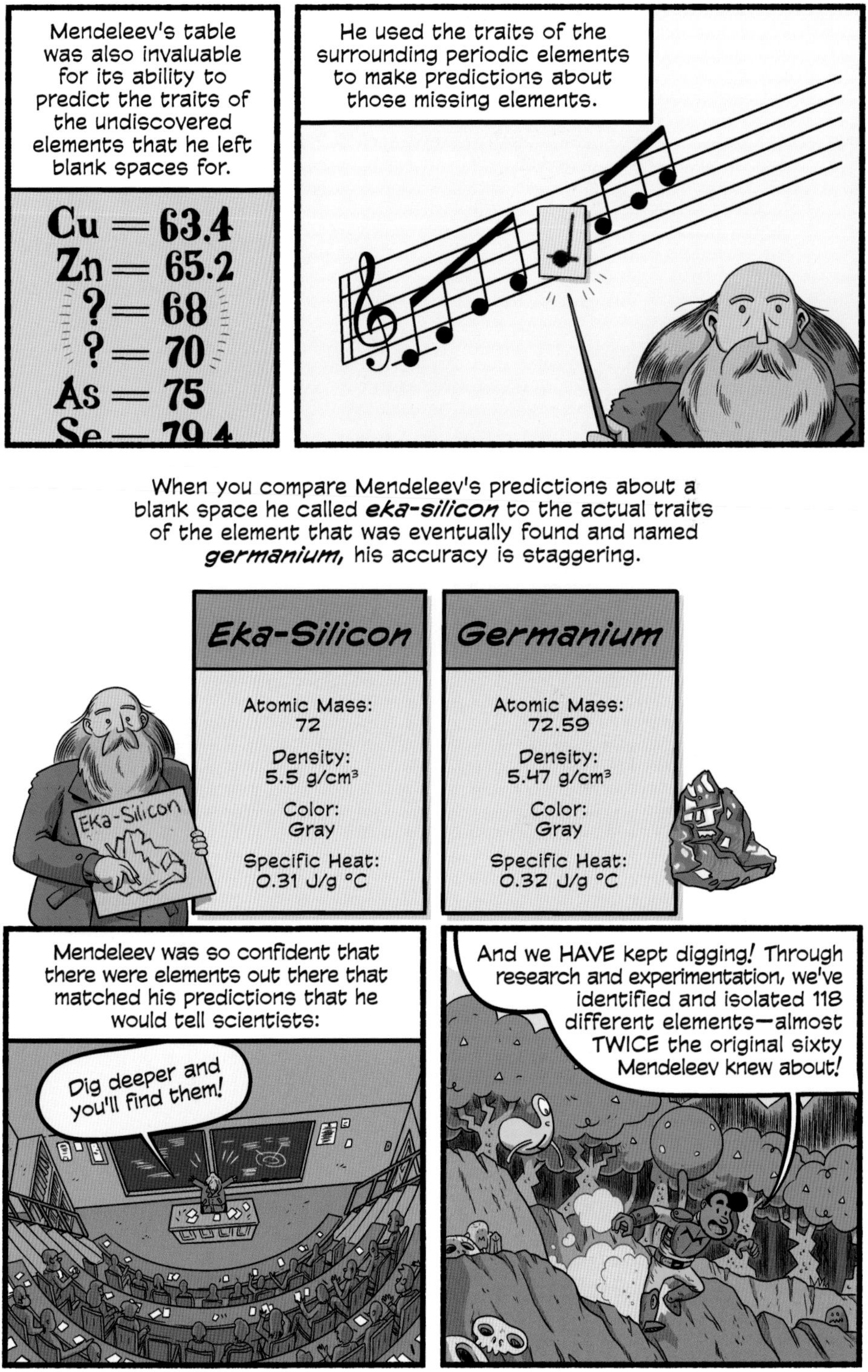
Mendeleev's table was also invaluable for its ability to predict the traits of the undiscovered elements that he left blank spaces for.
Cu = 63.4
Zn = 65.2
? = 68
? = 70
As = 75
Se = 79.4
He used the traits of the surrounding periodic elements to make predictions about those missing elements.
When you compare Mendeleev's predictions about a blank space he called *eka-silicon* to the actual traits of the element that was eventually found and named *germanium*, his accuracy is staggering.
Eka-Silicon
Atomic Mass: 72
Density: 5.5 g/cm³
Color: Gray
Specific Heat: 0.31 J/g °C
Eka-Silicon
Germanium
Atomic Mass: 72.59
Density: 5.47 g/cm³
Color: Gray
Specific Heat: 0.32 J/g °C
Mendeleev was so confident that there were elements out there that matched his predictions that he would tell scientists:
Dig deeper and you'll find them!
And we HAVE kept digging! Through research and experimentation, we've identified and isolated 118 different elements—almost TWICE the original sixty Mendeleev knew about!

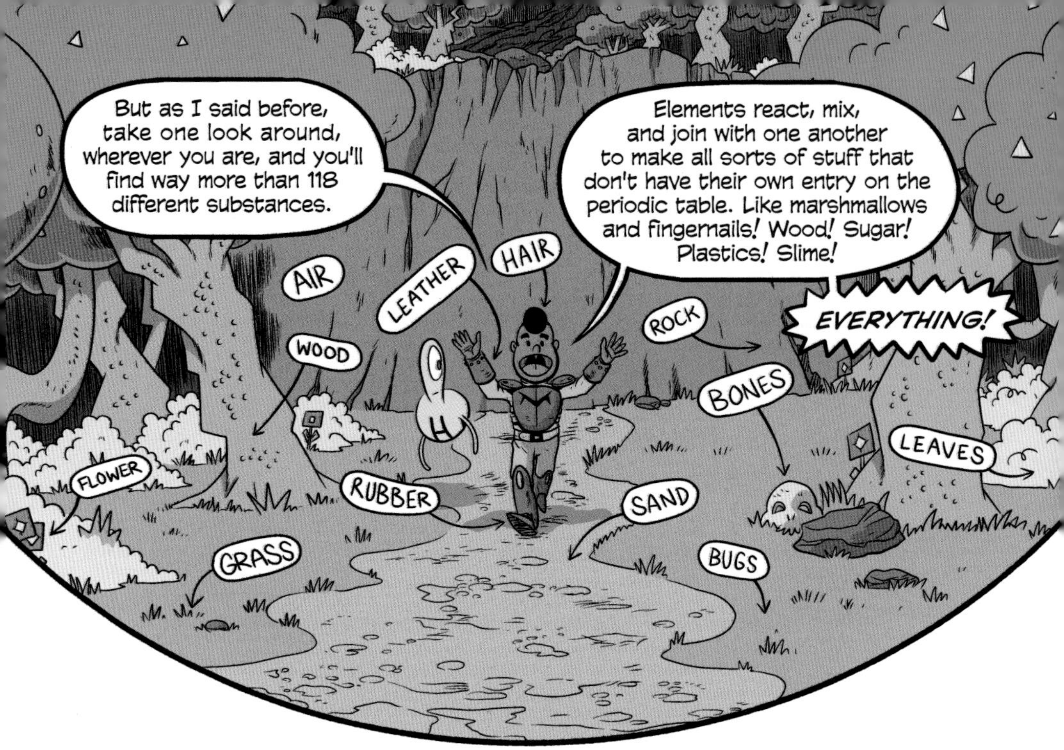

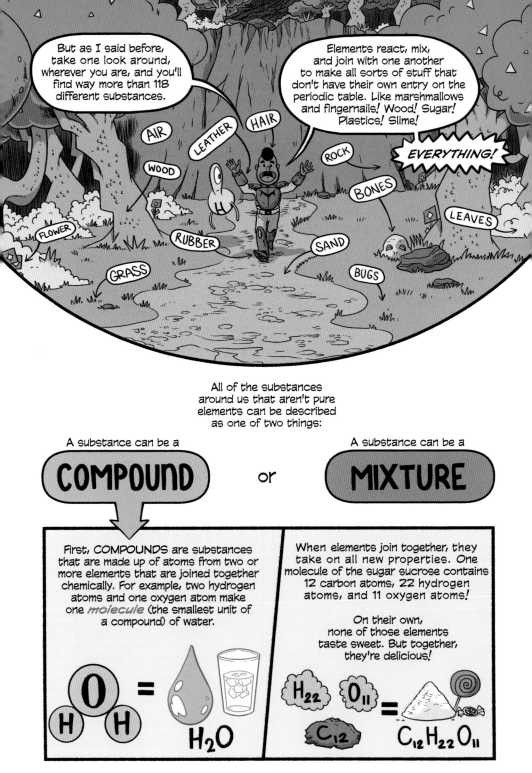

But as I said before, take one look around, wherever you are, and you'll find way more than 118 different substances.
Elements react, mix, and join with one another to make all sorts of stuff that don't have their own entry on the periodic table. Like marshmallows and fingernails! Wood! Sugar! Plastics! Slime!
EVERYTHING!
AIR
LEATHER
HAIR
WOOD
ROCK
BONES
FLOWER
RUBBER
LEAVES
SAND
GRASS
BUGS
H

All of the substances around us that aren't pure elements can be described as one of two things:

A substance can be a **COMPOUND** or A substance can be a **MIXTURE**

First, COMPOUNDS are substances that are made up of atoms from two or more elements that are joined together chemically. For example, two hydrogen atoms and one oxygen atom make one *molecule* (the smallest unit of a compound) of water.

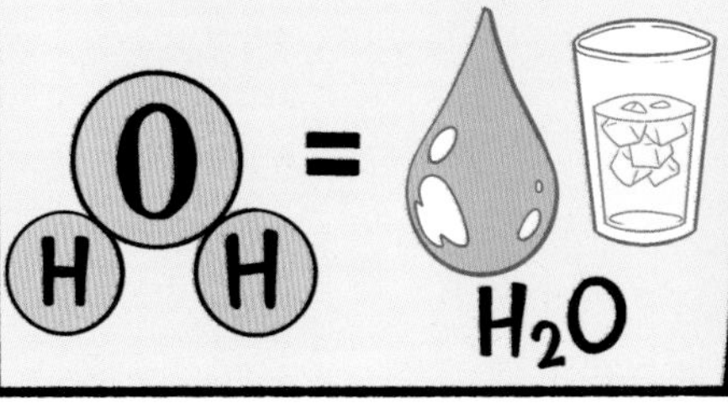

O
H
H
=
H_2O

When elements join together, they take on all new properties. One molecule of the sugar sucrose contains 12 carbon atoms, 22 hydrogen atoms, and 11 oxygen atoms!

On their own, none of those elements taste sweet. But together, they're delicious!

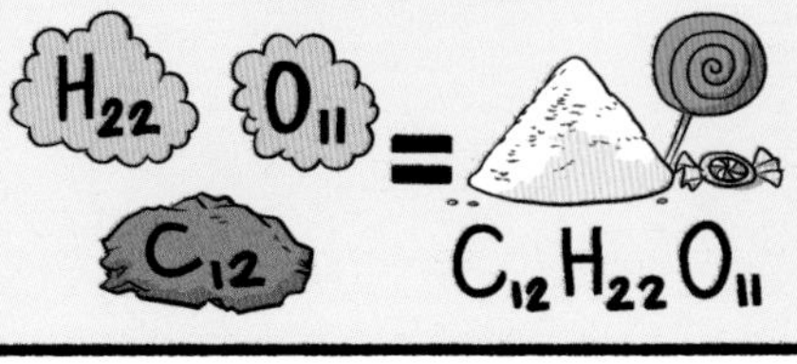

H_{22}
O_{11}
C_{12}
=
$C_{12}H_{22}O_{11}$

COMPOUND

water

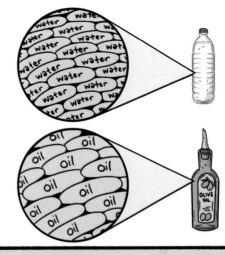

If you look at every single molecule of a compound, they will all be identical, with the same set of atoms—all bonded together the same way.

oil
OLIVE OIL

There are more than **10 MILLION** different types of compounds!
What about mixtures?

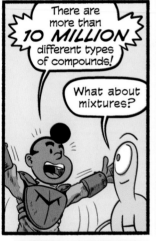

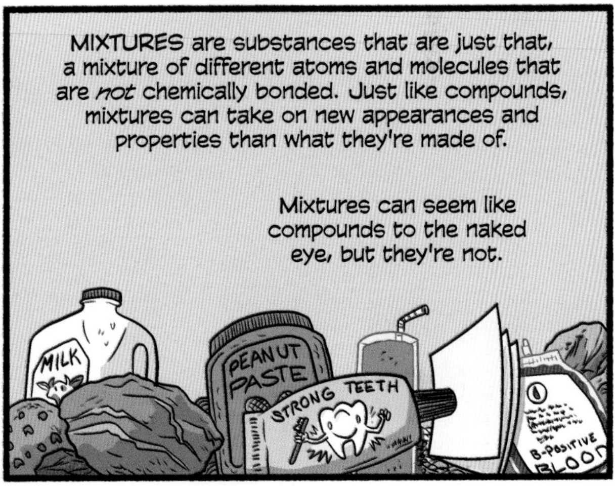

MIXTURES are substances that are just that, a mixture of different atoms and molecules that are *not* chemically bonded. Just like compounds, mixtures can take on new appearances and properties than what they're made of.
Mixtures can seem like compounds to the naked eye, but they're not.
MILK
PEANUT PASTE
STRONG TEETH
B-POSITIVE

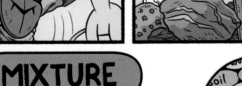

MIXTURE

When you look closely at the molecules that make up a mixture, you will see that *not* every molecule is the same. Some mixtures are substances floating in liquids like water or oil (for example: milk, salad dressing, peanut butter, or oil paints).

soil
water

Other mixtures are tightly packed together and seem like they would be the same throughout, like paper, sand, or chocolate, but look closely and you'll still see the differences in the molecules.

sizing
dye
pulp
glue

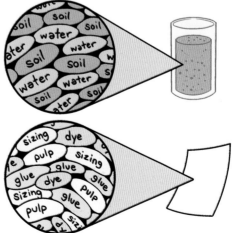

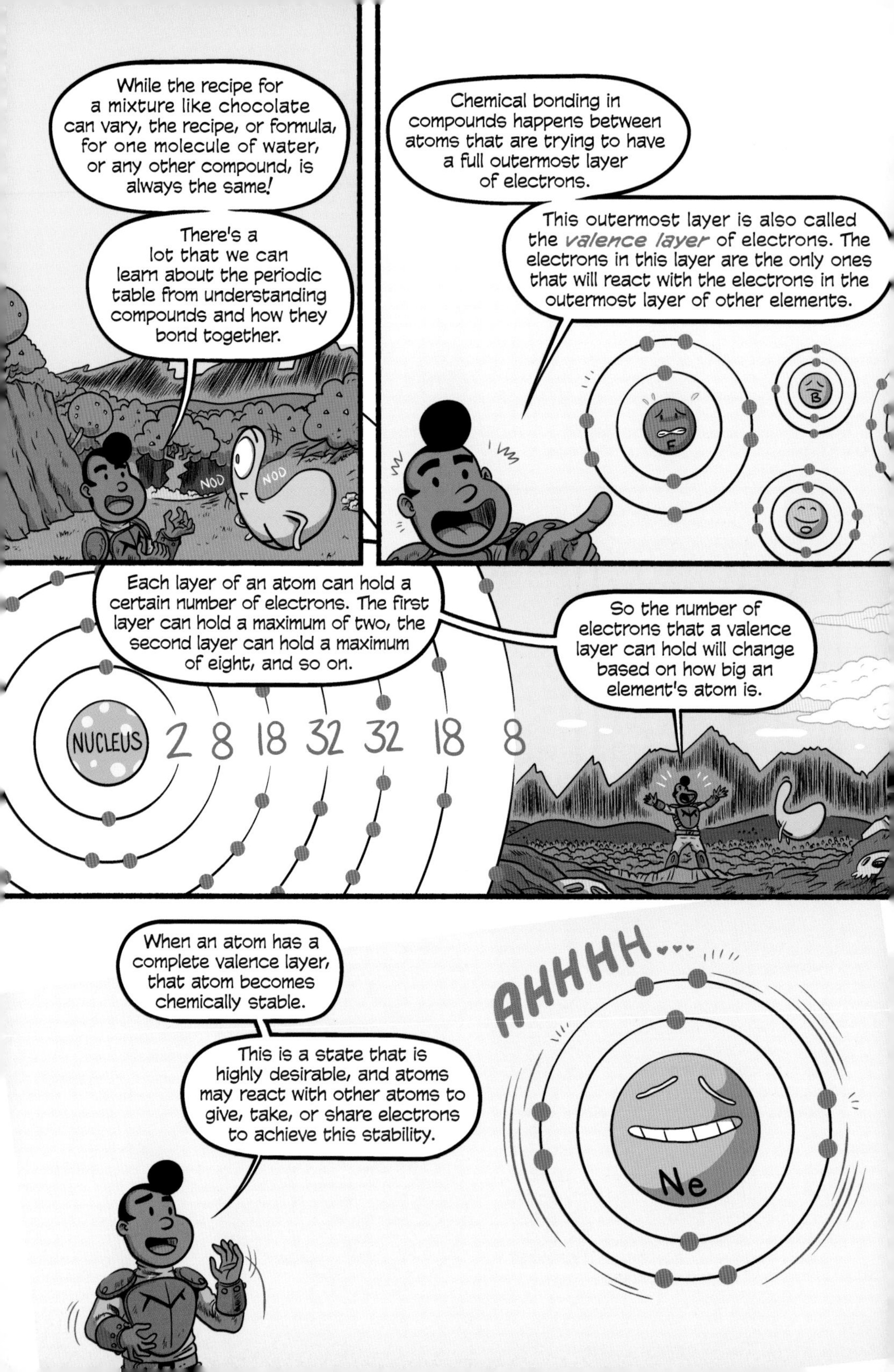
While the recipe for a mixture like chocolate can vary, the recipe, or formula, for one molecule of water, or any other compound, is always the same!
There's a lot that we can learn about the periodic table from understanding compounds and how they bond together.
NOD
NOD
Chemical bonding in compounds happens between atoms that are trying to have a full outermost layer of electrons.
This outermost layer is also called the *valence layer* of electrons. The electrons in this layer are the only ones that will react with the electrons in the outermost layer of other elements.
F
B
Each layer of an atom can hold a certain number of electrons. The first layer can hold a maximum of two, the second layer can hold a maximum of eight, and so on.
NUCLEUS
2 8 18 32 32 18 8
So the number of electrons that a valence layer can hold will change based on how big an element's atom is.
When an atom has a complete valence layer, that atom becomes chemically stable.
This is a state that is highly desirable, and atoms may react with other atoms to give, take, or share electrons to achieve this stability.
AHHHH...
Ne

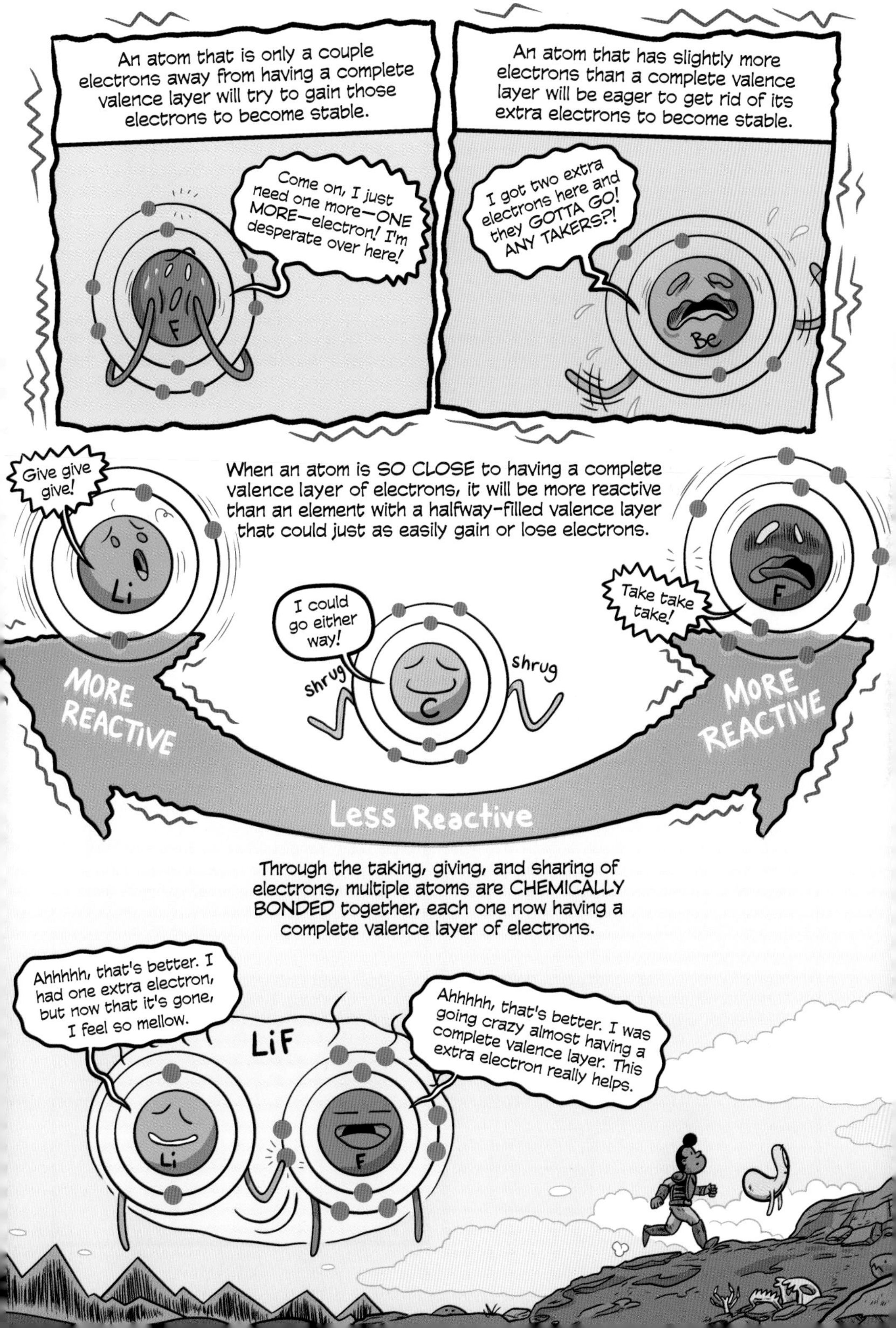

An atom that is only a couple electrons away from having a complete valence layer will try to gain those electrons to become stable.
Come on, I just need one more—ONE MORE—electron! I'm desperate over here!
F
An atom that has slightly more electrons than a complete valence layer will be eager to get rid of its extra electrons to become stable.
I got two extra electrons here and they GOTTA GO! ANY TAKERS?!
Be
When an atom is SO CLOSE to having a complete valence layer of electrons, it will be more reactive than an element with a halfway-filled valence layer that could just as easily gain or lose electrons.
Give give give!
Li
I could go either way!
shrug
C
shrug
Take take take!
F
MORE REACTIVE
MORE REACTIVE
Less Reactive
Through the taking, giving, and sharing of electrons, multiple atoms are CHEMICALLY BONDED together, each one now having a complete valence layer of electrons.
Ahhhhh, that's better. I had one extra electron, but now that it's gone, I feel so mellow.
LiF
Ahhhhh, that's better. I was going crazy almost having a complete valence layer. This extra electron really helps.
Li
F

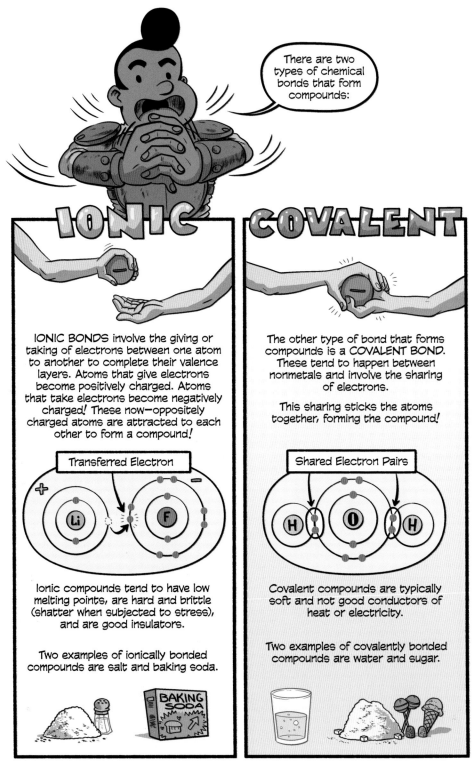

There are two types of chemical bonds that form compounds:

IONIC

IONIC BONDS involve the giving or taking of electrons between one atom to another to complete their valence layers. Atoms that give electrons become positively charged. Atoms that take electrons become negatively charged! These now-oppositely charged atoms are attracted to each other to form a compound!

Transferred Electron

Li   F

Ionic compounds tend to have low melting points, are hard and brittle (shatter when subjected to stress), and are good insulators.

Two examples of ionically bonded compounds are salt and baking soda.

BAKING SODA

COVALENT

The other type of bond that forms compounds is a COVALENT BOND. These tend to happen between nonmetals and involve the sharing of electrons.

This sharing sticks the atoms together, forming the compound!

Shared Electron Pairs

H   O   H

Covalent compounds are typically soft and not good conductors of heat or electricity.

Two examples of covalently bonded compounds are water and sugar.

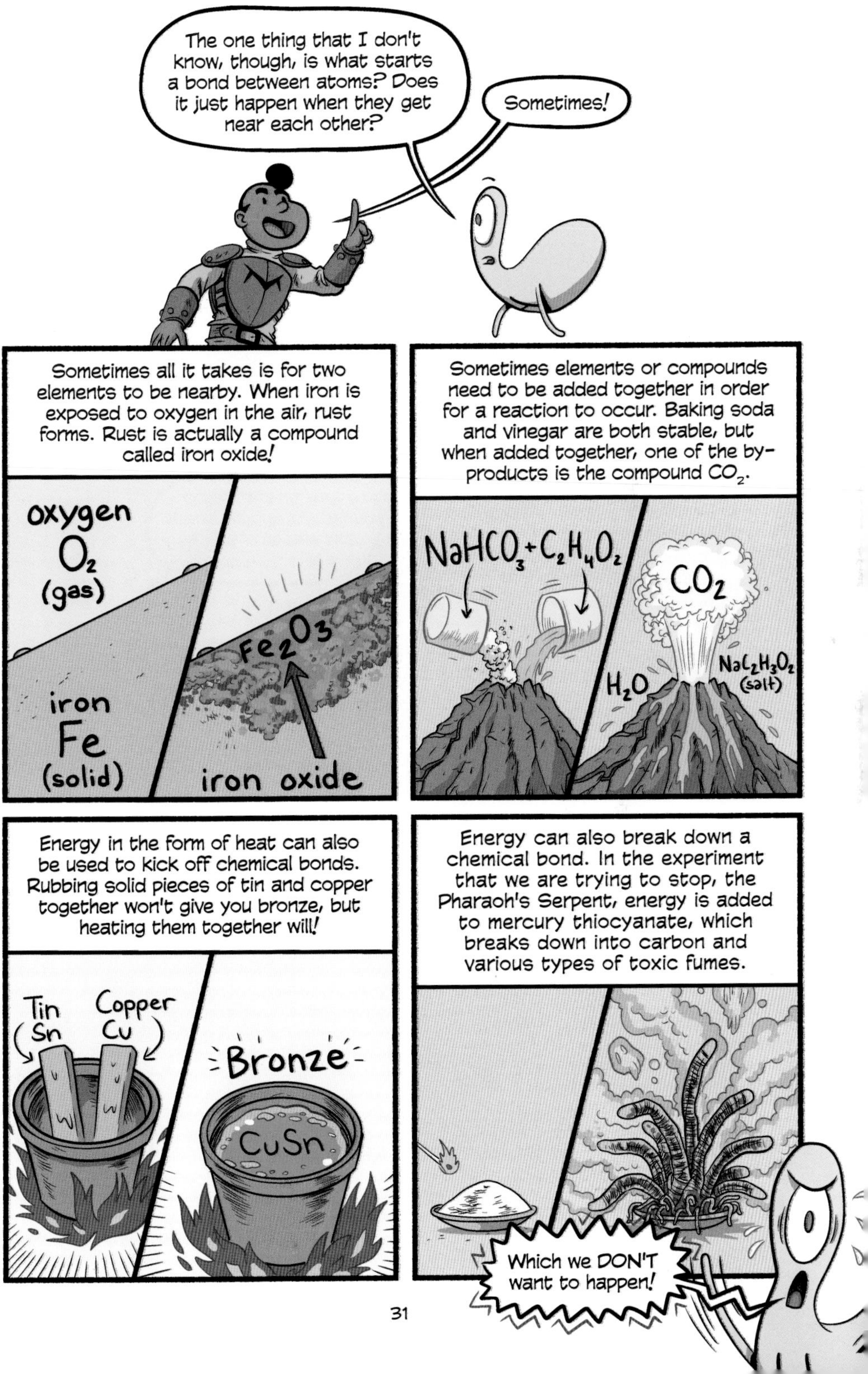
The one thing that I don't know, though, is what starts a bond between atoms? Does it just happen when they get near each other?
Sometimes!
Sometimes all it takes is for two elements to be nearby. When iron is exposed to oxygen in the air, rust forms. Rust is actually a compound called iron oxide!
oxygen
O_2
(gas)
iron
Fe
(solid)
Fe_2O_3
iron oxide
Sometimes elements or compounds need to be added together in order for a reaction to occur. Baking soda and vinegar are both stable, but when added together, one of the by-products is the compound CO_2.
$NaHCO_3 + C_2H_4O_2$
CO_2
H_2O
$NaC_2H_3O_2$
(salt)
Energy in the form of heat can also be used to kick off chemical bonds. Rubbing solid pieces of tin and copper together won't give you bronze, but heating them together will!
Tin
Sn
Copper
Cu
Bronze
CuSn
Energy can also break down a chemical bond. In the experiment that we are trying to stop, the Pharaoh's Serpent, energy is added to mercury thiocyanate, which breaks down into carbon and various types of toxic fumes.
Which we DON'T want to happen!

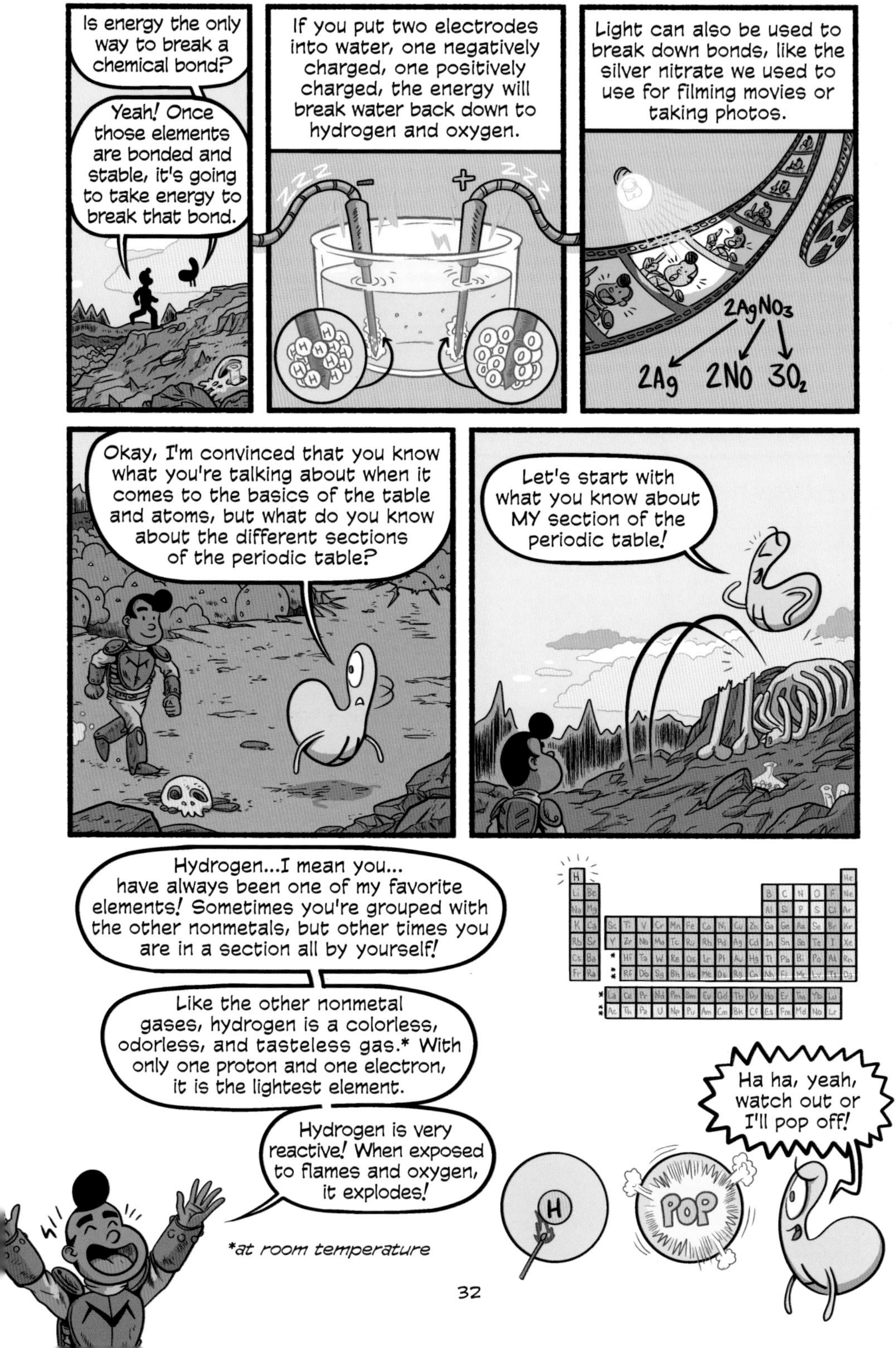

Is energy the only way to break a chemical bond?
Yeah! Once those elements are bonded and stable, it's going to take energy to break that bond.
If you put two electrodes into water, one negatively charged, one positively charged, the energy will break water back down to hydrogen and oxygen.
ZZZ
ZZZ
H
O
Light can also be used to break down bonds, like the silver nitrate we used to use for filming movies or taking photos.
2AgNO3
2Ag 2NO 3O2
Okay, I'm convinced that you know what you're talking about when it comes to the basics of the table and atoms, but what do you know about the different sections of the periodic table?
Let's start with what you know about MY section of the periodic table!
Hydrogen...I mean you... have always been one of my favorite elements! Sometimes you're grouped with the other nonmetals, but other times you are in a section all by yourself!
Like the other nonmetal gases, hydrogen is a colorless, odorless, and tasteless gas.* With only one proton and one electron, it is the lightest element.
Hydrogen is very reactive! When exposed to flames and oxygen, it explodes!
H
POP
Ha ha, yeah, watch out or I'll pop off!
*at room temperature

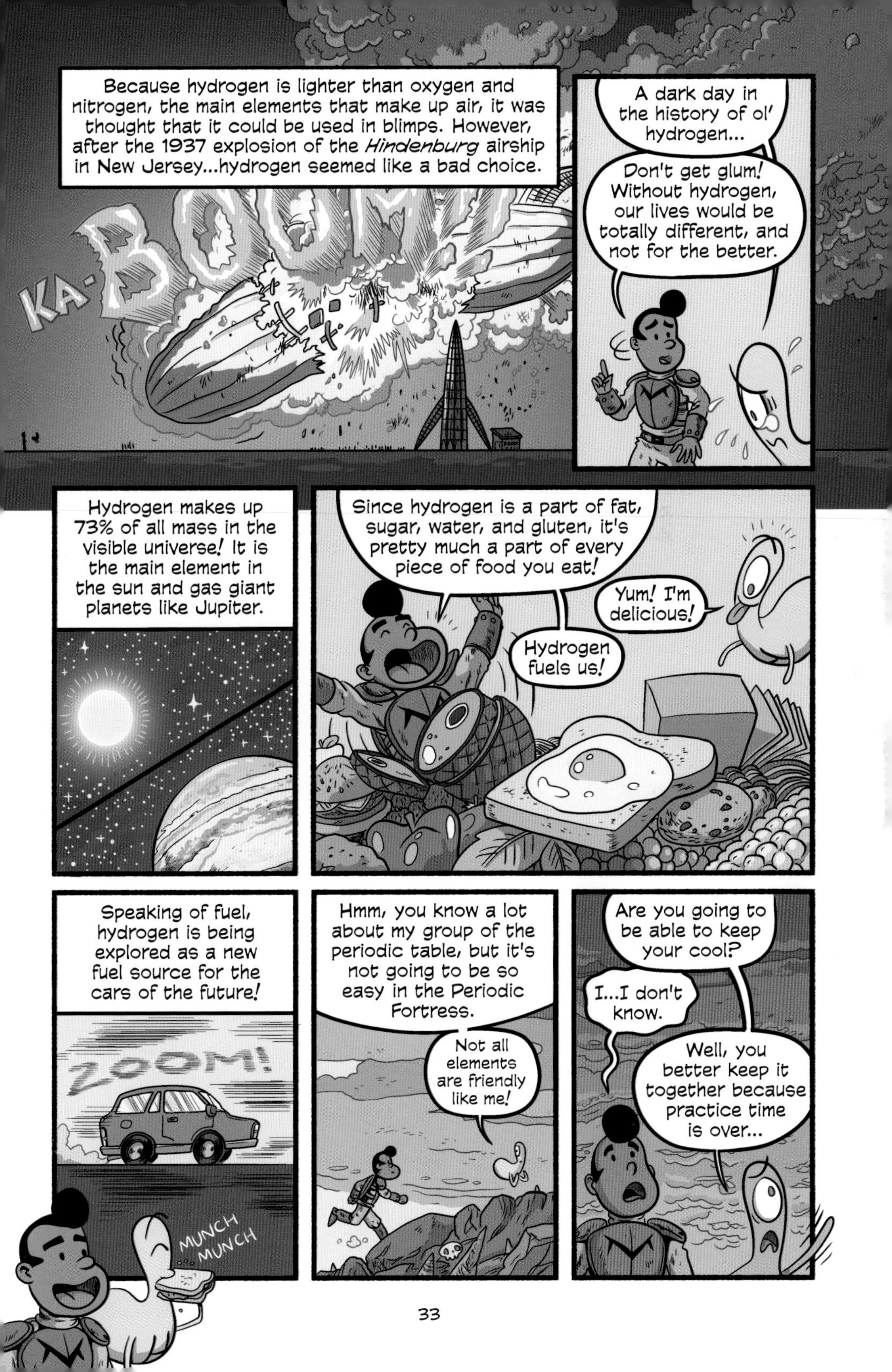
Because hydrogen is lighter than oxygen and nitrogen, the main elements that make up air, it was thought that it could be used in blimps. However, after the 1937 explosion of the *Hindenburg* airship in New Jersey...hydrogen seemed like a bad choice.
KA-BOOM!
A dark day in the history of ol' hydrogen...
Don't get glum! Without hydrogen, our lives would be totally different, and not for the better.
Hydrogen makes up 73% of all mass in the visible universe! It is the main element in the sun and gas giant planets like Jupiter.
Since hydrogen is a part of fat, sugar, water, and gluten, it's pretty much a part of every piece of food you eat!
Yum! I'm delicious!
Hydrogen fuels us!
Speaking of fuel, hydrogen is being explored as a new fuel source for the cars of the future!
ZOOM!
MUNCH MUNCH
Hmm, you know a lot about my group of the periodic table, but it's not going to be so easy in the Periodic Fortress.
Not all elements are friendly like me!
Are you going to be able to keep your cool?
I...I don't know.
Well, you better keep it together because practice time is over...

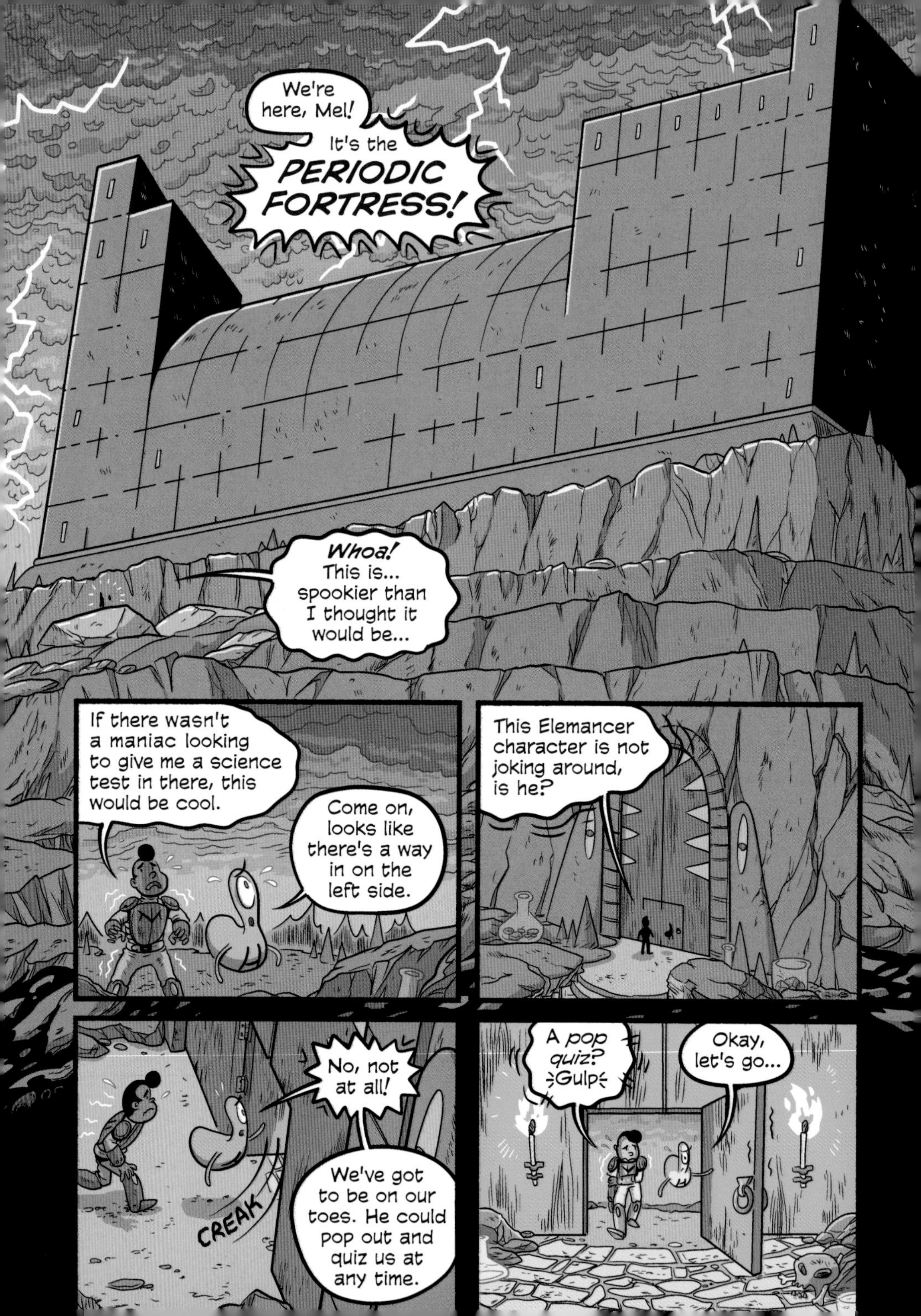
We're here, Mel!
It's the PERIODIC FORTRESS!
Whoa! This is... spookier than I thought it would be...
If there wasn't a maniac looking to give me a science test in there, this would be cool.
Come on, looks like there's a way in on the left side.
This Elemancer character is not joking around, is he?
No, not at all!
We've got to be on our toes. He could pop out and quiz us at any time.
CREAK
A pop quiz? Gulp
Okay, let's go...

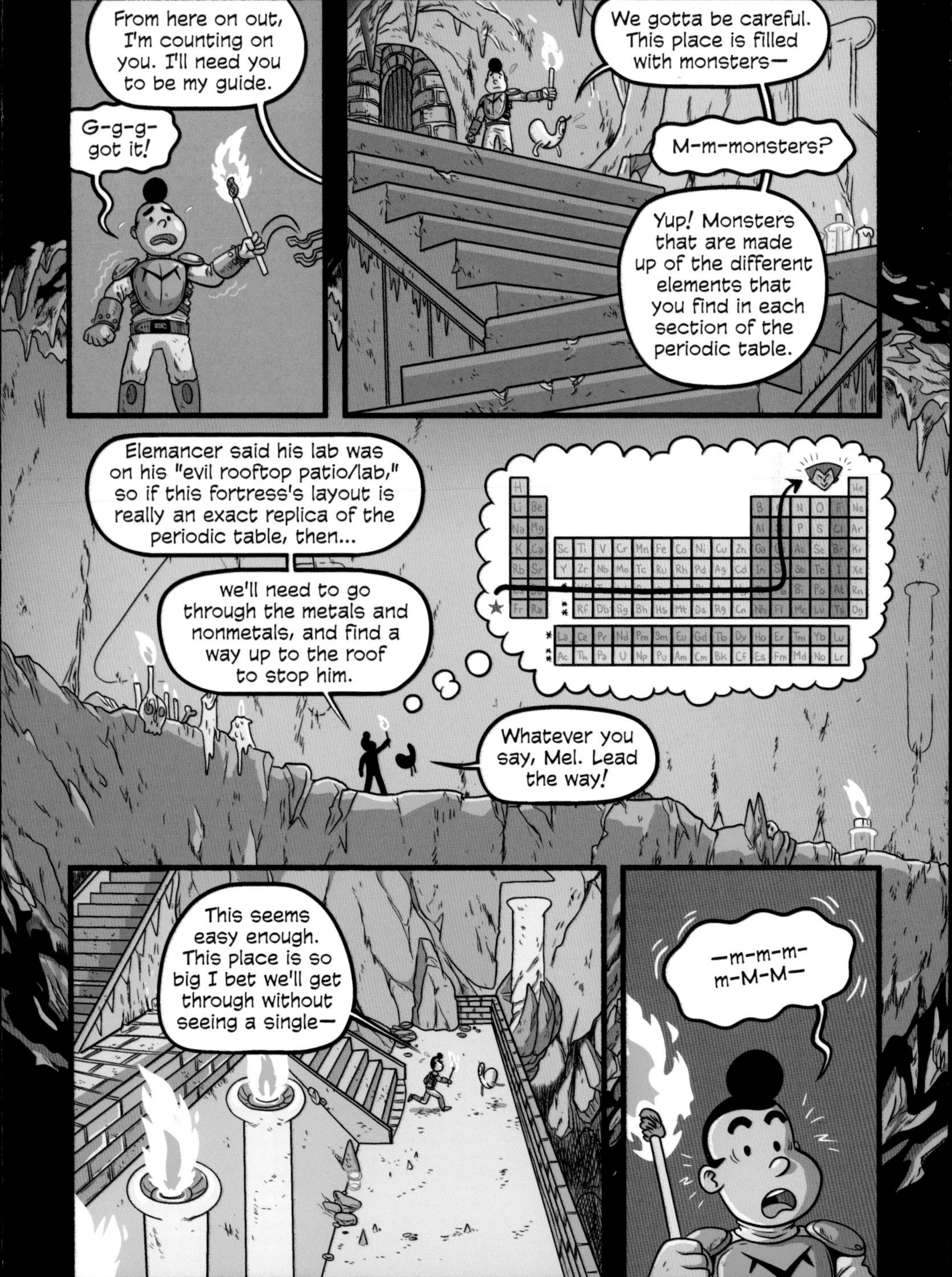
From here on out, I'm counting on you. I'll need you to be my guide.
G-g-g-got it!
We gotta be careful. This place is filled with monsters—
M-m-monsters?
Yup! Monsters that are made up of the different elements that you find in each section of the periodic table.
Elemancer said his lab was on his "evil rooftop patio/lab," so if this fortress's layout is really an exact replica of the periodic table, then...
we'll need to go through the metals and nonmetals, and find a way up to the roof to stop him.
Whatever you say, Mel. Lead the way!
This seems easy enough. This place is so big I bet we'll get through without seeing a single—
—m-m-m-m-M-M—

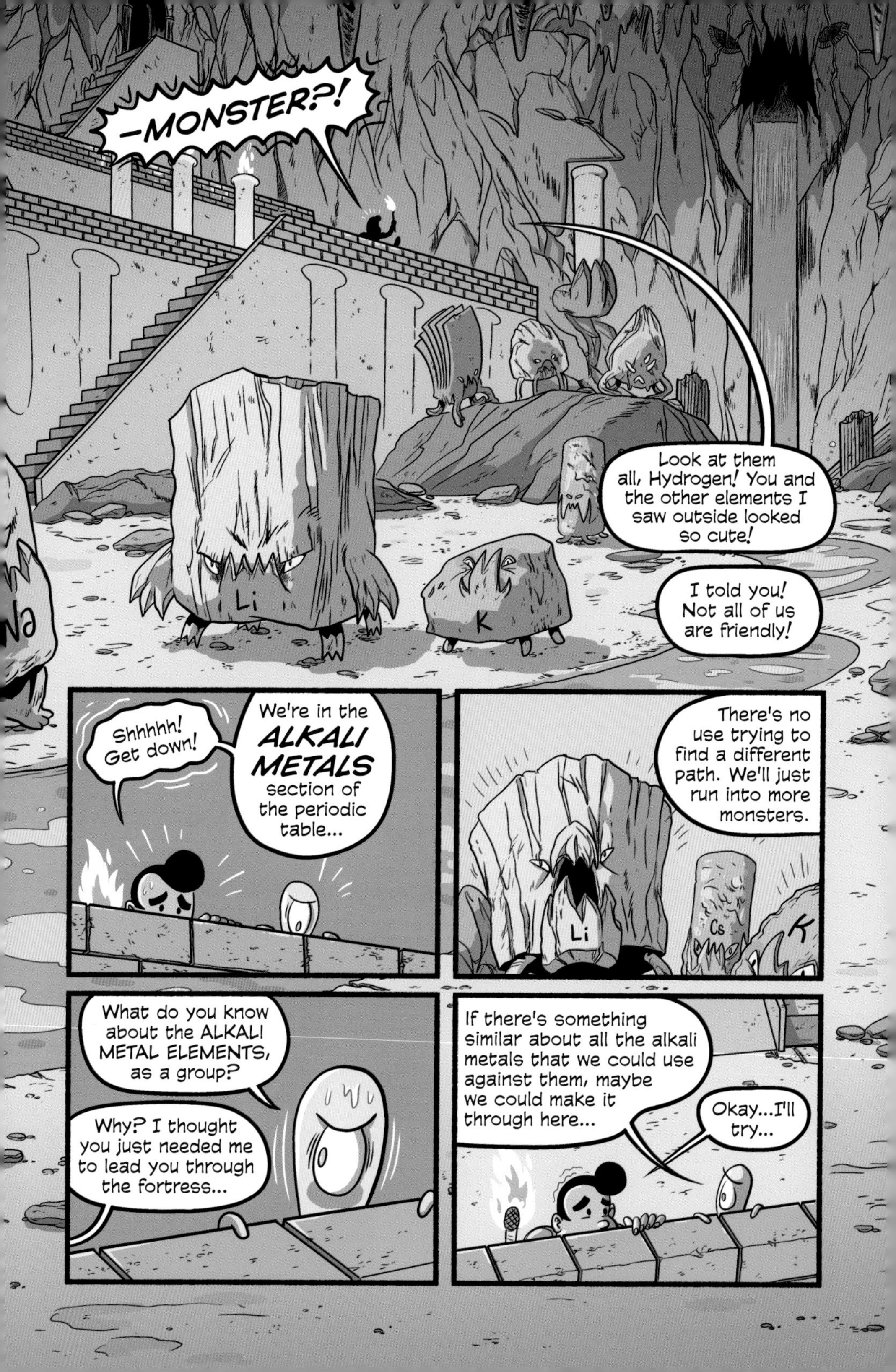
—MONSTER?!
Look at them all, Hydrogen! You and the other elements I saw outside looked so cute!
I told you! Not all of us are friendly!
Li
K
Na
Shhhhh! Get down!
We're in the ALKALI METALS section of the periodic table...
There's no use trying to find a different path. We'll just run into more monsters.
Li
Cs
K
What do you know about the ALKALI METAL ELEMENTS, as a group?
Why? I thought you just needed me to lead you through the fortress...
If there's something similar about all the alkali metals that we could use against them, maybe we could make it through here...
Okay...I'll try...

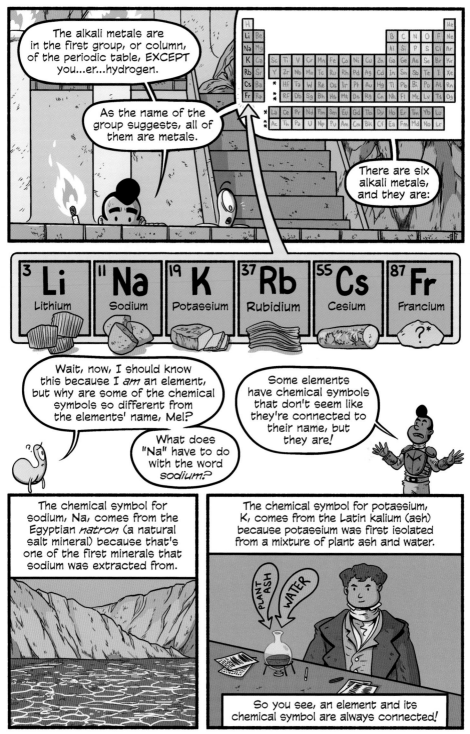

The alkali metals are in the first group, or column, of the periodic table, EXCEPT you...er...hydrogen.

As the name of the group suggests, all of them are metals.

There are six alkali metals, and they are:

3 Li Lithium

11 Na Sodium

19 K Potassium

37 Rb Rubidium

55 Cs Cesium

87 Fr Francium ?*

Wait, now, I should know this because I *am* an element, but why are some of the chemical symbols so different from the elements' name, Mel?

What does "Na" have to do with the word *sodium*?

Some elements have chemical symbols that don't seem like they're connected to their name, but they are!

The chemical symbol for sodium, Na, comes from the Egyptian *natron* (a natural salt mineral) because that's one of the first minerals that sodium was extracted from.

The chemical symbol for potassium, K, comes from the Latin kalium (ash) because potassium was first isolated from a mixture of plant ash and water.

PLANT ASH   WATER

So you see, an element and its chemical symbol are always connected!

*So little of this element has ever existed that we don't even really know what it looks like!

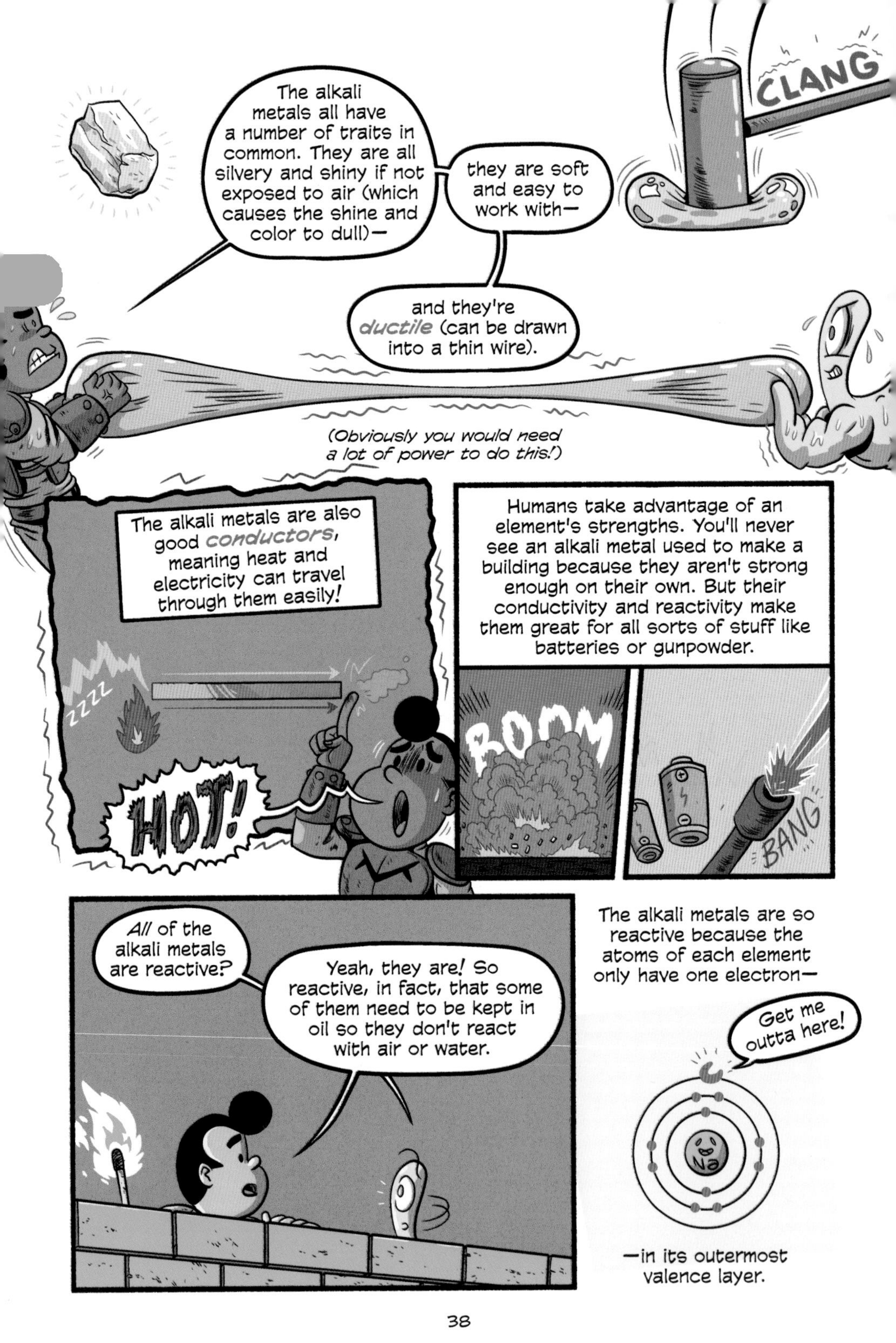
The alkali metals all have a number of traits in common. They are all silvery and shiny if not exposed to air (which causes the shine and color to dull)—
they are soft and easy to work with—
CLANG
and they're *ductile* (can be drawn into a thin wire).
(Obviously you would need a lot of power to do this!)
The alkali metals are also good *conductors*, meaning heat and electricity can travel through them easily!
ZZZZ
HOT!
Humans take advantage of an element's strengths. You'll never see an alkali metal used to make a building because they aren't strong enough on their own. But their conductivity and reactivity make them great for all sorts of stuff like batteries or gunpowder.
BOOM
BANG
All of the alkali metals are reactive?
Yeah, they are! So reactive, in fact, that some of them need to be kept in oil so they don't react with air or water.
The alkali metals are so reactive because the atoms of each element only have one electron—
Get me outta here!
Na
—in its outermost valence layer.

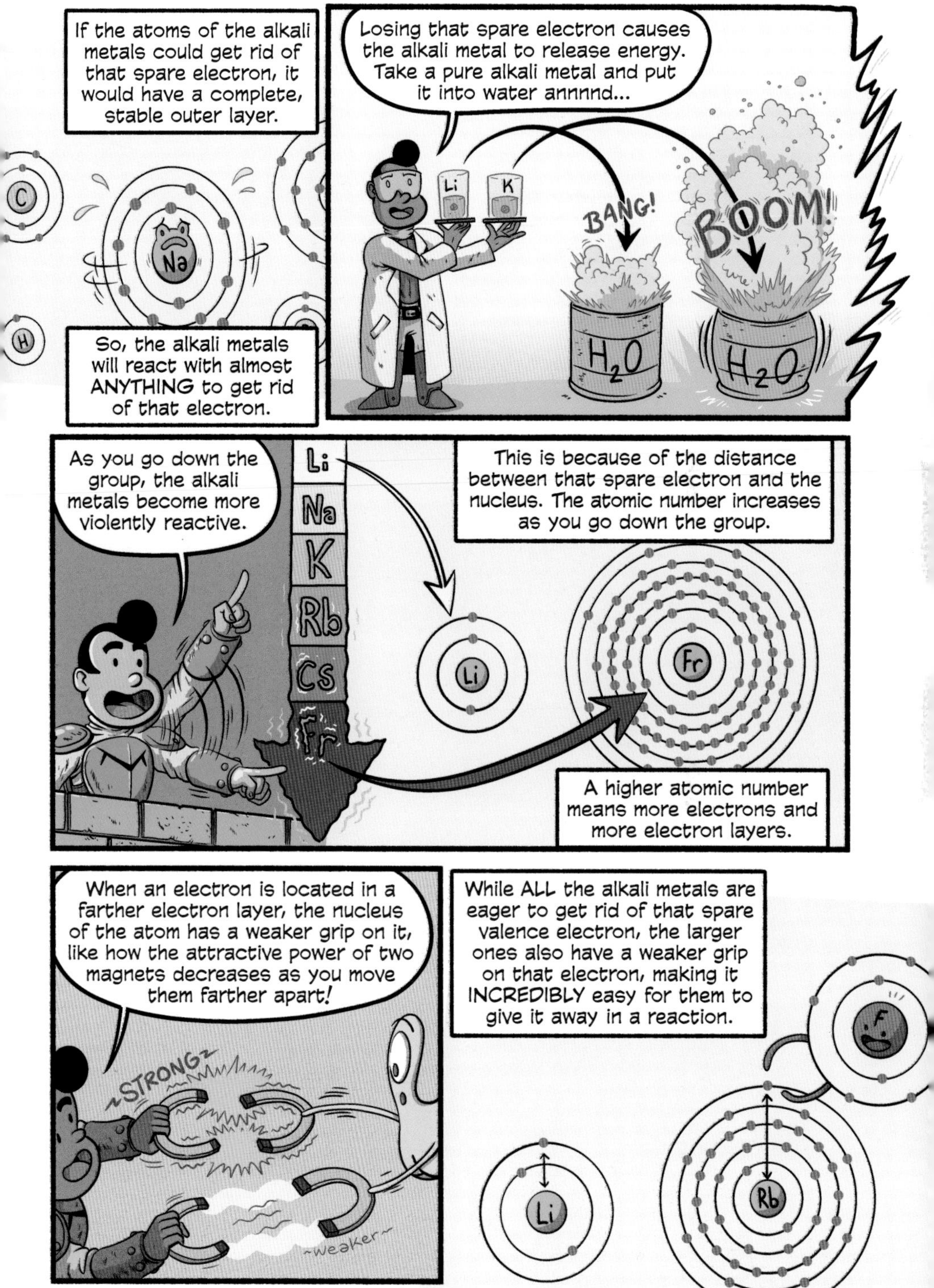
If the atoms of the alkali metals could get rid of that spare electron, it would have a complete, stable outer layer.
C
Na
H
So, the alkali metals will react with almost ANYTHING to get rid of that electron.
Losing that spare electron causes the alkali metal to release energy. Take a pure alkali metal and put it into water annnnd...
Li
K
BANG!
BOOM!
H2O
H2O
As you go down the group, the alkali metals become more violently reactive.
Li
Na
K
Rb
Cs
Fr
This is because of the distance between that spare electron and the nucleus. The atomic number increases as you go down the group.
Li
Fr
A higher atomic number means more electrons and more electron layers.
When an electron is located in a farther electron layer, the nucleus of the atom has a weaker grip on it, like how the attractive power of two magnets decreases as you move them farther apart!
STRONG
~Weaker~
While ALL the alkali metals are eager to get rid of that spare valence electron, the larger ones also have a weaker grip on that electron, making it INCREDIBLY easy for them to give it away in a reaction.
F
Li
Rb

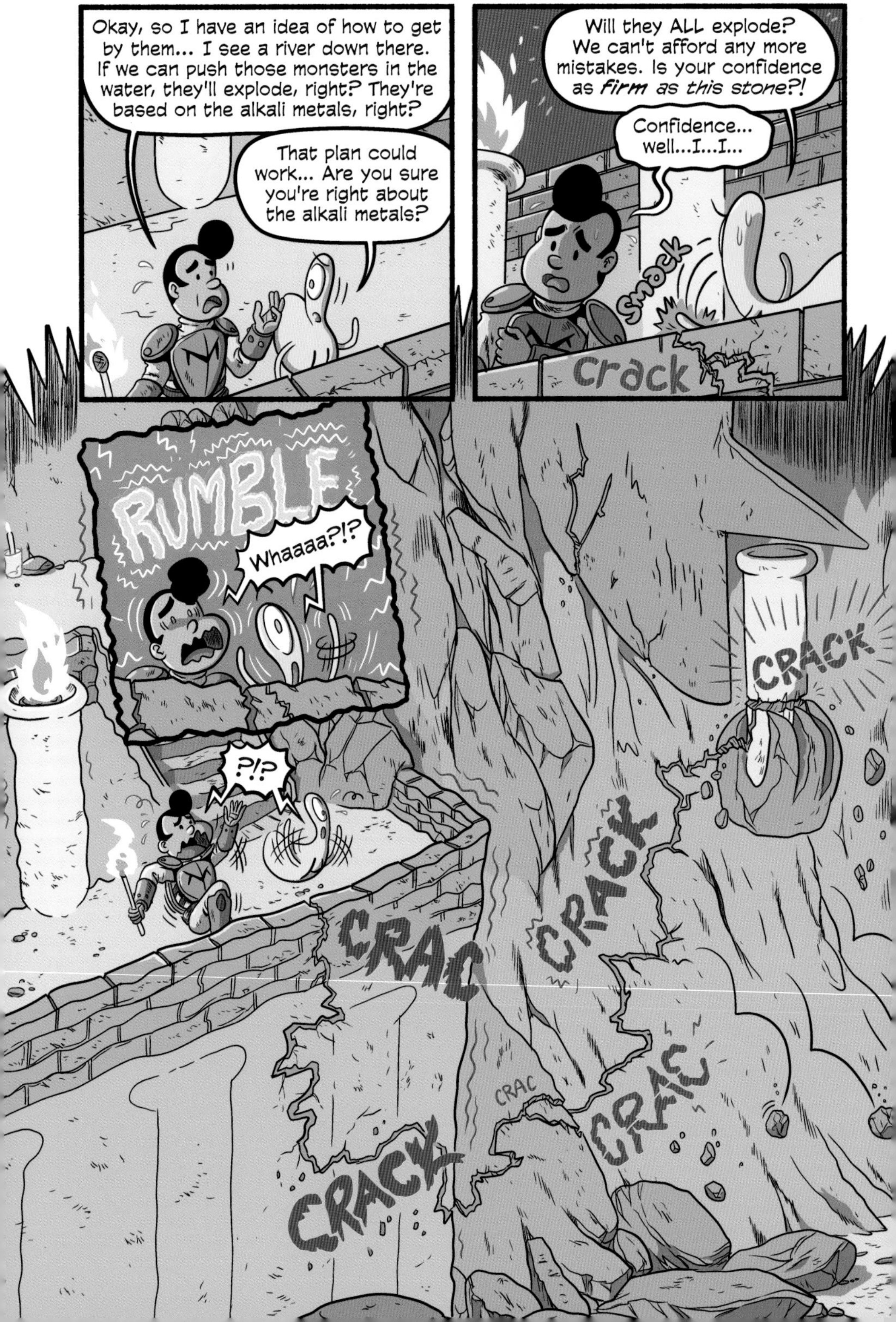

Okay, so I have an idea of how to get by them... I see a river down there. If we can push those monsters in the water, they'll explode, right? They're based on the alkali metals, right?
That plan could work... Are you sure you're right about the alkali metals?
Will they ALL explode? We can't afford any more mistakes. Is your confidence as *firm as this stone*?!
Confidence... well...I...I...
Smack
crack
RUMBLE
Whaaaa?!?
?!?
CRACK
CRAC
CRACK
CRACK
CRAC
CRAC
CRACK

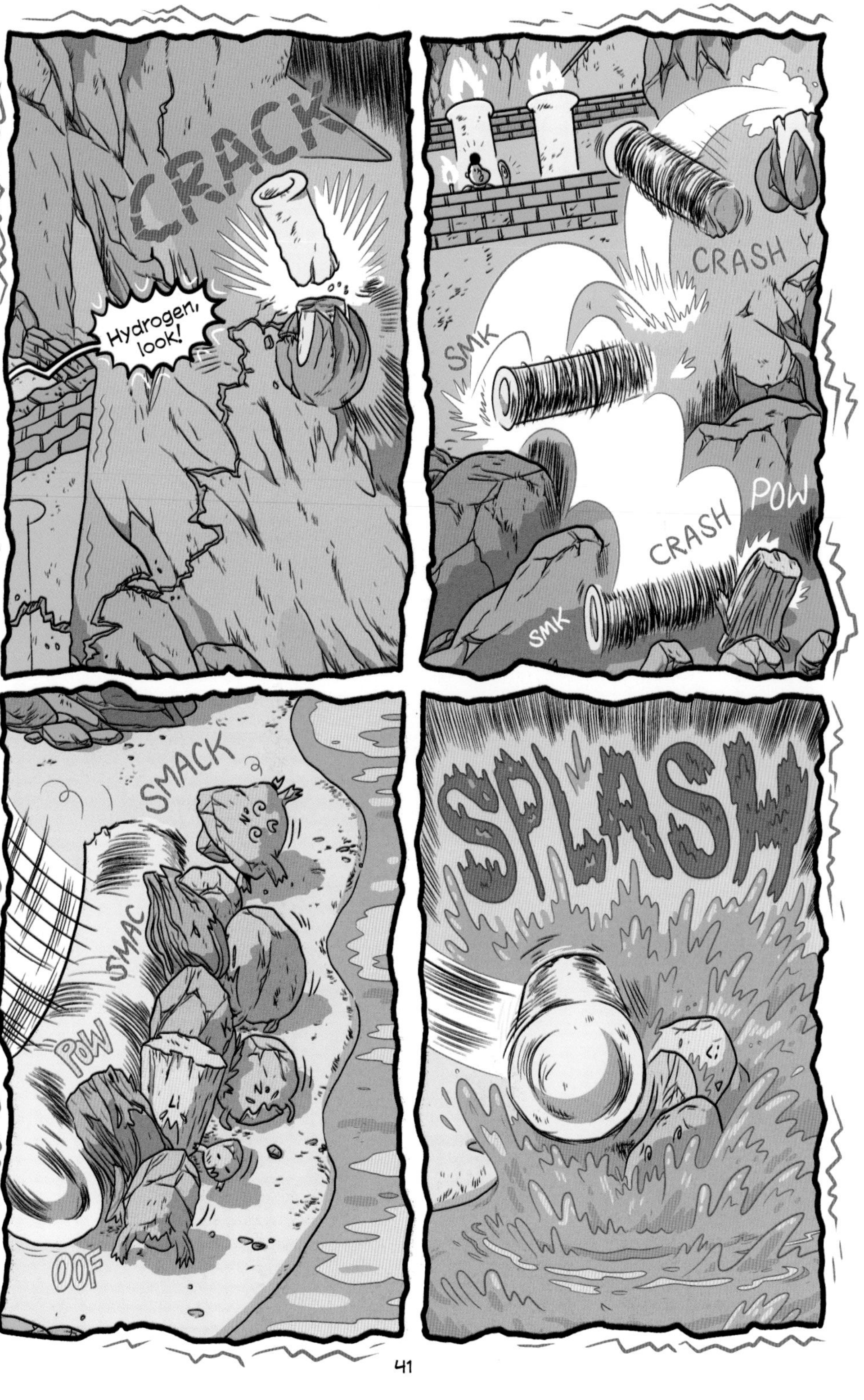
CRACK
Hydrogen, look!
CRASH
SMK
CRASH
POW
SMK
SMACK
SMAC
POW
OOF
SPLASH

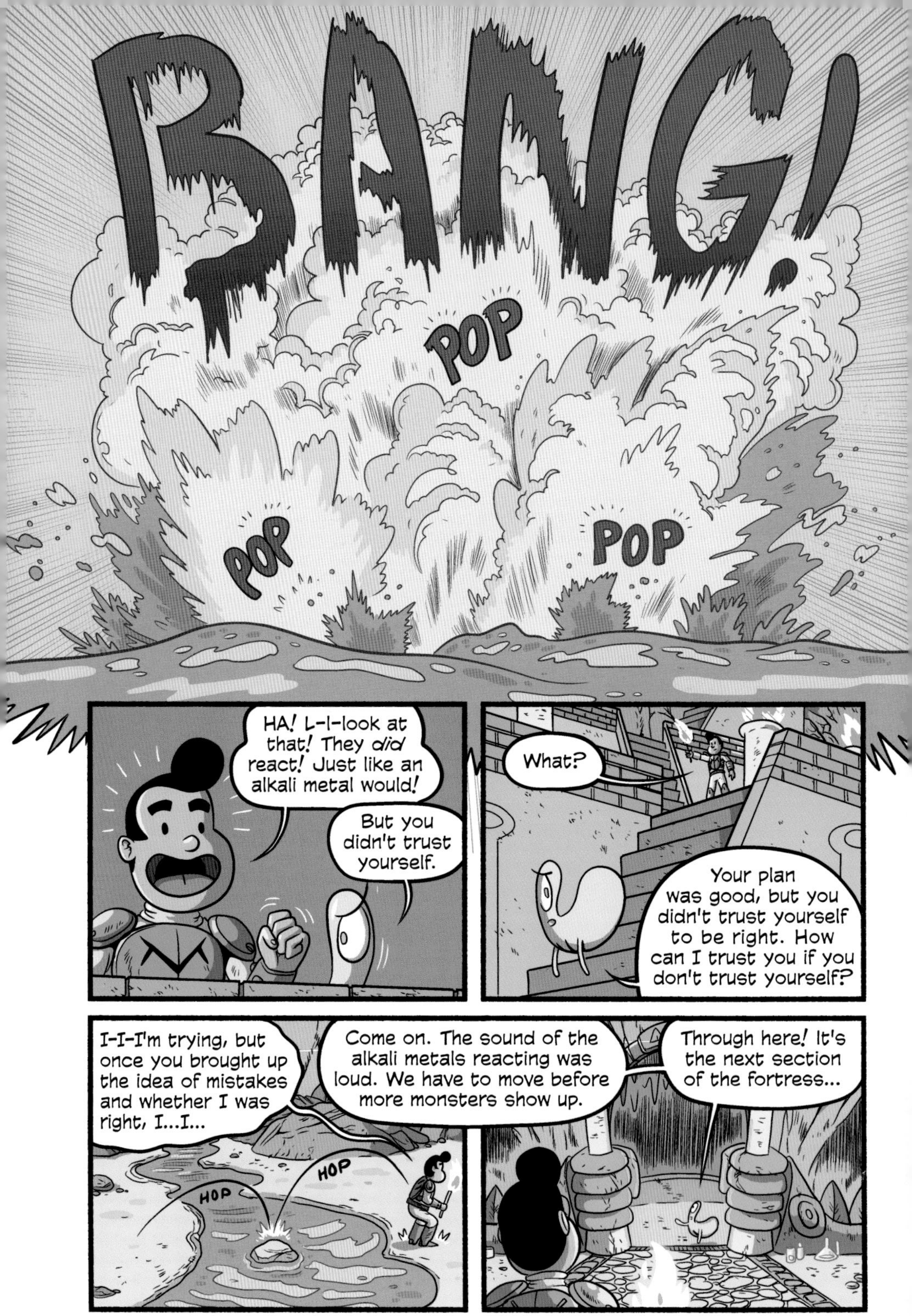
BANG!
POP
POP
POP
HA! L-l-look at that! They did react! Just like an alkali metal would!
But you didn't trust yourself.
What?
Your plan was good, but you didn't trust yourself to be right. How can I trust you if you don't trust yourself?
I-I-I'm trying, but once you brought up the idea of mistakes and whether I was right, I...I...
HOP
HOP
Come on. The sound of the alkali metals reacting was loud. We have to move before more monsters show up.
Through here! It's the next section of the fortress...

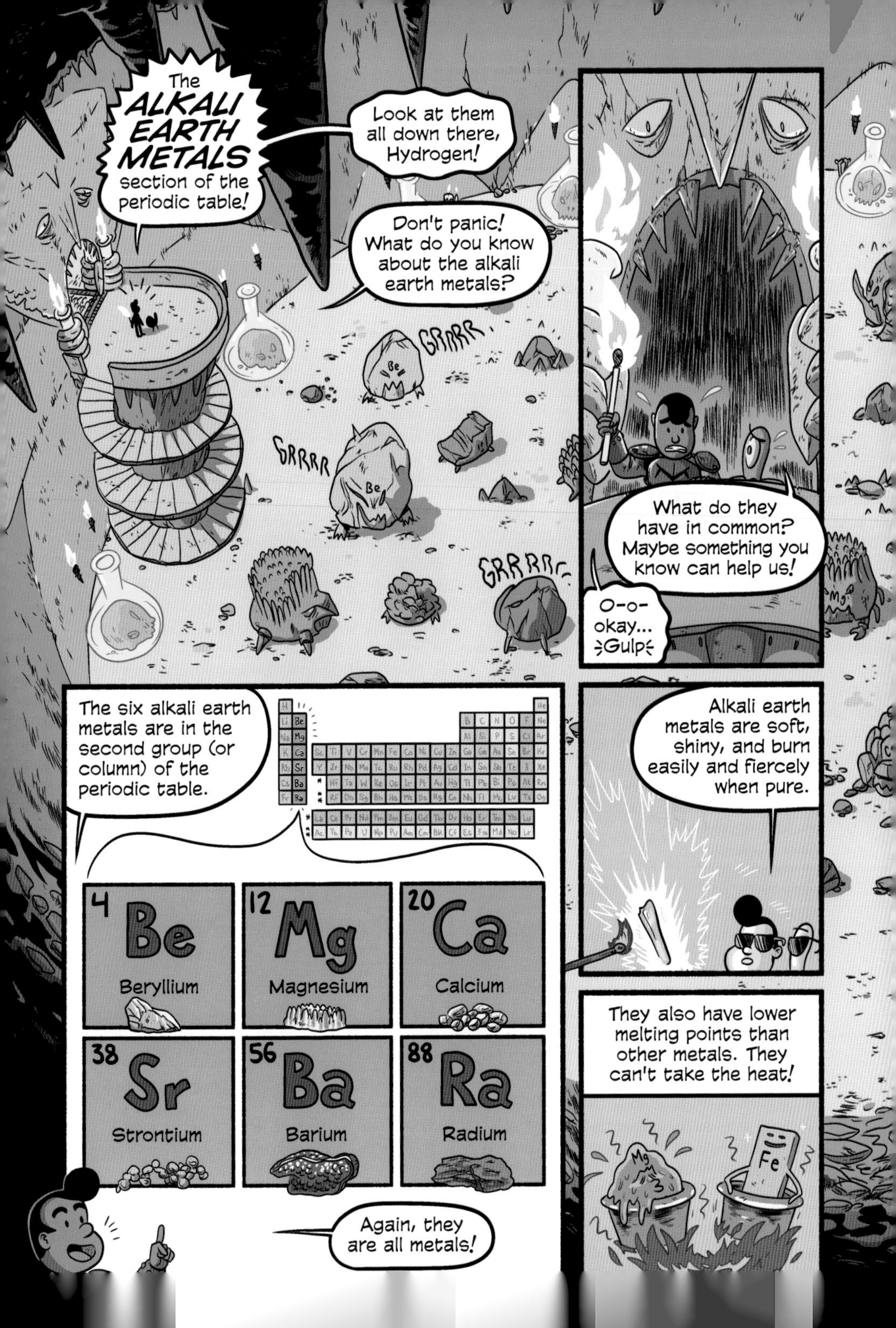
The ALKALI EARTH METALS section of the periodic table!
Look at them all down there, Hydrogen!
Don't panic! What do you know about the alkali earth metals?
GRRRR
Be
GRRRR
Be
GRRRRR
What do they have in common? Maybe something you know can help us!
O-o-okay... Gulp
The six alkali earth metals are in the second group (or column) of the periodic table.
4 Be Beryllium
12 Mg Magnesium
20 Ca Calcium
38 Sr Strontium
56 Ba Barium
88 Ra Radium
Again, they are all metals!
Alkali earth metals are soft, shiny, and burn easily and fiercely when pure.
They also have lower melting points than other metals. They can't take the heat!
Mg
Fe

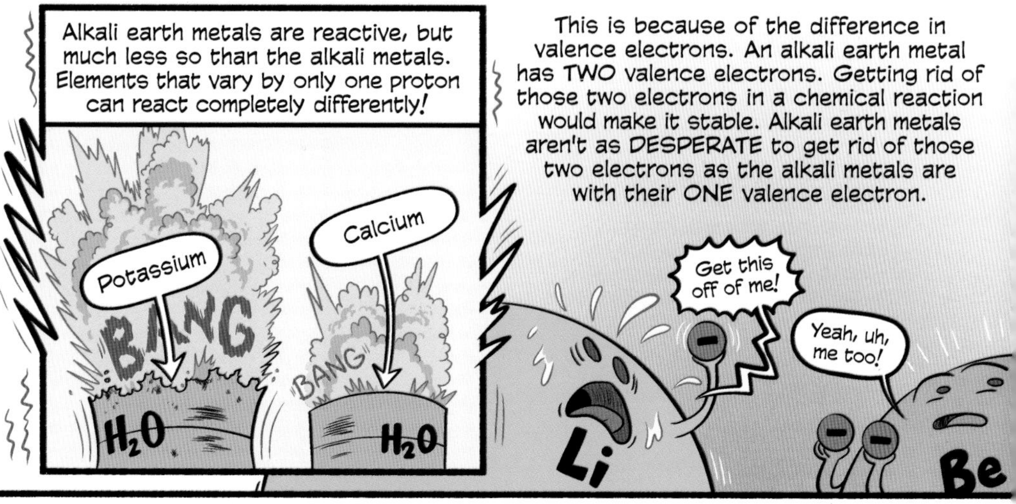
Alkali earth metals are reactive, but much less so than the alkali metals. Elements that vary by only one proton can react completely differently!
Potassium
BANG
H_2O
Calcium
BANG
H_2O
This is because of the difference in valence electrons. An alkali earth metal has TWO valence electrons. Getting rid of those two electrons in a chemical reaction would make it stable. Alkali earth metals aren't as DESPERATE to get rid of those two electrons as the alkali metals are with their ONE valence electron.
Get this off of me!
Yeah, uh, me too!
Li
Be

And the alkali earth metals hold those two valence electrons a little tighter than the alkali metals do to their one electron. A tighter grip on your valence electrons means an element is less reactive.

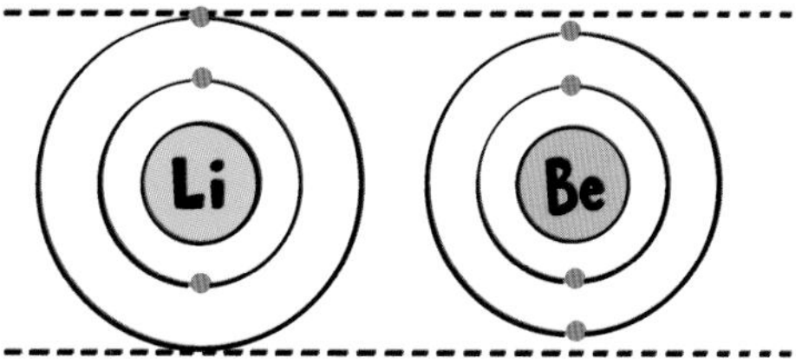
Li
Be
Lithium
Beryllium

Also, because of that grip, the alkali earth metals are slightly smaller than the alkali metals, despite having more protons and electrons.

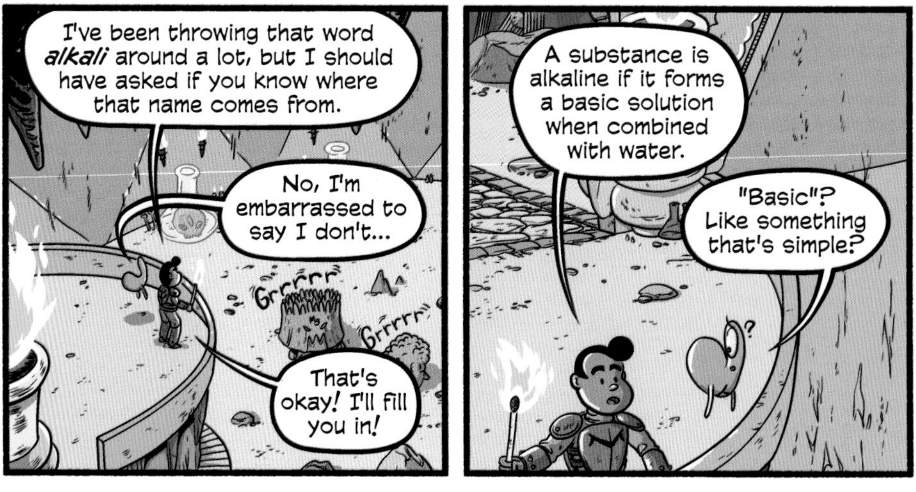
I've been throwing that word *alkali* around a lot, but I should have asked if you know where that name comes from.
No, I'm embarrassed to say I don't...
Grrrrr
Grrrr
That's okay! I'll fill you in!
A substance is alkaline if it forms a basic solution when combined with water.
"Basic"? Like something that's simple?
?

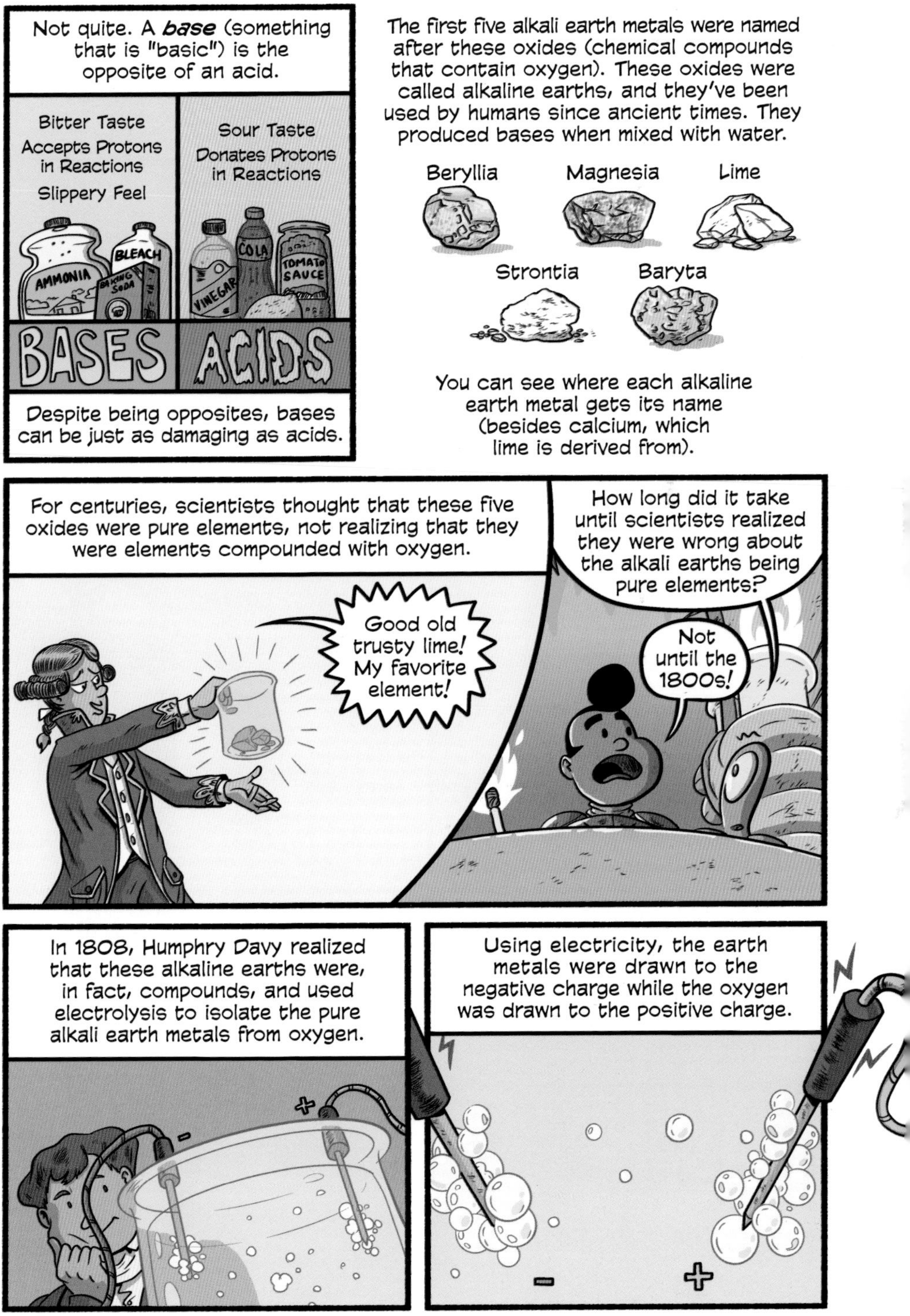
Not quite. A *base* (something that is "basic") is the opposite of an acid.
Bitter Taste
Accepts Protons in Reactions
Slippery Feel
AMMONIA
BAKING SODA
BLEACH
Sour Taste
Donates Protons in Reactions
VINEGAR
COLA
TOMATO SAUCE
BASES
ACIDS
Despite being opposites, bases can be just as damaging as acids.
The first five alkali earth metals were named after these oxides (chemical compounds that contain oxygen). These oxides were called alkaline earths, and they've been used by humans since ancient times. They produced bases when mixed with water.
Beryllia
Magnesia
Lime
Strontia
Baryta
You can see where each alkaline earth metal gets its name (besides calcium, which lime is derived from).
For centuries, scientists thought that these five oxides were pure elements, not realizing that they were elements compounded with oxygen.
Good old trusty lime! My favorite element!
How long did it take until scientists realized they were wrong about the alkali earths being pure elements?
Not until the 1800s!
In 1808, Humphry Davy realized that these alkaline earths were, in fact, compounds, and used electrolysis to isolate the pure alkali earth metals from oxygen.
Using electricity, the earth metals were drawn to the negative charge while the oxygen was drawn to the positive charge.

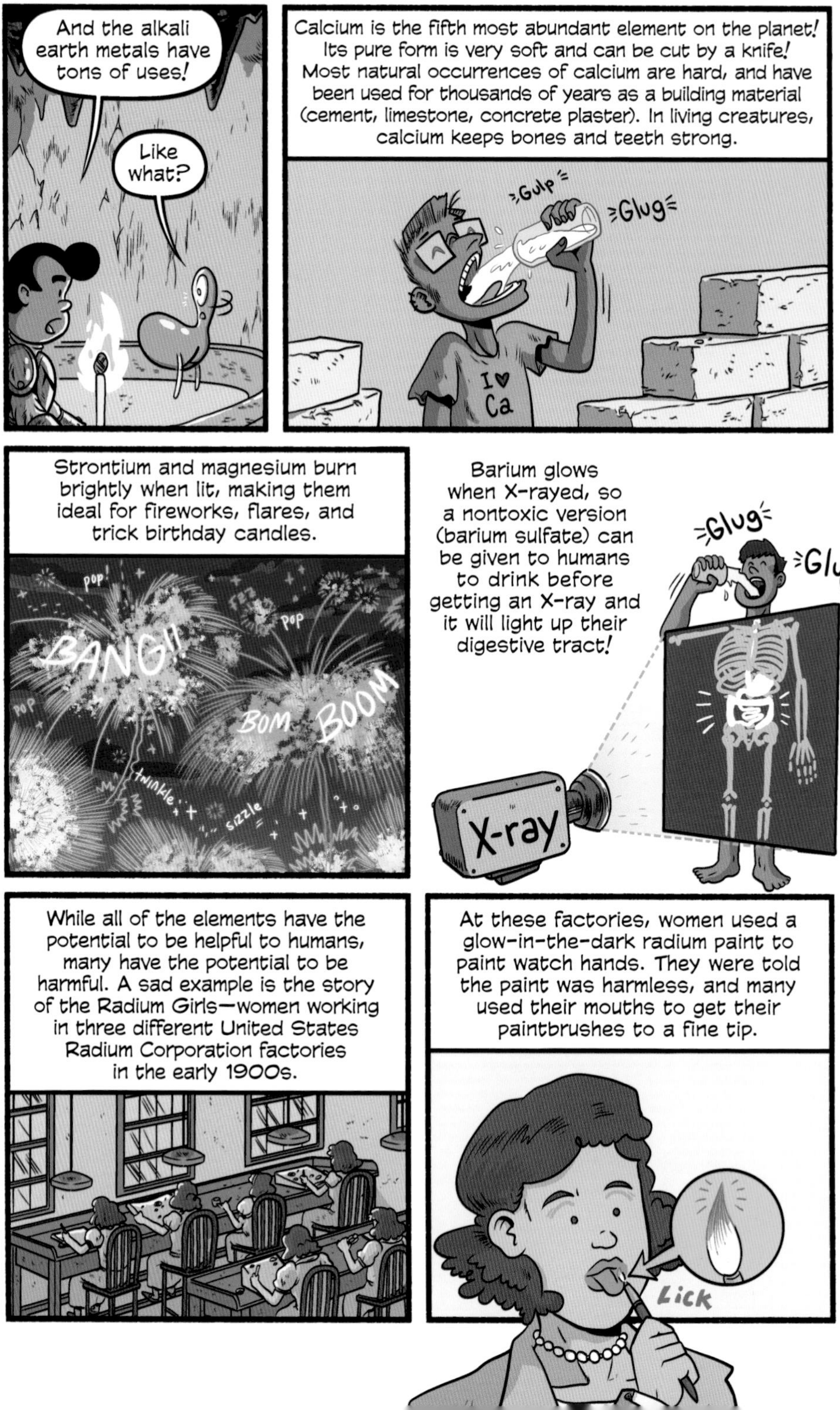

And the alkali earth metals have tons of uses!
Like what?
Calcium is the fifth most abundant element on the planet! Its pure form is very soft and can be cut by a knife! Most natural occurrences of calcium are hard, and have been used for thousands of years as a building material (cement, limestone, concrete plaster). In living creatures, calcium keeps bones and teeth strong.
Gulp
Glug
I ♥ Ca
Strontium and magnesium burn brightly when lit, making them ideal for fireworks, flares, and trick birthday candles.
pop
pop
BANG!!
pop
BOM
BOOM
twinkle
sizzle
Barium glows when X-rayed, so a nontoxic version (barium sulfate) can be given to humans to drink before getting an X-ray and it will light up their digestive tract!
Glug
Glug
X-ray
While all of the elements have the potential to be helpful to humans, many have the potential to be harmful. A sad example is the story of the Radium Girls—women working in three different United States Radium Corporation factories in the early 1900s.
At these factories, women used a glow-in-the-dark radium paint to paint watch hands. They were told the paint was harmless, and many used their mouths to get their paintbrushes to a fine tip.
Lick

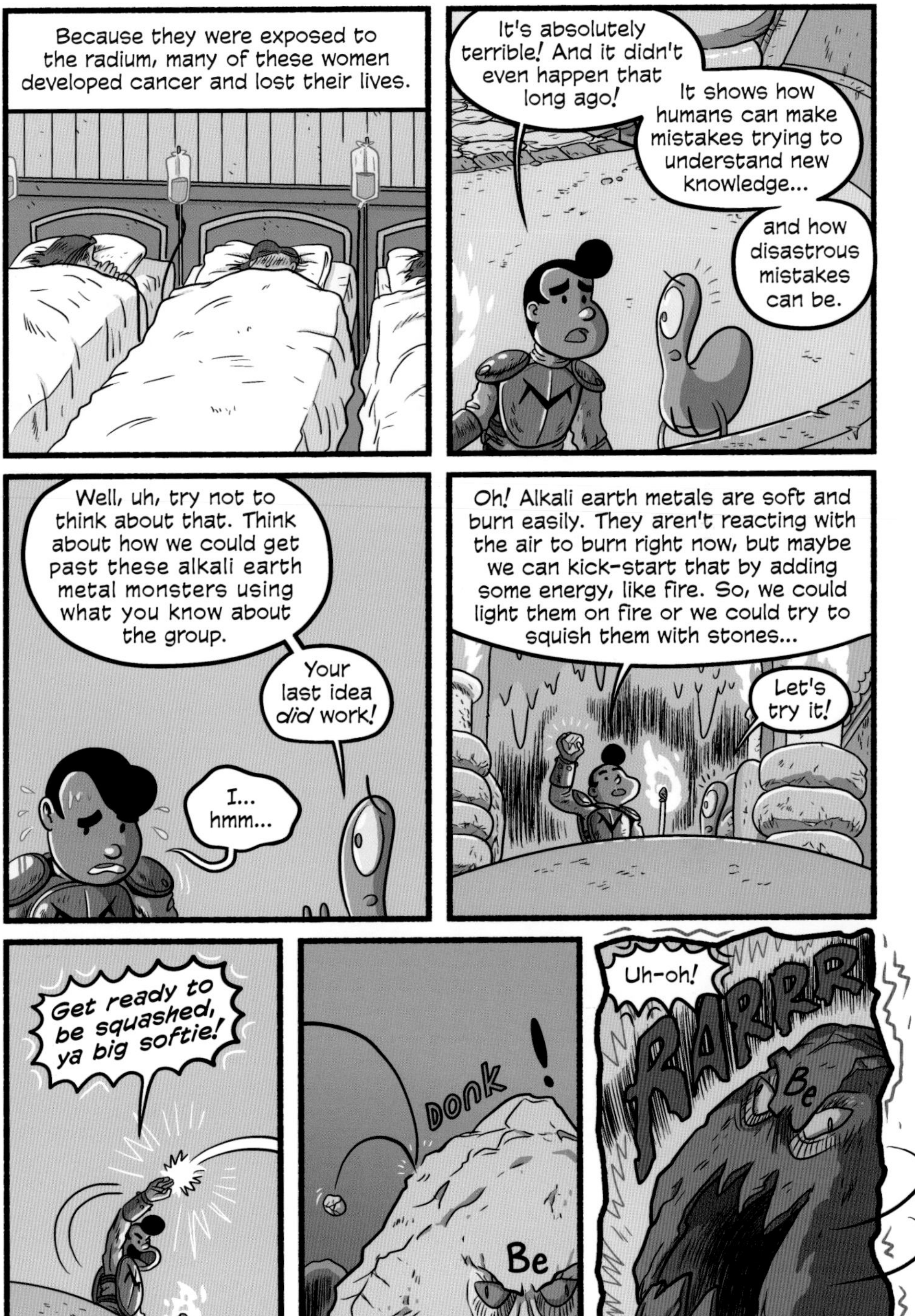

Because they were exposed to the radium, many of these women developed cancer and lost their lives.
It's absolutely terrible! And it didn't even happen that long ago!
It shows how humans can make mistakes trying to understand new knowledge...
and how disastrous mistakes can be.
Well, uh, try not to think about that. Think about how we could get past these alkali earth metal monsters using what you know about the group.
Your last idea did work!
I... hmm...
Oh! Alkali earth metals are soft and burn easily. They aren't reacting with the air to burn right now, but maybe we can kick-start that by adding some energy, like fire. So, we could light them on fire or we could try to squish them with stones...
Let's try it!
Get ready to be squashed, ya big softie!
DONK
!
Be
Uh-oh!
RARRR
Be

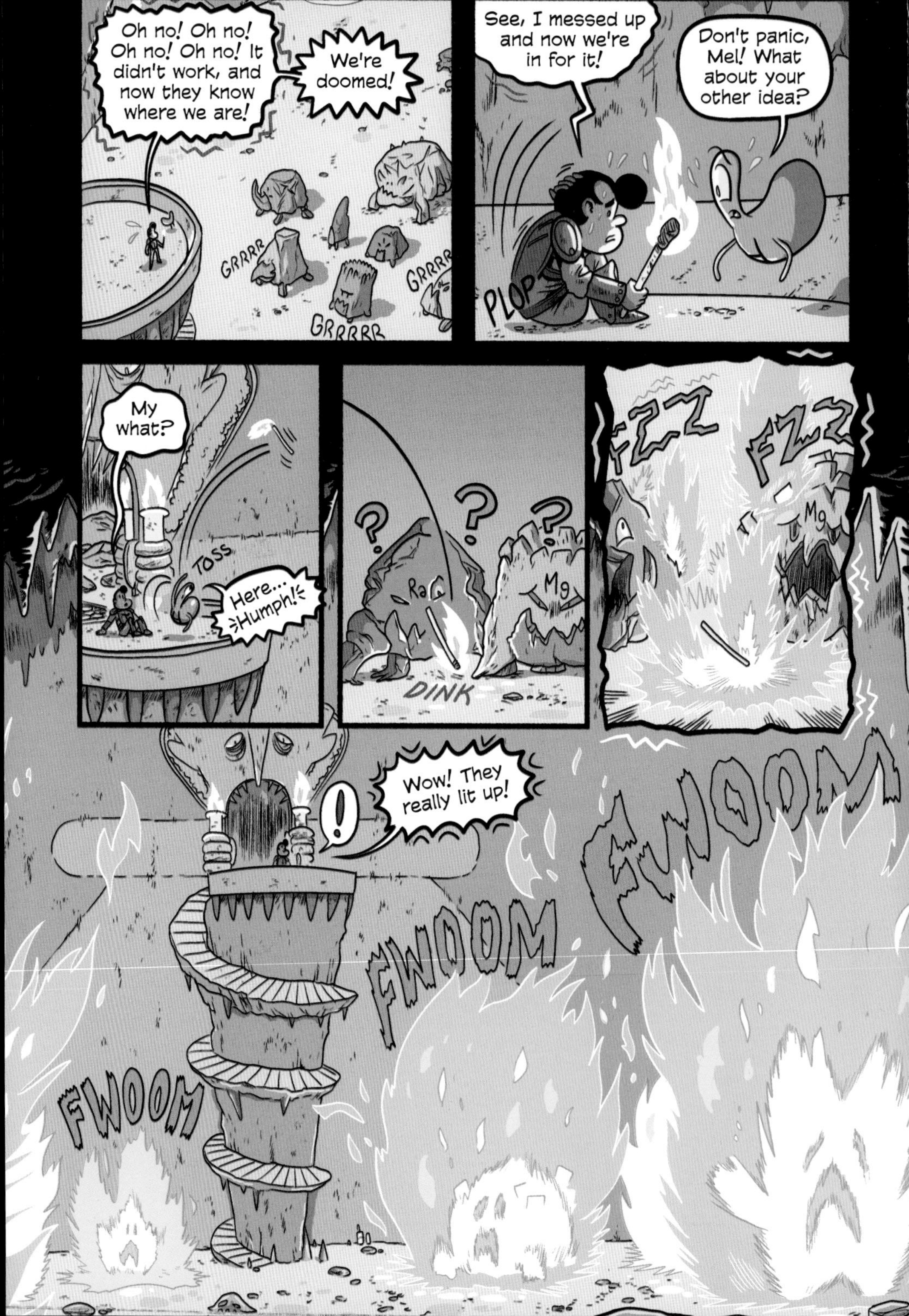

Oh no! Oh no! Oh no! Oh no! It didn't work, and now they know where we are!
We're doomed!
GRRRR
GRRRR
GRRRRRR
See, I messed up and now we're in for it!
Don't panic, Mel! What about your other idea?
PLOP
My what?
TOSS
Here... Humph!
?
?
?
Ra
Mg
DINK
FZZ
FZZ
Mg
!
Wow! They really lit up!
FWOOM
FWOOM
FWOOM

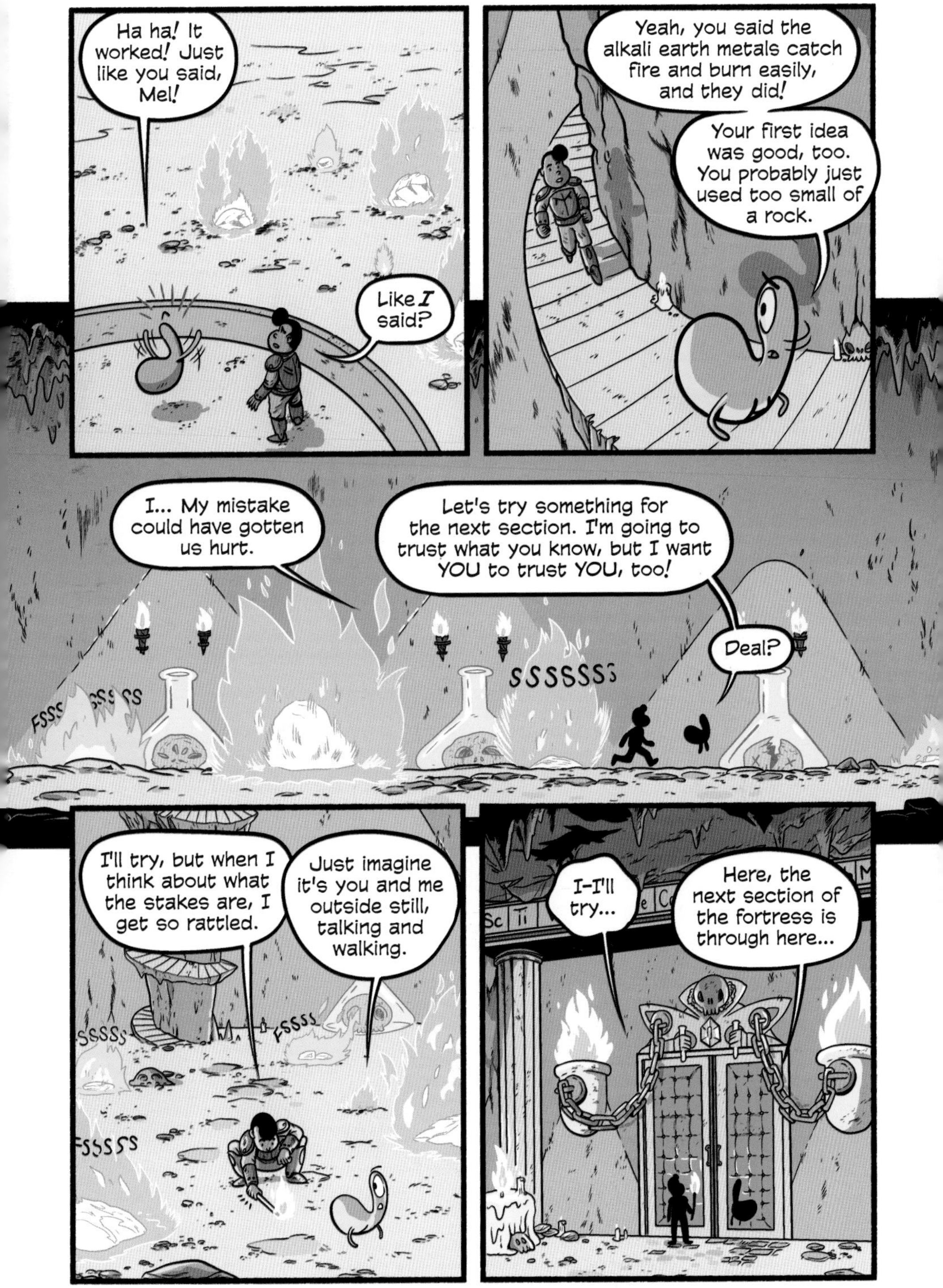

Ha ha! It worked! Just like you said, Mel!
Like *I* said?
Yeah, you said the alkali earth metals catch fire and burn easily, and they did!
Your first idea was good, too. You probably just used too small of a rock.
I... My mistake could have gotten us hurt.
Let's try something for the next section. I'm going to trust what you know, but I want YOU to trust YOU, too!
Deal?
FSSS
SSSSS
SSSSSSS
I'll try, but when I think about what the stakes are, I get so rattled.
Just imagine it's you and me outside still, talking and walking.
SSSSS
FSSSS
FSSSSS
I-I'll try...
Here, the next section of the fortress is through here...

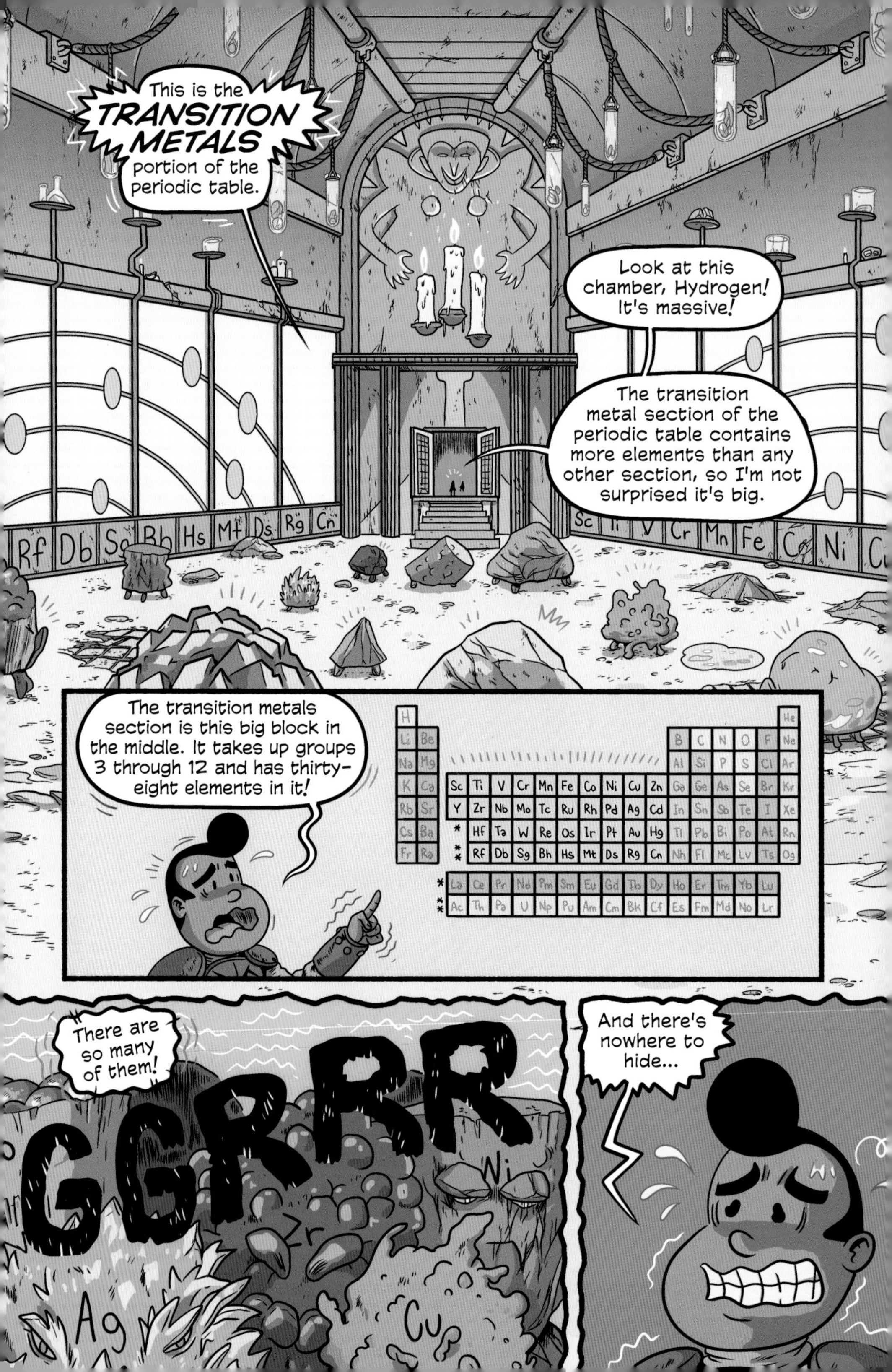
This is the TRANSITION METALS portion of the periodic table.
Look at this chamber, Hydrogen! It's massive!
The transition metal section of the periodic table contains more elements than any other section, so I'm not surprised it's big.
The transition metals section is this big block in the middle. It takes up groups 3 through 12 and has thirty-eight elements in it!
H He
Li Be B C N O F Ne
Na Mg Al Si P S Cl Ar
K Ca Sc Ti V Cr Mn Fe Co Ni Cu Zn Ga Ge As Se Br Kr
Rb Sr Y Zr Nb Mo Tc Ru Rh Pd Ag Cd In Sn Sb Te I Xe
Cs Ba * Hf Ta W Re Os Ir Pt Au Hg Tl Pb Bi Po At Rn
Fr Ra ** Rf Db Sg Bh Hs Mt Ds Rg Cn Nh Fl Mc Lv Ts Og
* La Ce Pr Nd Pm Sm Eu Gd Tb Dy Ho Er Tm Yb Lu
** Ac Th Pa U Np Pu Am Cm Bk Cf Es Fm Md No Lr
There are so many of them!
GGRR
Ni
Zr
Ag
Cu
And there's nowhere to hide...

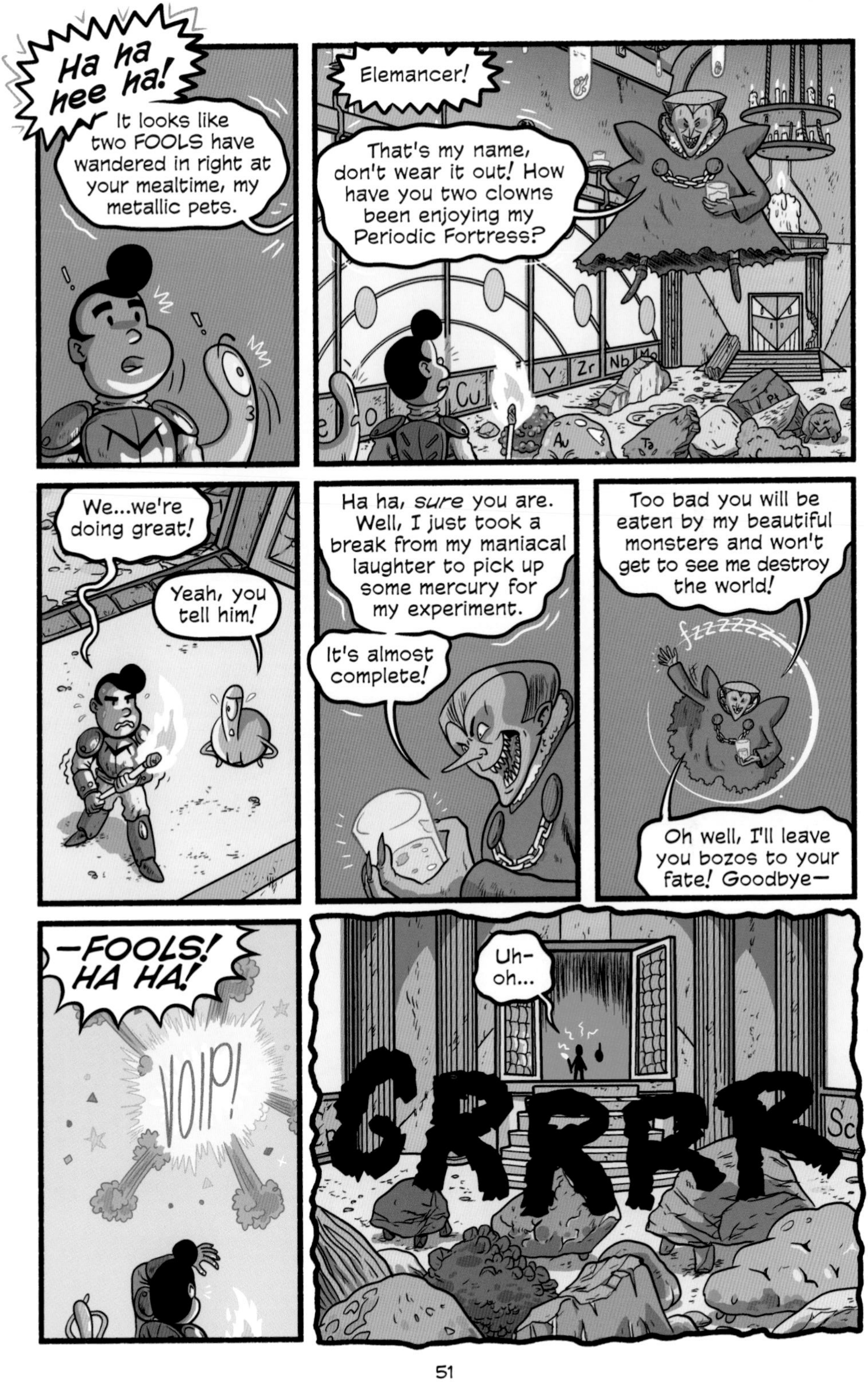
Ha ha hee ha!
It looks like two FOOLS have wandered in right at your mealtime, my metallic pets.
Elemancer!
That's my name, don't wear it out! How have you two clowns been enjoying my Periodic Fortress?
We...we're doing great!
Yeah, you tell him!
Ha ha, *sure* you are. Well, I just took a break from my maniacal laughter to pick up some mercury for my experiment.
It's almost complete!
Too bad you will be eaten by my beautiful monsters and won't get to see me destroy the world!
fzzzzzz
Oh well, I'll leave you bozos to your fate! Goodbye—
—FOOLS! HA HA!
VOIP!
Uh-oh...
GRRRR

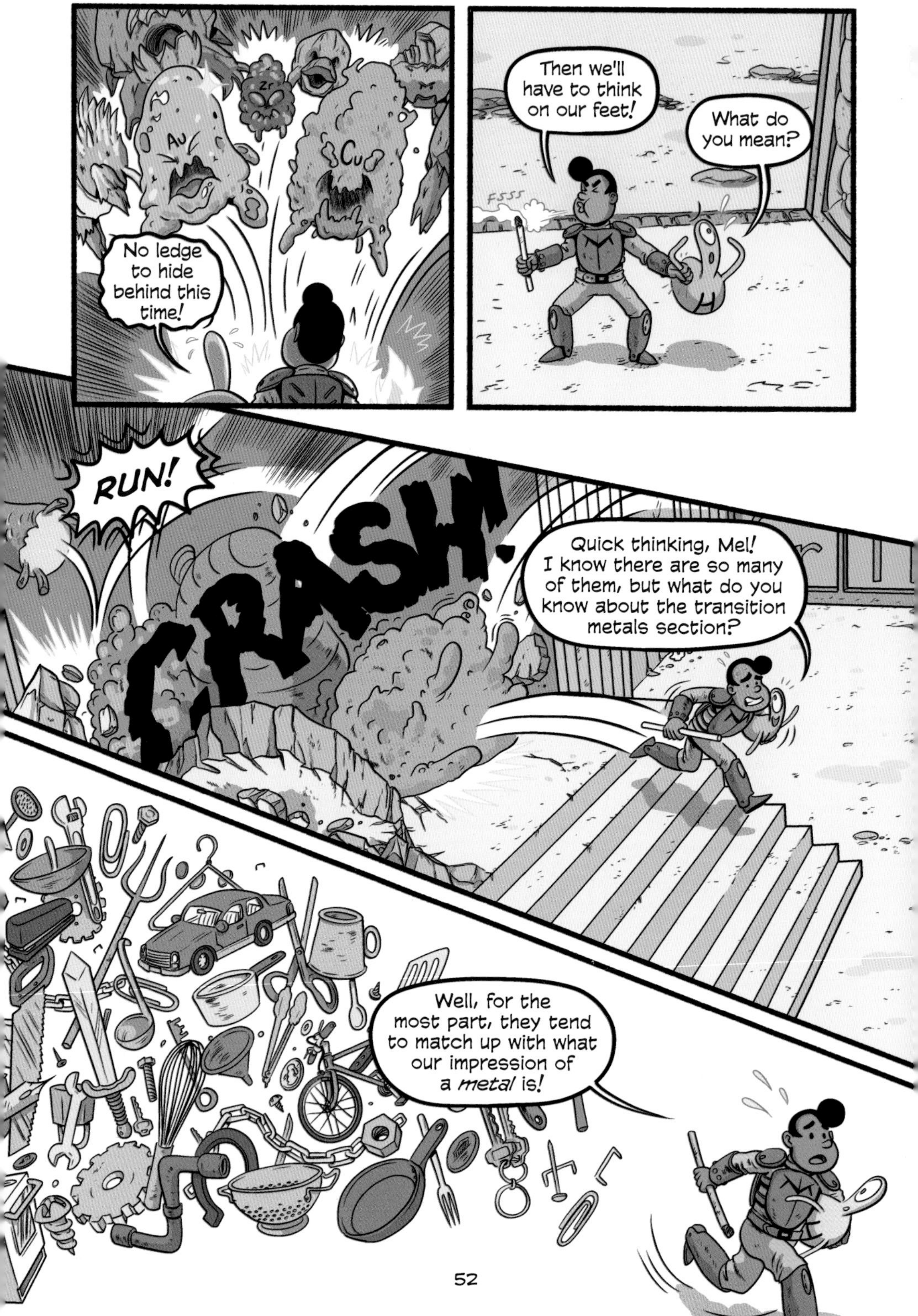
Zr
Au
Cu
No ledge to hide behind this time!
Then we'll have to think on our feet!
FSSS
What do you mean?
RUN!
CRASH!
Quick thinking, Mel! I know there are so many of them, but what do you know about the transition metals section?
Well, for the most part, they tend to match up with what our impression of a *metal* is!

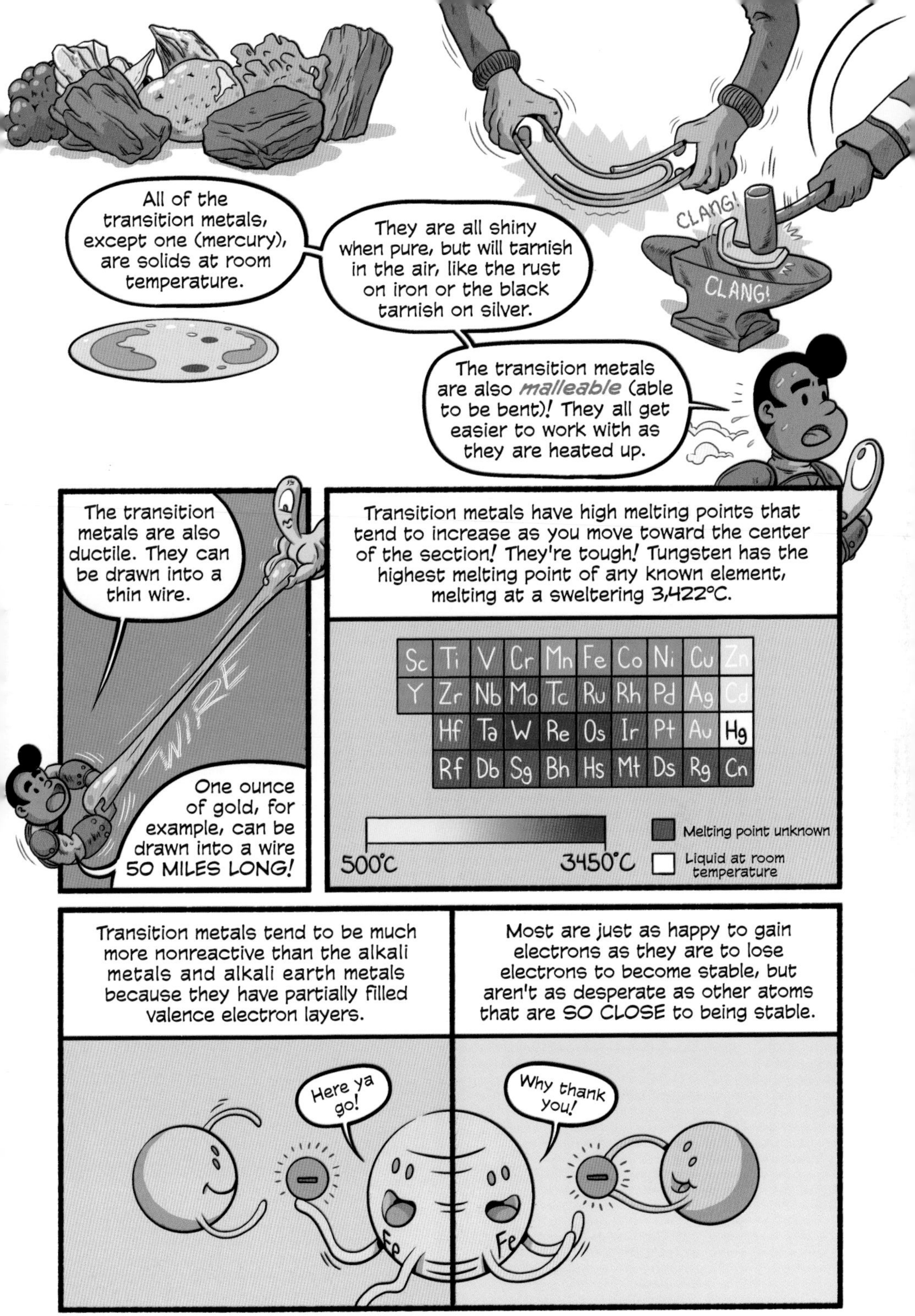
All of the transition metals, except one (mercury), are solids at room temperature.
They are all shiny when pure, but will tarnish in the air, like the rust on iron or the black tarnish on silver.
CLANG!
CLANG!
The transition metals are also *malleable* (able to be bent)! They all get easier to work with as they are heated up.
The transition metals are also ductile. They can be drawn into a thin wire.
WIRE
One ounce of gold, for example, can be drawn into a wire 50 MILES LONG!
Transition metals have high melting points that tend to increase as you move toward the center of the section! They're tough! Tungsten has the highest melting point of any known element, melting at a sweltering 3,422°C.
Sc Ti V Cr Mn Fe Co Ni Cu Zn
Y Zr Nb Mo Tc Ru Rh Pd Ag Cd
Hf Ta W Re Os Ir Pt Au Hg
Rf Db Sg Bh Hs Mt Ds Rg Cn
500°C
3450°C
Melting point unknown
Liquid at room temperature
Transition metals tend to be much more nonreactive than the alkali metals and alkali earth metals because they have partially filled valence electron layers.
Most are just as happy to gain electrons as they are to lose electrons to become stable, but aren't as desperate as other atoms that are SO CLOSE to being stable.
Here ya go!
Fe
Fe
Why thank you!

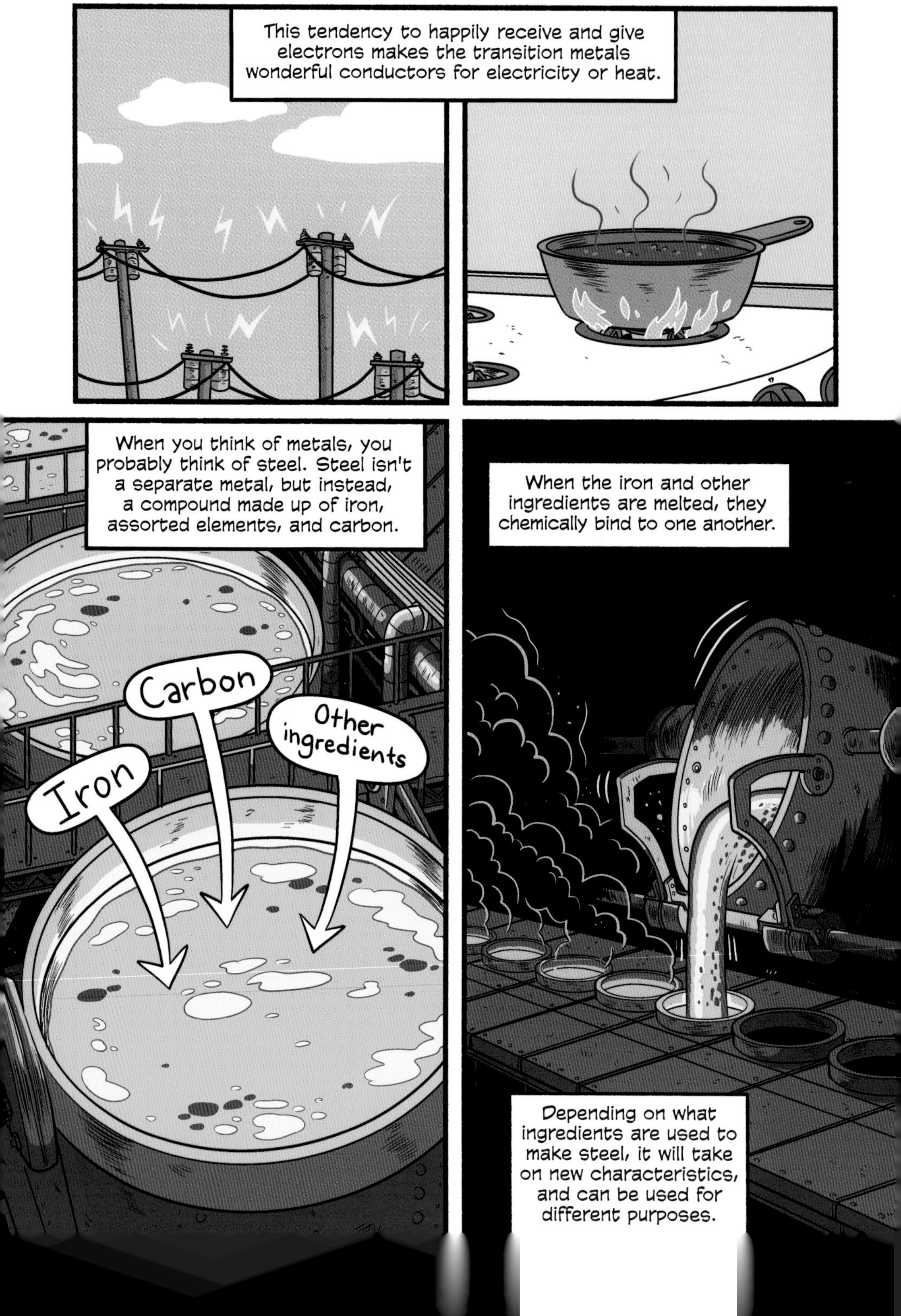
This tendency to happily receive and give electrons makes the transition metals wonderful conductors for electricity or heat.
When you think of metals, you probably think of steel. Steel isn't a separate metal, but instead, a compound made up of iron, assorted elements, and carbon.
Carbon
Other ingredients
Iron
When the iron and other ingredients are melted, they chemically bind to one another.
Depending on what ingredients are used to make steel, it will take on new characteristics, and can be used for different purposes.

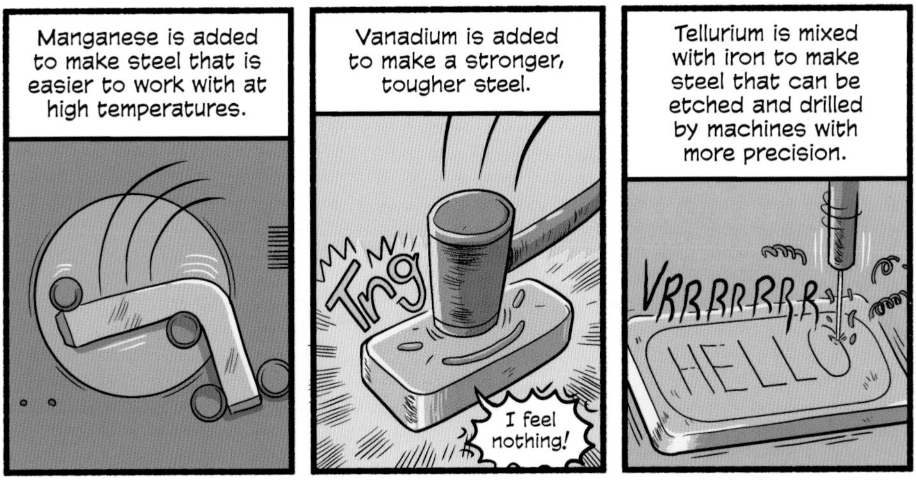
Manganese is added to make steel that is easier to work with at high temperatures.
Vanadium is added to make a stronger, tougher steel.
Trng
I feel nothing!
Tellurium is mixed with iron to make steel that can be etched and drilled by machines with more precision.
VRRRRRRR
HELLO

When metals are compounded together, the substance is called an *alloy*. There are a lot of metal substances that you might think are their own elements, but they are actually alloys.

Just like different mixtures of steel, different alloys serve different purposes.

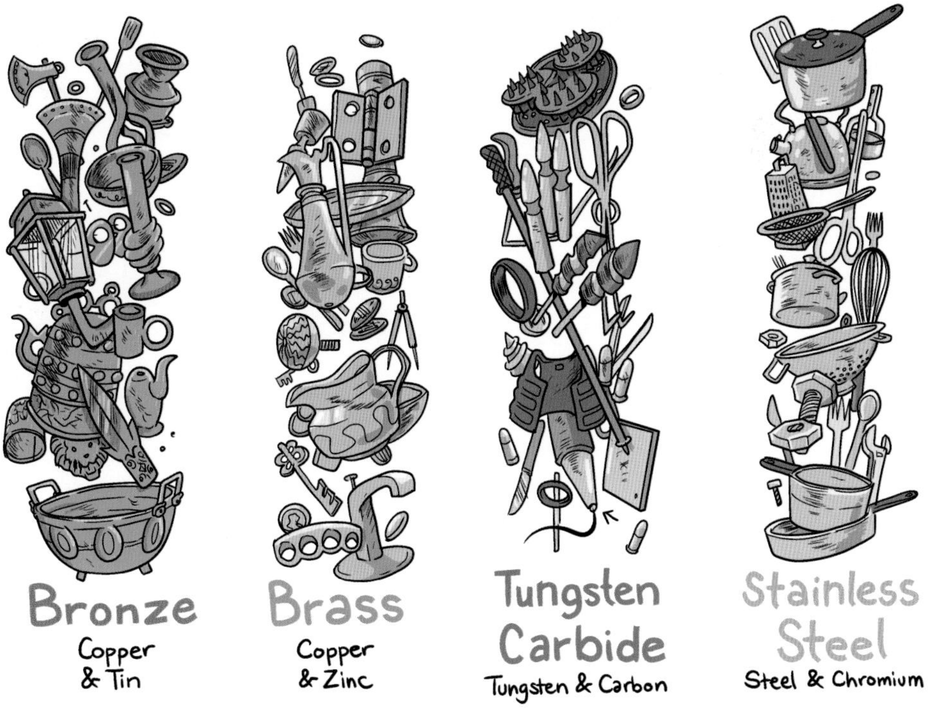
Bronze
Copper & Tin
Brass
Copper & Zinc
Tungsten Carbide
Tungsten & Carbon
Stainless Steel
Steel & Chromium

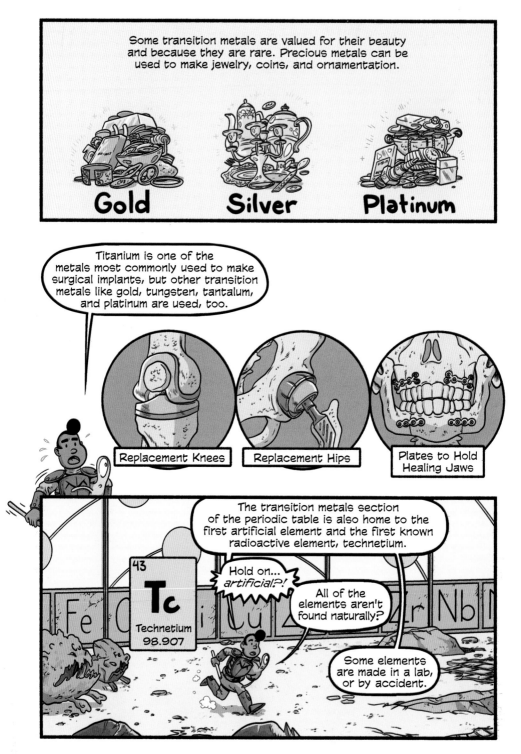

Some transition metals are valued for their beauty and because they are rare. Precious metals can be used to make jewelry, coins, and ornamentation.

Gold

Silver

Platinum

Titanium is one of the metals most commonly used to make surgical implants, but other transition metals like gold, tungsten, tantalum, and platinum are used, too.

Replacement Knees

Replacement Hips

Plates to Hold Healing Jaws

The transition metals section of the periodic table is also home to the first artificial element and the first known radioactive element, technetium.

43

Tc

Technetium
98.907

Hold on... *artificial!?!*

All of the elements aren't found naturally?

Some elements are made in a lab, or by accident.

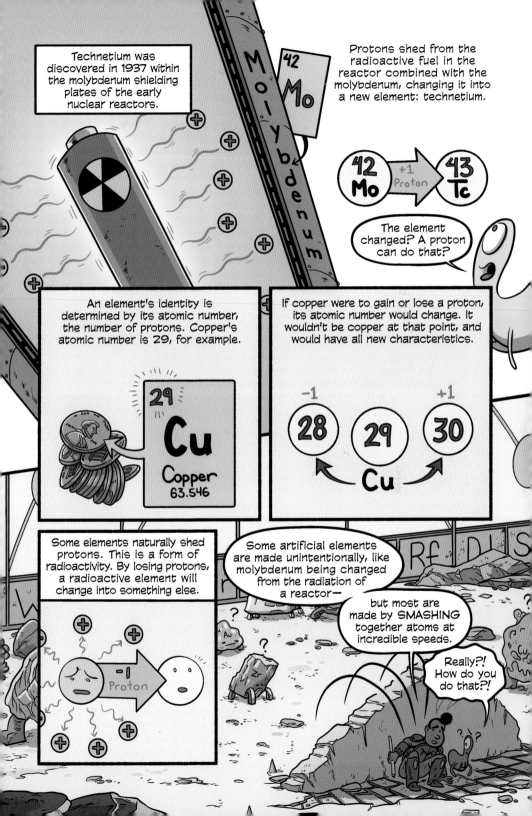

Technetium was discovered in 1937 within the molybdenum shielding plates of the early nuclear reactors.

42 Mo

M o l y b d e n u m

Protons shed from the radioactive fuel in the reactor combined with the molybdenum, changing it into a new element: technetium.

42 Mo +1 Proton 43 Tc

The element changed? A proton can do that?

An element's identity is determined by its atomic number, the number of protons. Copper's atomic number is 29, for example.

29 Cu Copper 63.546

If copper were to gain or lose a proton, its atomic number would change. It wouldn't be copper at that point, and would have all new characteristics.

−1 28   29   30 +1
Cu

Some elements naturally shed protons. This is a form of radioactivity. By losing protons, a radioactive element will change into something else.

−1 Proton

Some artificial elements are made unintentionally, like molybdenum being changed from the radiation of a reactor—

but most are made by SMASHING together atoms at incredible speeds.

Really?! How do you do that?!

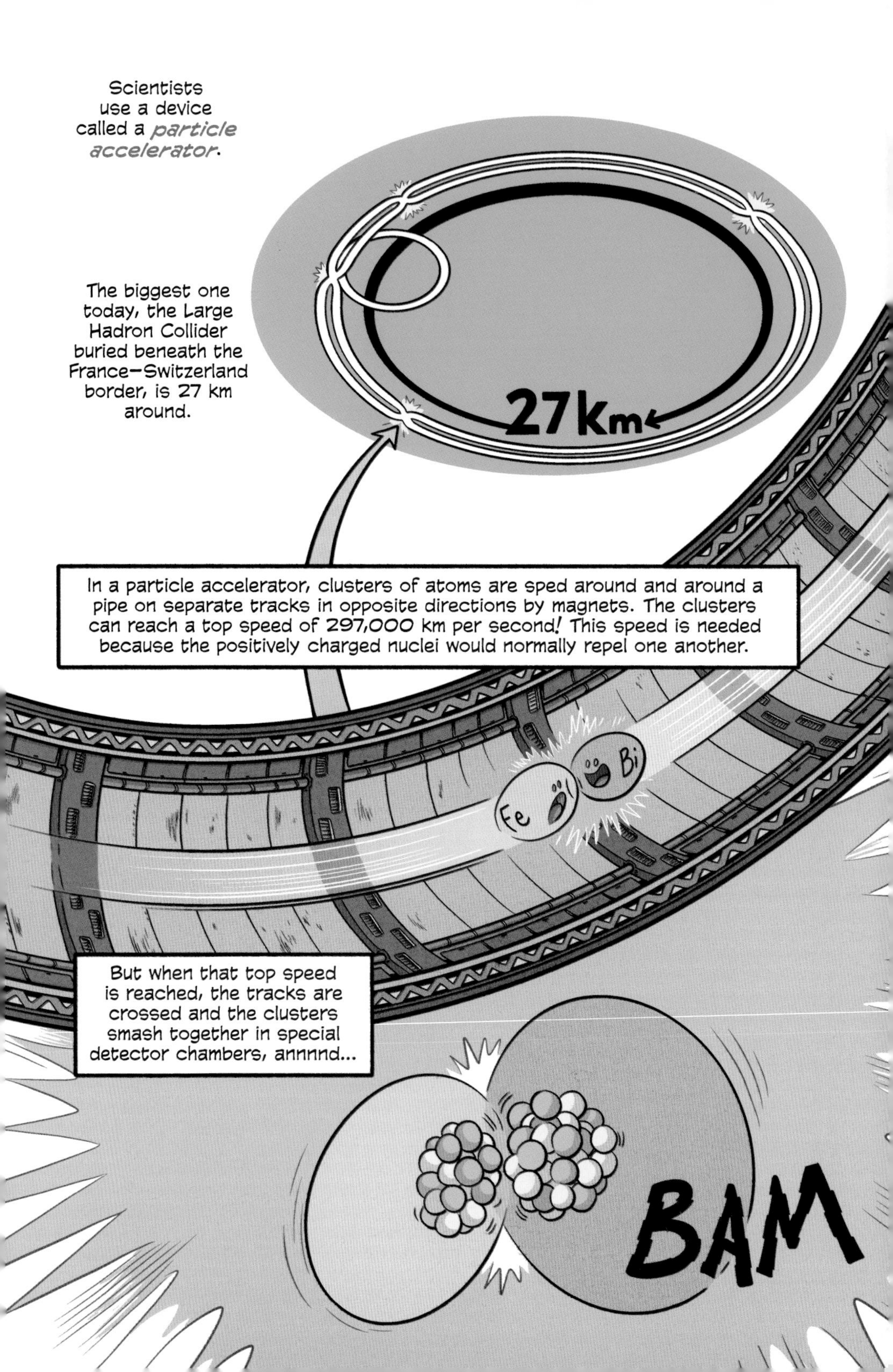
Scientists use a device called a *particle accelerator*.
The biggest one today, the Large Hadron Collider buried beneath the France—Switzerland border, is 27 km around.
27Km
In a particle accelerator, clusters of atoms are sped around and around a pipe on separate tracks in opposite directions by magnets. The clusters can reach a top speed of 297,000 km per second! This speed is needed because the positively charged nuclei would normally repel one another.
Fe
Bi
But when that top speed is reached, the tracks are crossed and the clusters smash together in special detector chambers, annnnd...
BAM

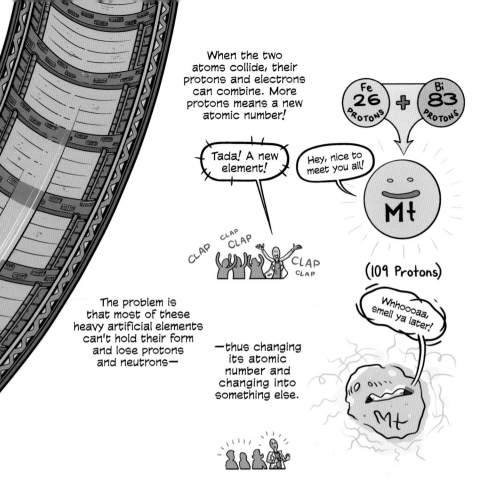

When the two atoms collide, their protons and electrons can combine. More protons means a new atomic number!

Fe 26 PROTONS + Bi 83 PROTONS

Tada! A new element!

Hey, nice to meet you all!

Mt

CLAP CLAP CLAP CLAP CLAP CLAP

(109 Protons)

The problem is that most of these heavy artificial elements can't hold their form and lose protons and neutrons—

—thus changing its atomic number and changing into something else.

Whhooooaa, smell ya later!

Mt

As I mentioned earlier, shedding protons is one form of *radioactivity*.

In fiction, we think of radioactivity as mysterious waves that can turn people into superheroes or mutants.

And so is born Crabclaw™!

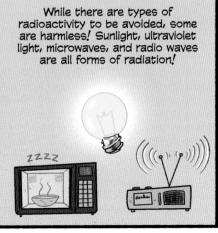

While there are types of radioactivity to be avoided, some are harmless! Sunlight, ultraviolet light, microwaves, and radio waves are all forms of radiation!

ZZZZ

Elements that are considered radioactive experience three different types of decay and release different types of energy.

Alpha Decay

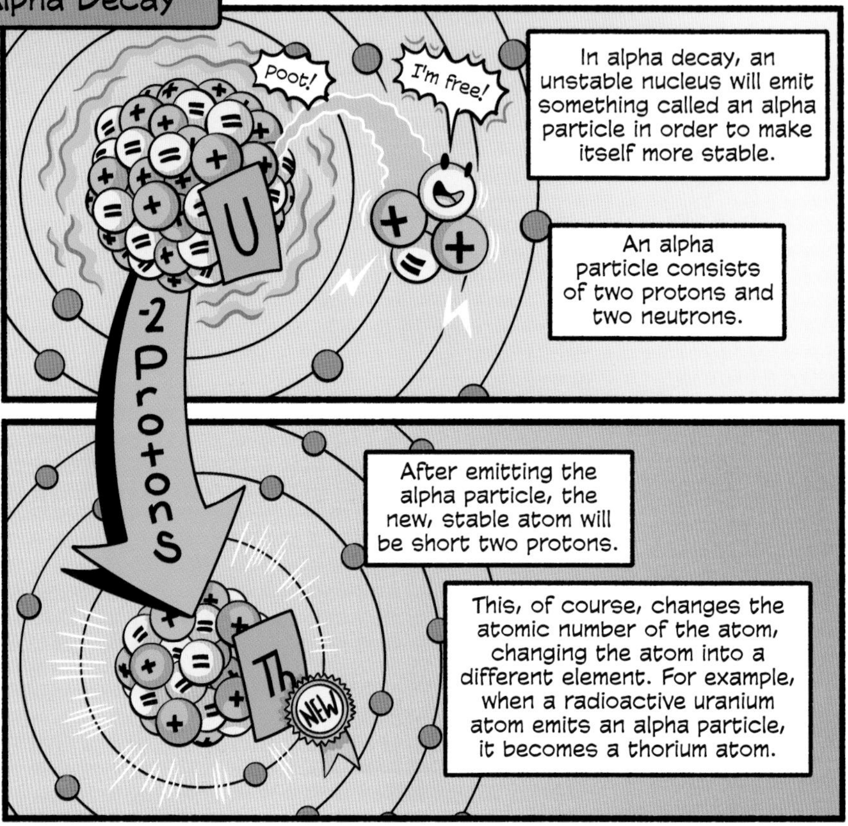

Poot!
I'm free!
In alpha decay, an unstable nucleus will emit something called an alpha particle in order to make itself more stable.
An alpha particle consists of two protons and two neutrons.
U
-2 Protons
After emitting the alpha particle, the new, stable atom will be short two protons.
Th
NEW
This, of course, changes the atomic number of the atom, changing the atom into a different element. For example, when a radioactive uranium atom emits an alpha particle, it becomes a thorium atom.

Beta Decay

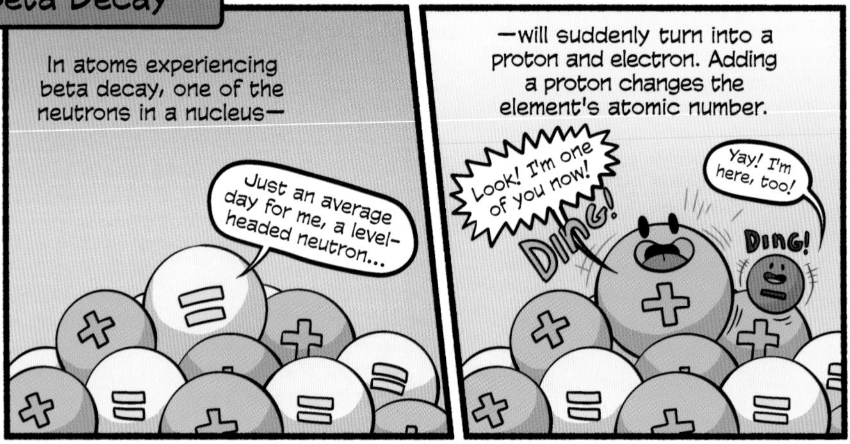

In atoms experiencing beta decay, one of the neutrons in a nucleus—
Just an average day for me, a level-headed neutron...
—will suddenly turn into a proton and electron. Adding a proton changes the element's atomic number.
Look! I'm one of you now!
DING!
Yay! I'm here, too!
DING!

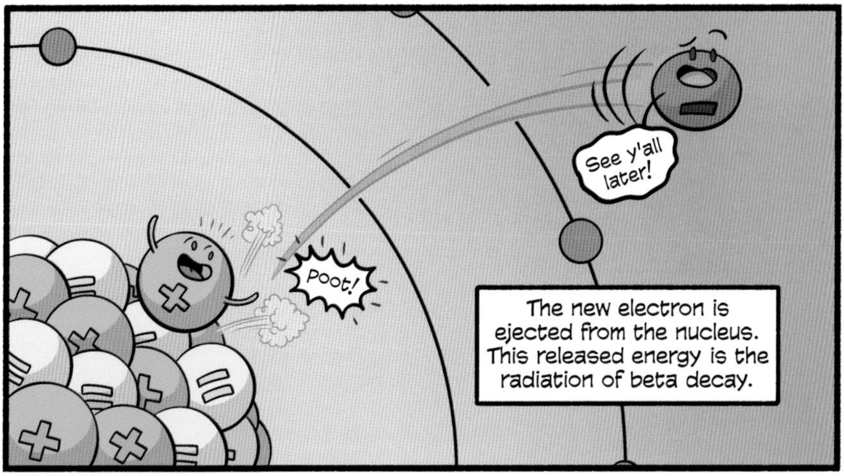
See y'all later!
Poot!
The new electron is ejected from the nucleus. This released energy is the radiation of beta decay.

Gamma Decay

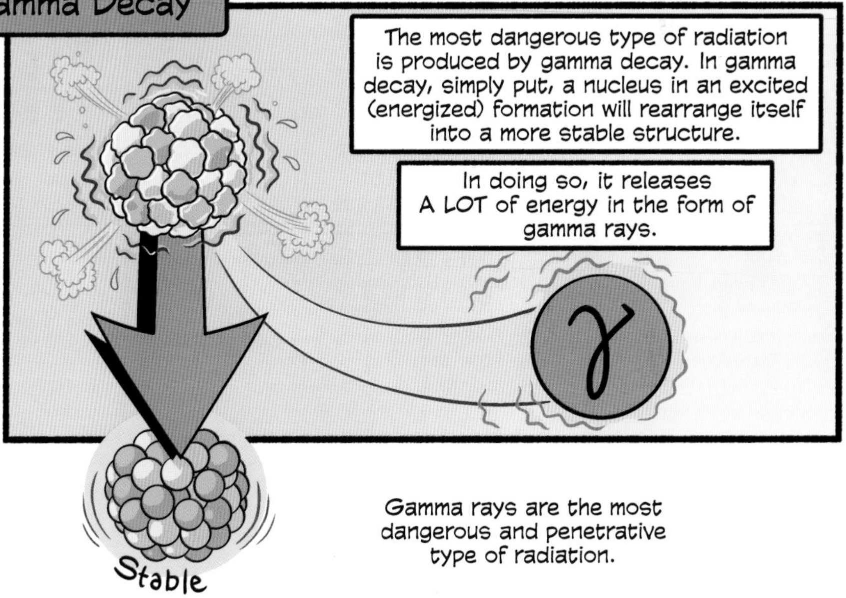
The most dangerous type of radiation is produced by gamma decay. In gamma decay, simply put, a nucleus in an excited (energized) formation will rearrange itself into a more stable structure.
In doing so, it releases A LOT of energy in the form of gamma rays.
γ
Stable
Gamma rays are the most dangerous and penetrative type of radiation.

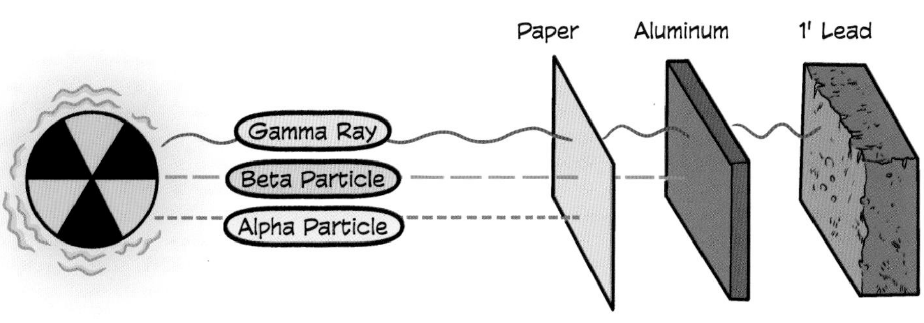
Paper
Aluminum
1' Lead
Gamma Ray
Beta Particle
Alpha Particle

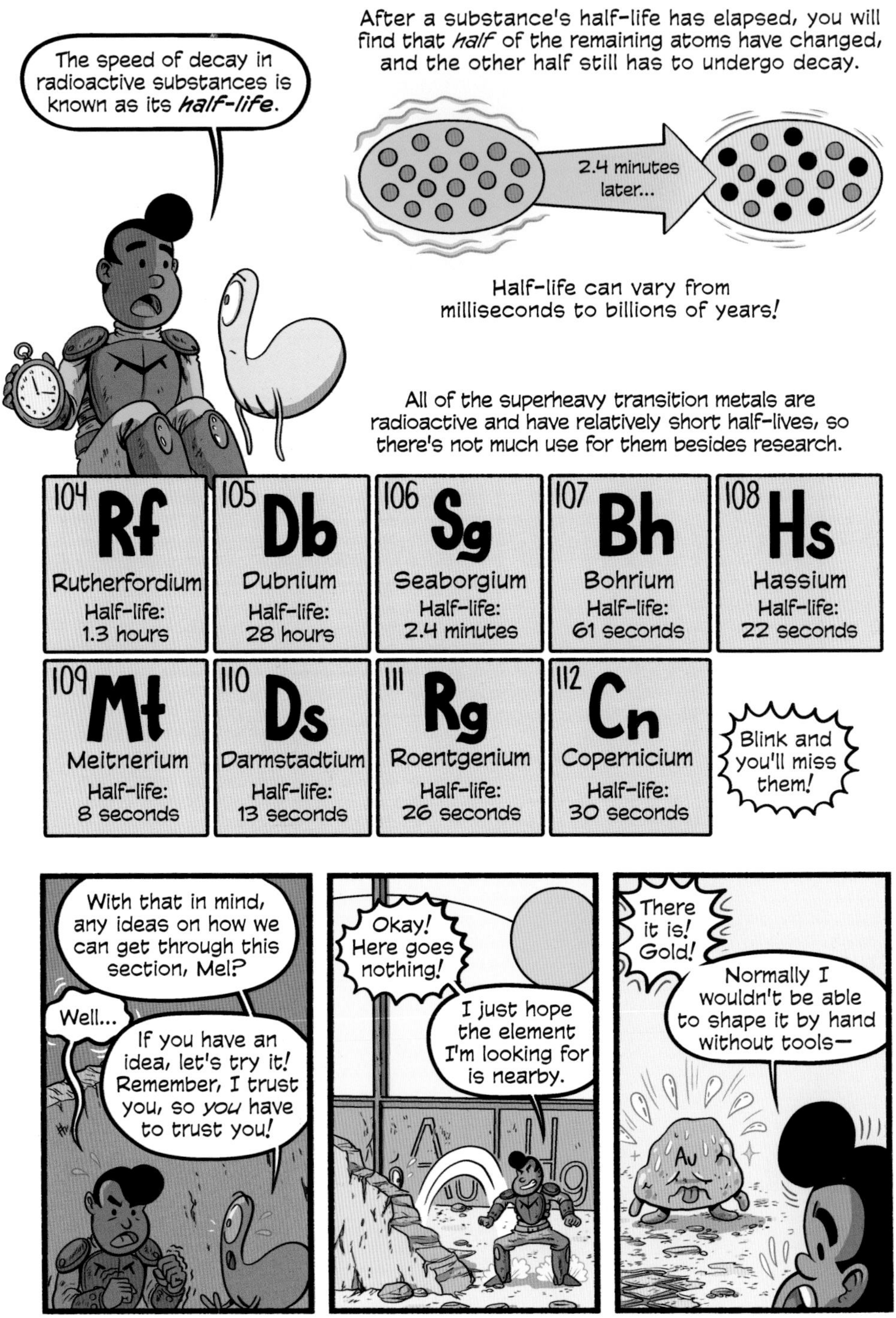
The speed of decay in radioactive substances is known as its *half-life*.
After a substance's half-life has elapsed, you will find that *half* of the remaining atoms have changed, and the other half still has to undergo decay.
2.4 minutes later...
Half-life can vary from milliseconds to billions of years!
All of the superheavy transition metals are radioactive and have relatively short half-lives, so there's not much use for them besides research.
104 Rf Rutherfordium Half-life: 1.3 hours
105 Db Dubnium Half-life: 28 hours
106 Sg Seaborgium Half-life: 2.4 minutes
107 Bh Bohrium Half-life: 61 seconds
108 Hs Hassium Half-life: 22 seconds
109 Mt Meitnerium Half-life: 8 seconds
110 Ds Darmstadtium Half-life: 13 seconds
111 Rg Roentgenium Half-life: 26 seconds
112 Cn Copernicium Half-life: 30 seconds
Blink and you'll miss them!
With that in mind, any ideas on how we can get through this section, Mel?
Well...
If you have an idea, let's try it! Remember, I trust you, so *you* have to trust you!
Okay! Here goes nothing!
I just hope the element I'm looking for is nearby.
There it is! Gold!
Normally I wouldn't be able to shape it by hand without tools—
Au

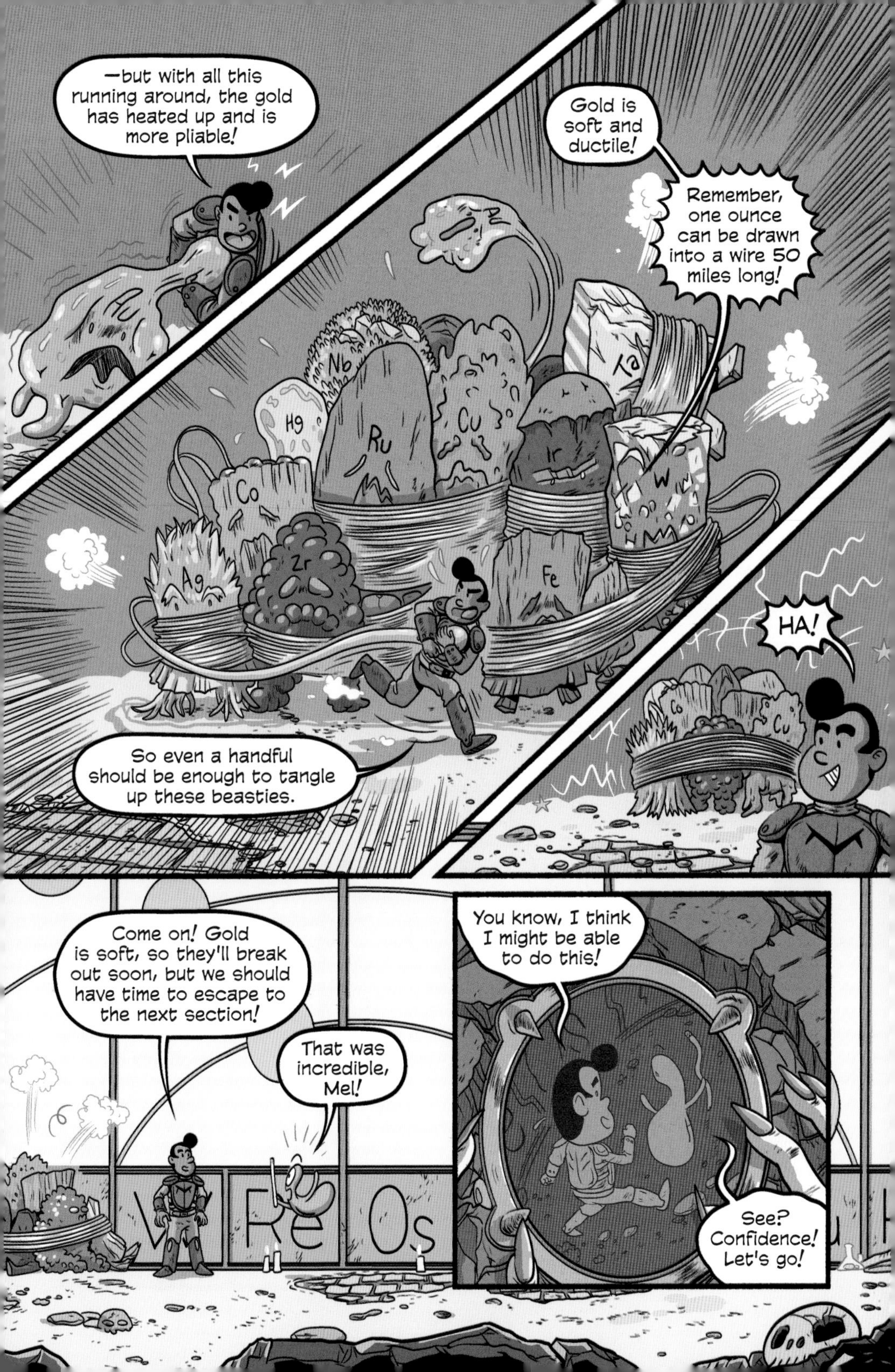

—but with all this running around, the gold has heated up and is more pliable!
Gold is soft and ductile!
Remember, one ounce can be drawn into a wire 50 miles long!
Au
Nb
Hg
Ru
Cu
Ta
Co
Ir
W
Zr
Ag
Fe
HA!
Co
Cu
So even a handful should be enough to tangle up these beasties.
Come on! Gold is soft, so they'll break out soon, but we should have time to escape to the next section!
That was incredible, Mel!
V
Re
Os
You know, I think I might be able to do this!
See? Confidence! Let's go!

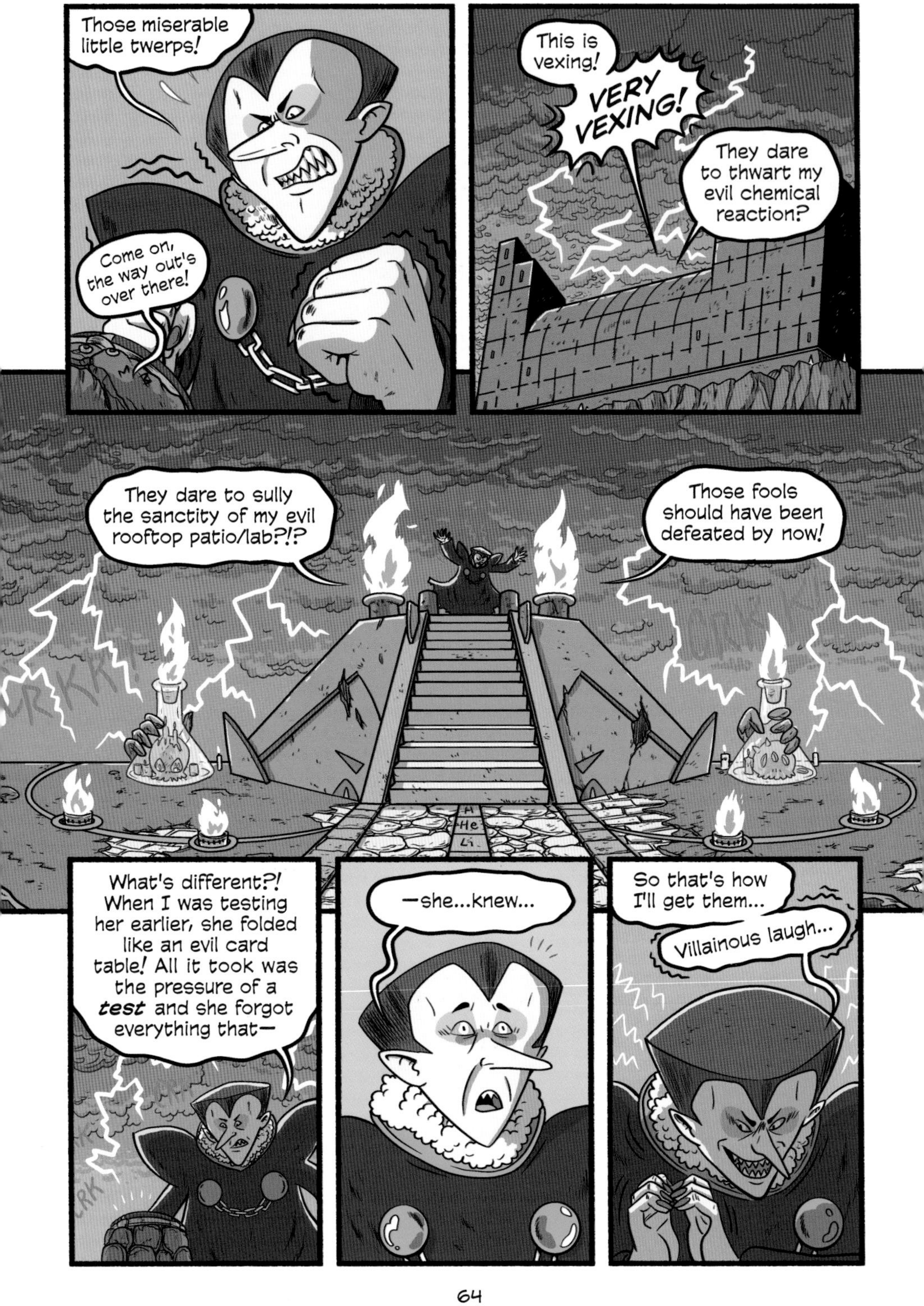
Those miserable little twerps!
Come on, the way out's over there!
This is vexing!
VERY VEXING!
They dare to thwart my evil chemical reaction?
They dare to sully the sanctity of my evil rooftop patio/lab?!?
Those fools should have been defeated by now!
What's different?! When I was testing her earlier, she folded like an evil card table! All it took was the pressure of a *test* and she forgot everything that—
—she...knew...
So that's how I'll get them...
Villainous laugh...

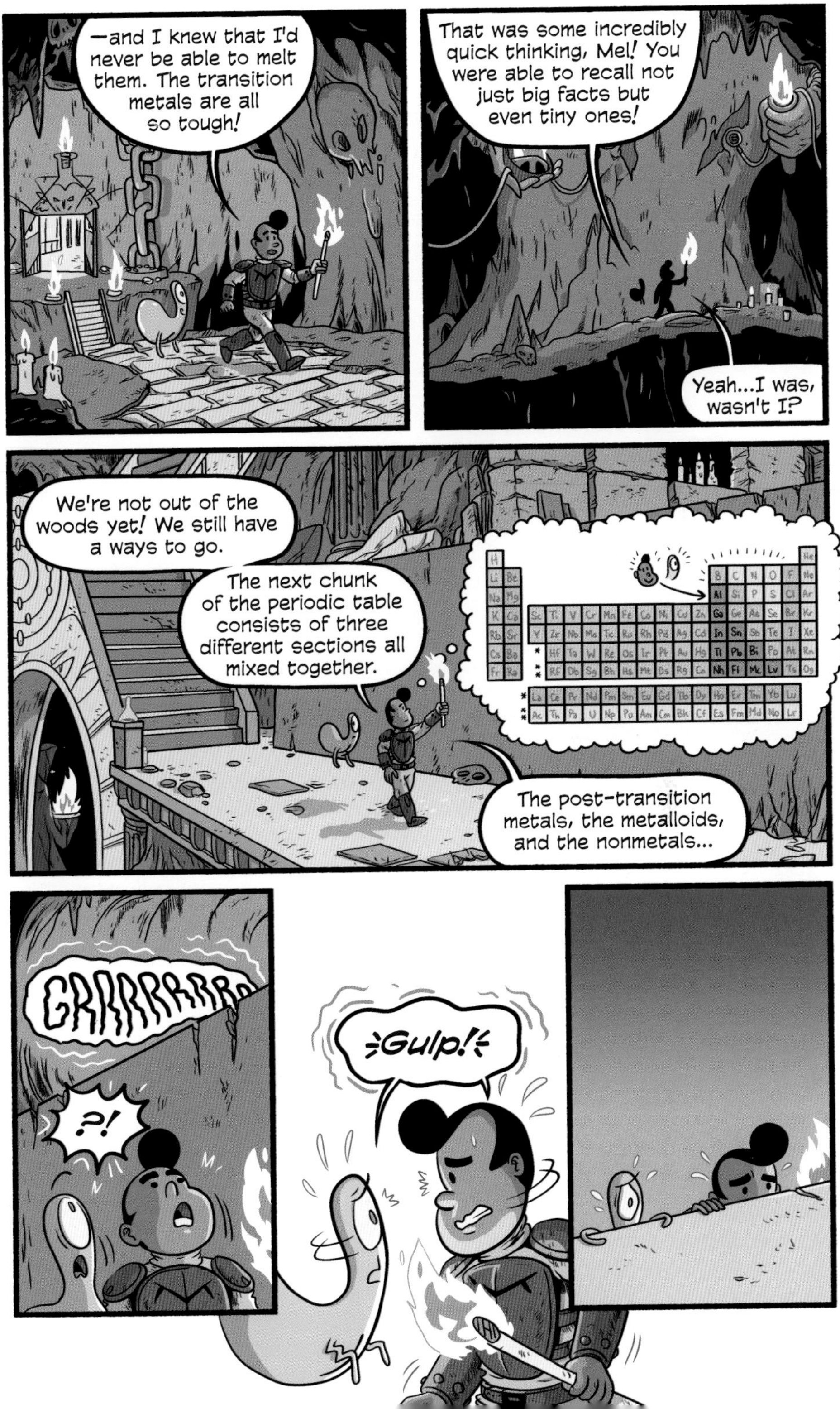
—and I knew that I'd never be able to melt them. The transition metals are all so tough!
That was some incredibly quick thinking, Mel! You were able to recall not just big facts but even tiny ones!
Yeah...I was, wasn't I?
We're not out of the woods yet! We still have a ways to go.
The next chunk of the periodic table consists of three different sections all mixed together.
The post-transition metals, the metalloids, and the nonmetals...
GRRRRRRR
?!
Gulp!

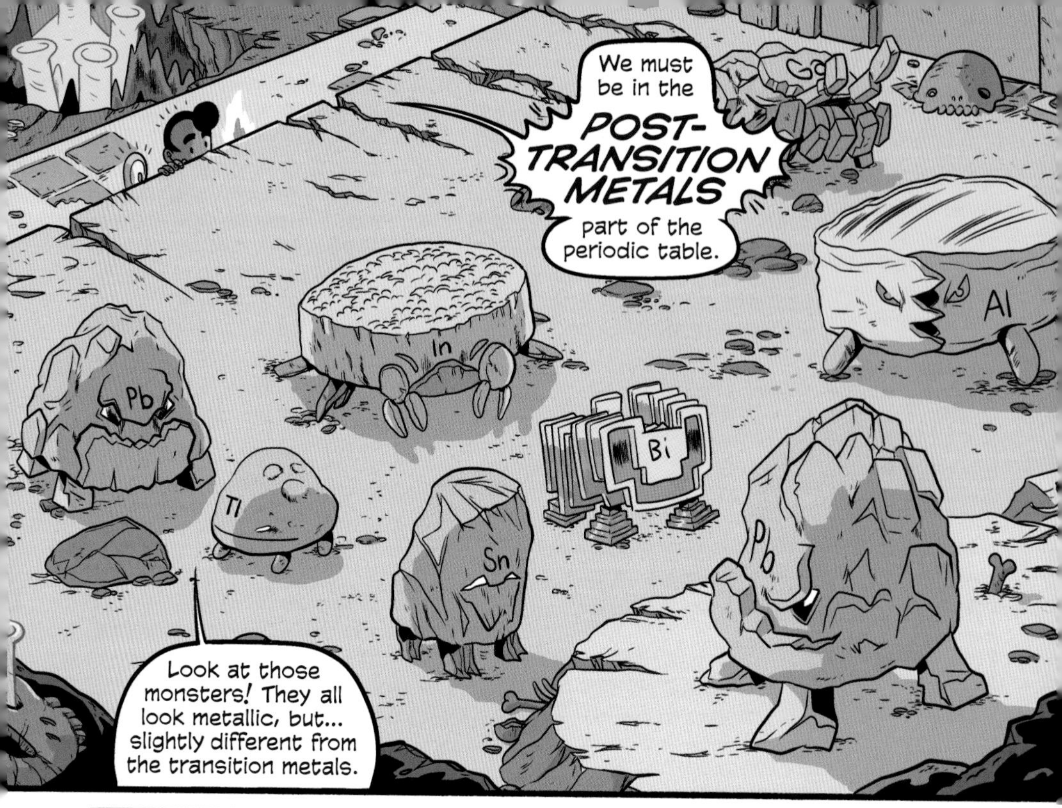
We must be in the
POST-TRANSITION METALS
part of the periodic table.
In
Al
Pb
Bi
Tl
Sn
Pb
Look at those monsters! They all look metallic, but... slightly different from the transition metals.

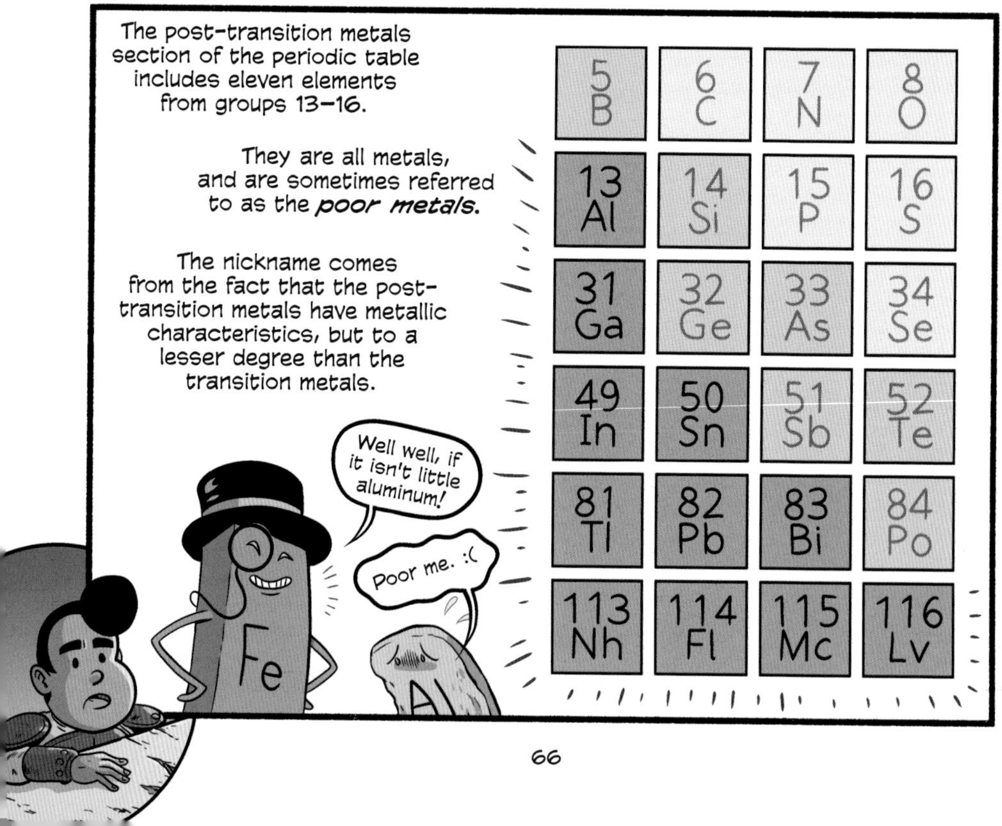
The post-transition metals section of the periodic table includes eleven elements from groups 13–16.
They are all metals, and are sometimes referred to as the *poor metals.*
The nickname comes from the fact that the post-transition metals have metallic characteristics, but to a lesser degree than the transition metals.
Well well, if it isn't little aluminum!
Poor me. :(
Fe
Al

5 B	6 C	7 N	8 O
13 Al	14 Si	15 P	16 S
31 Ga	32 Ge	33 As	34 Se
49 In	50 Sn	51 Sb	52 Te
81 Tl	82 Pb	83 Bi	84 Po
113 Nh	114 Fl	115 Mc	116 Lv

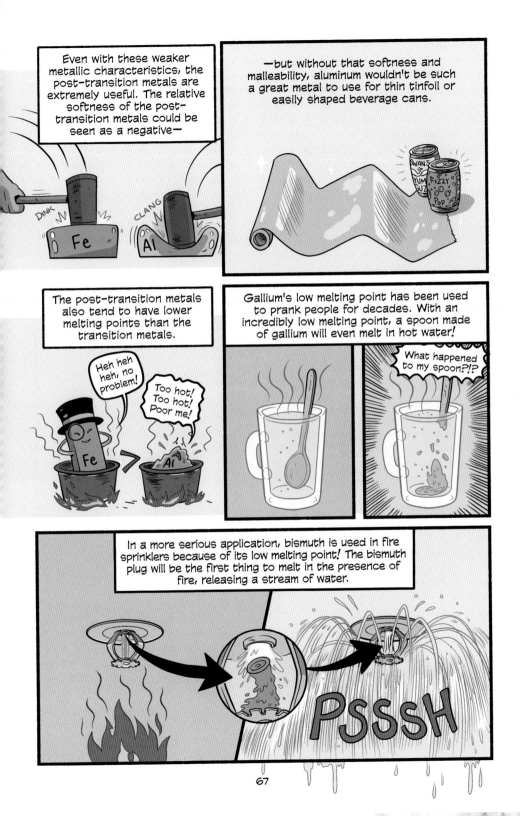

Even with these weaker metallic characteristics, the post-transition metals are extremely useful. The relative softness of the post-transition metals could be seen as a negative—

DINK

CLANG

Fe

Al

—but without that softness and malleability, aluminum wouldn't be such a great metal to use for thin tinfoil or easily shaped beverage cans.

SWANS

YUM JUZ

FIZZY POP

The post-transition metals also tend to have lower melting points than the transition metals.

Heh heh heh, no problem!

Too hot! Too hot! Poor me!

Fe

Al

Gallium's low melting point has been used to prank people for decades. With an incredibly low melting point, a spoon made of gallium will even melt in hot water!

What happened to my spoon?!?

In a more serious application, bismuth is used in fire sprinklers because of its low melting point! The bismuth plug will be the first thing to melt in the presence of fire, releasing a stream of water.

PSSSH

Post-transition metals are rarely used for anything structural because they are softer, but they can be used as a coating or as an ingredient to give different benefits to steel. Tin is extremely anticorrosive, and so it is used as a coating for copper cookware and "tin" cans.

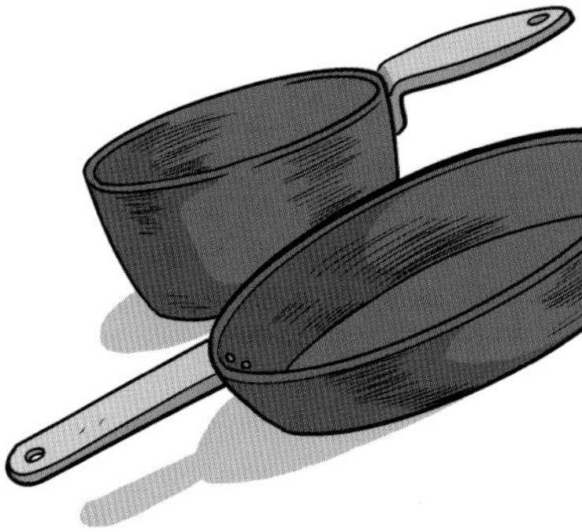

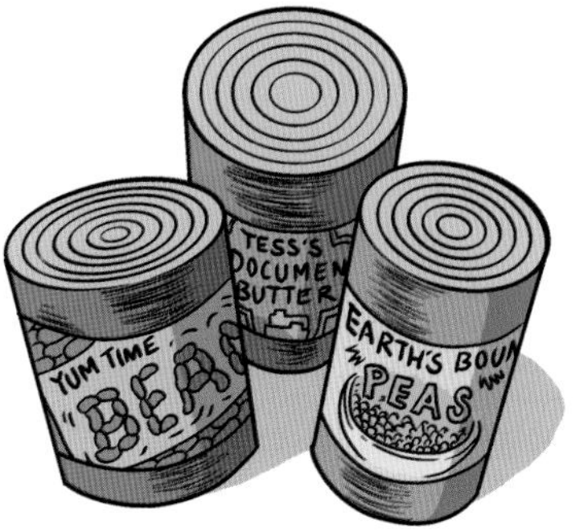
TESS'S
YUM TIME
PEAS

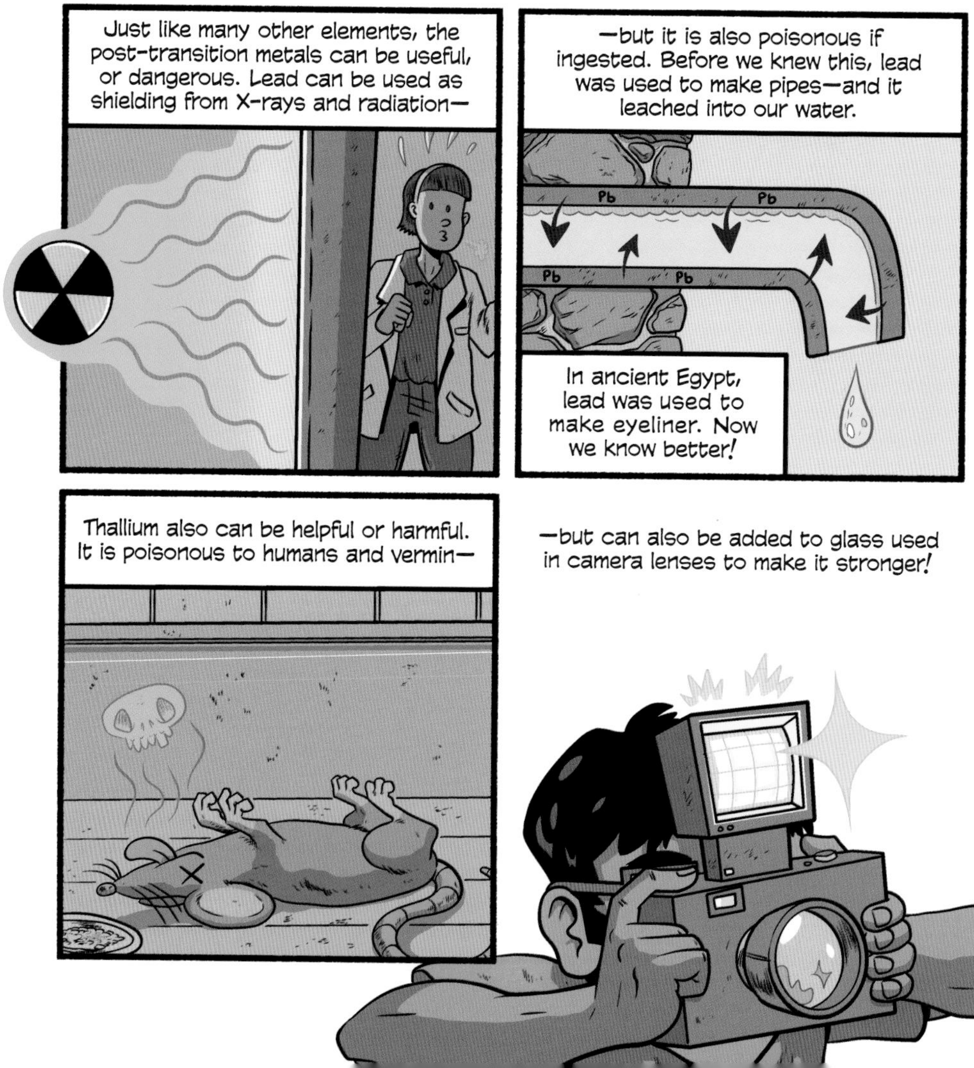
Just like many other elements, the post-transition metals can be useful, or dangerous. Lead can be used as shielding from X-rays and radiation—
—but it is also poisonous if ingested. Before we knew this, lead was used to make pipes—and it leached into our water.
Pb
Pb
Pb
Pb
In ancient Egypt, lead was used to make eyeliner. Now we know better!
Thallium also can be helpful or harmful. It is poisonous to humans and vermin—
—but can also be added to glass used in camera lenses to make it stronger!

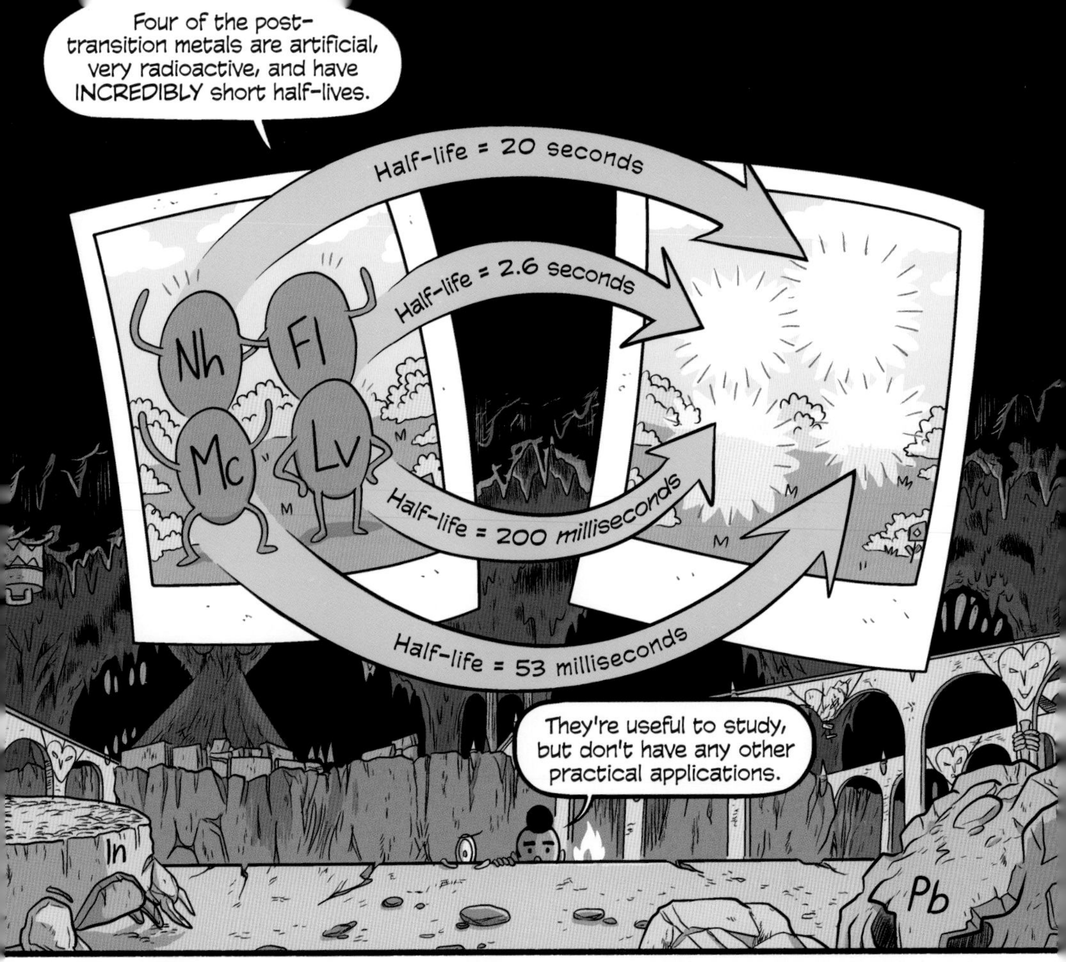
Four of the post-transition metals are artificial, very radioactive, and have INCREDIBLY short half-lives.
Half-life = 20 seconds
Half-life = 2.6 seconds
Nh
Fl
Mc
Lv
Half-life = 200 milliseconds
Half-life = 53 milliseconds
They're useful to study, but don't have any other practical applications.
In
Pb

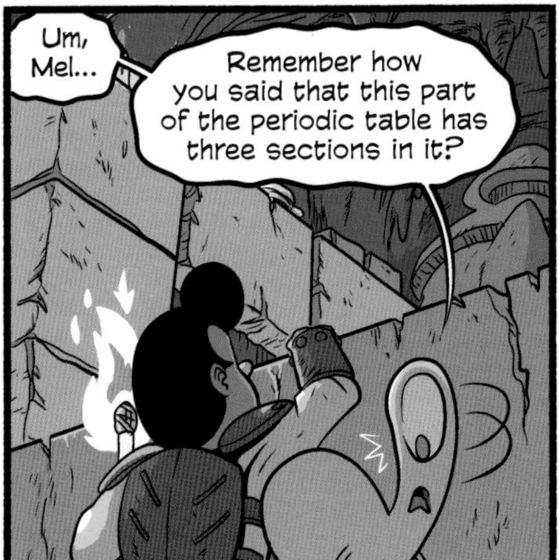
Um, Mel...
Remember how you said that this part of the periodic table has three sections in it?

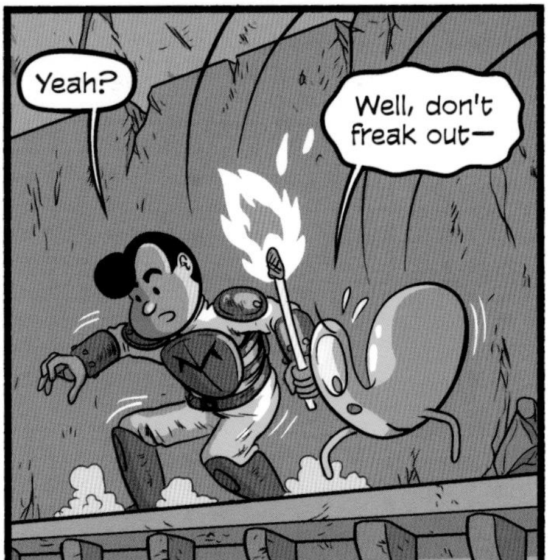
Yeah?
Well, don't freak out—

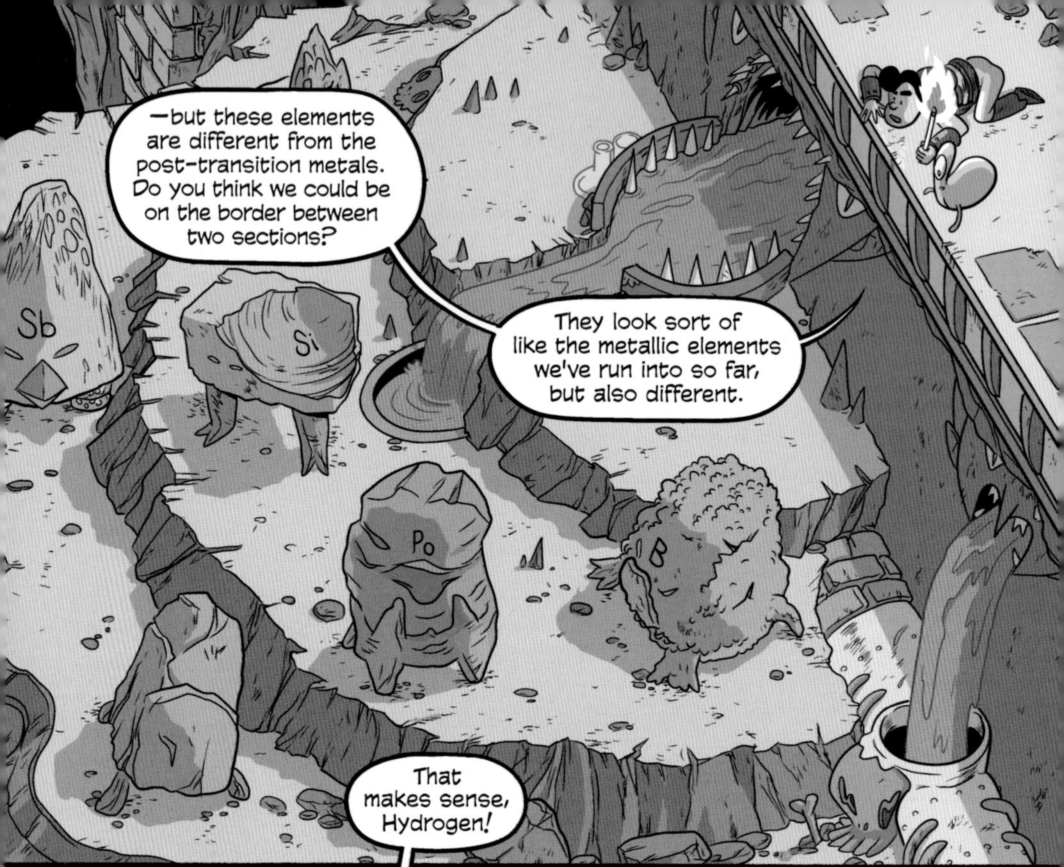
—but these elements are different from the post-transition metals. Do you think we could be on the border between two sections?
They look sort of like the metallic elements we've run into so far, but also different.
Sb
Si
Po
B
That makes sense, Hydrogen!

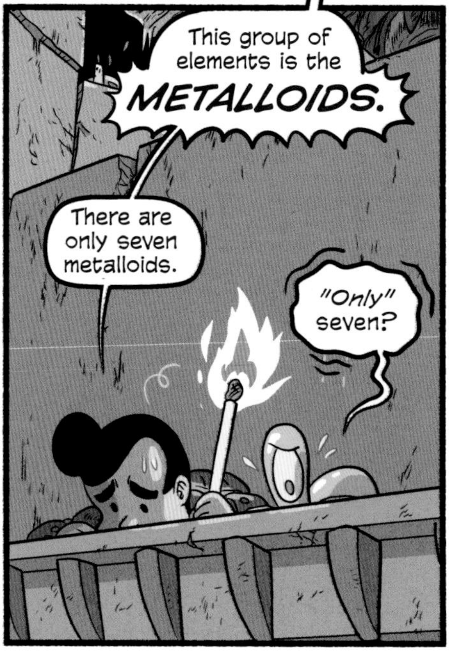
This group of elements is the METALLOIDS.
There are only seven metalloids.
"Only" seven?

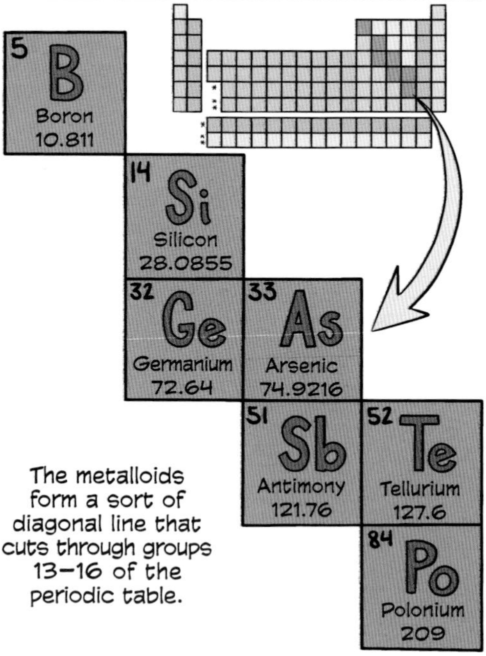
5 B Boron 10.811
14 Si Silicon 28.0855
32 Ge Germanium 72.64
33 As Arsenic 74.9216
51 Sb Antimony 121.76
52 Te Tellurium 127.6
84 Po Polonium 209

The metalloids form a sort of diagonal line that cuts through groups 13–16 of the periodic table.

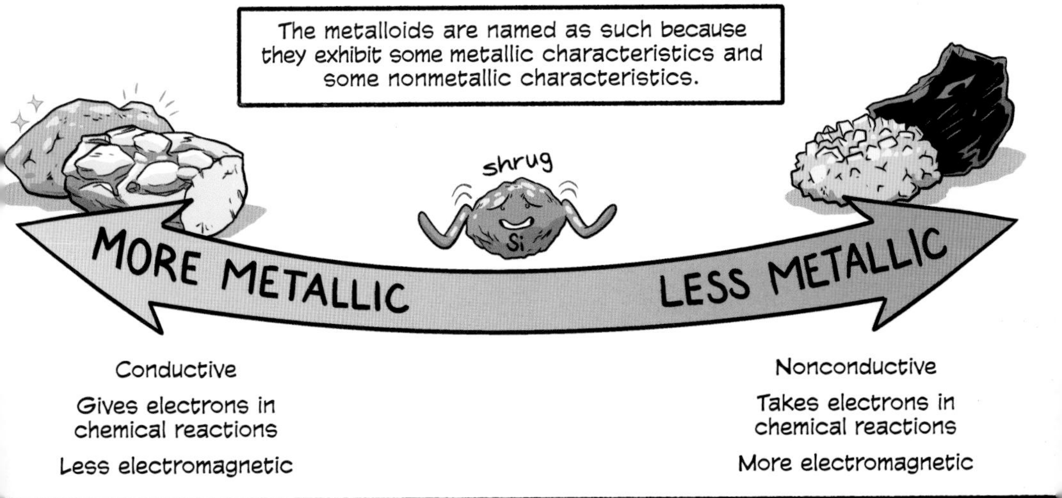
The metalloids are named as such because they exhibit some metallic characteristics and some nonmetallic characteristics.
shrug
Si
MORE METALLIC
LESS METALLIC
Conductive
Gives electrons in chemical reactions
Less electromagnetic
Nonconductive
Takes electrons in chemical reactions
More electromagnetic

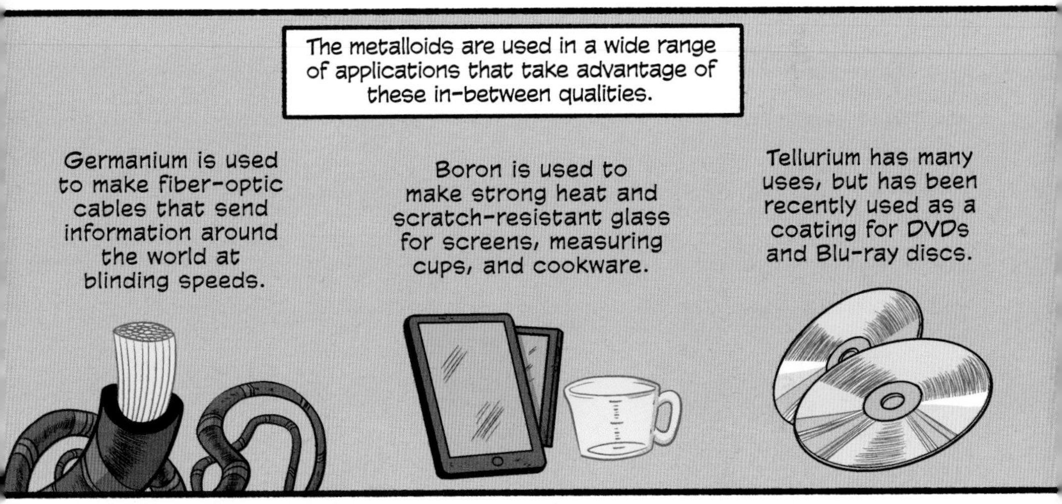
The metalloids are used in a wide range of applications that take advantage of these in-between qualities.
Germanium is used to make fiber-optic cables that send information around the world at blinding speeds.
Boron is used to make strong heat and scratch-resistant glass for screens, measuring cups, and cookware.
Tellurium has many uses, but has been recently used as a coating for DVDs and Blu-ray discs.

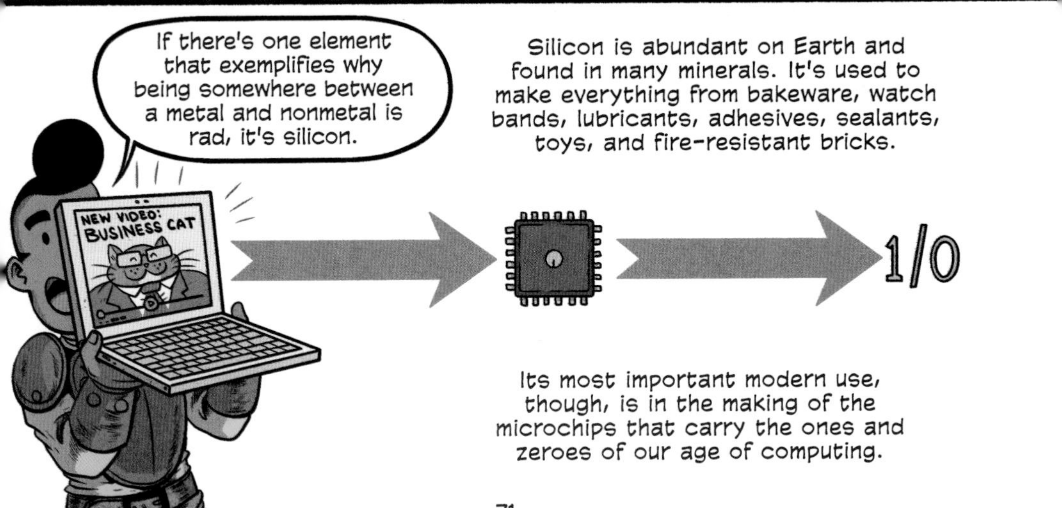
If there's one element that exemplifies why being somewhere between a metal and nonmetal is rad, it's silicon.
Silicon is abundant on Earth and found in many minerals. It's used to make everything from bakeware, watch bands, lubricants, adhesives, sealants, toys, and fire-resistant bricks.
NEW VIDEO: BUSINESS CAT
1/0
Its most important modern use, though, is in the making of the microchips that carry the ones and zeroes of our age of computing.

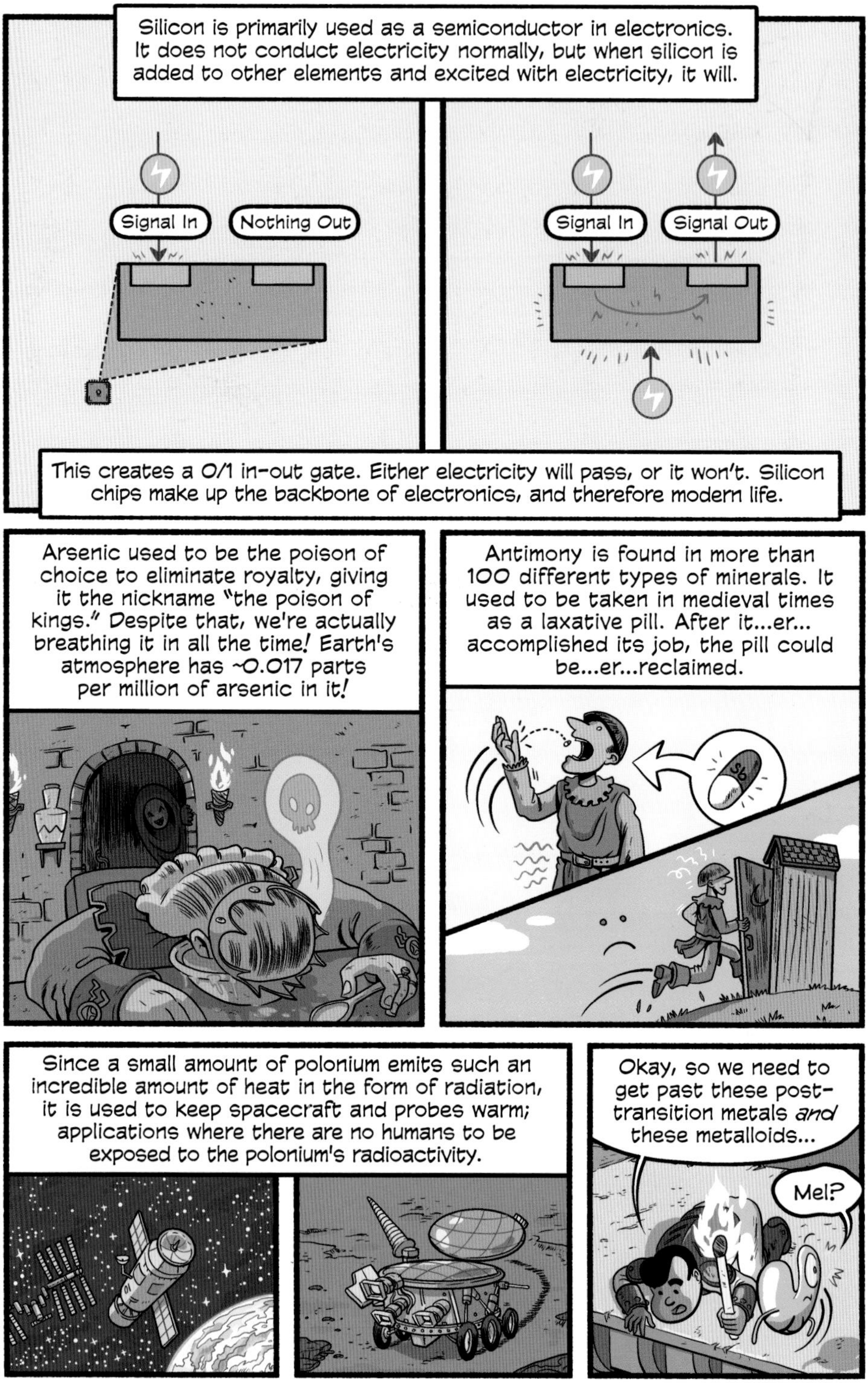
Silicon is primarily used as a semiconductor in electronics. It does not conduct electricity normally, but when silicon is added to other elements and excited with electricity, it will.
Signal In
Nothing Out
Signal In
Signal Out
This creates a 0/1 in-out gate. Either electricity will pass, or it won't. Silicon chips make up the backbone of electronics, and therefore modern life.
Arsenic used to be the poison of choice to eliminate royalty, giving it the nickname "the poison of kings." Despite that, we're actually breathing it in all the time! Earth's atmosphere has ~0.017 parts per million of arsenic in it!
Antimony is found in more than 100 different types of minerals. It used to be taken in medieval times as a laxative pill. After it...er... accomplished its job, the pill could be...er...reclaimed.
Sb
Since a small amount of polonium emits such an incredible amount of heat in the form of radiation, it is used to keep spacecraft and probes warm; applications where there are no humans to be exposed to the polonium's radioactivity.
Okay, so we need to get past these post-transition metals *and* these metalloids...
Mel?

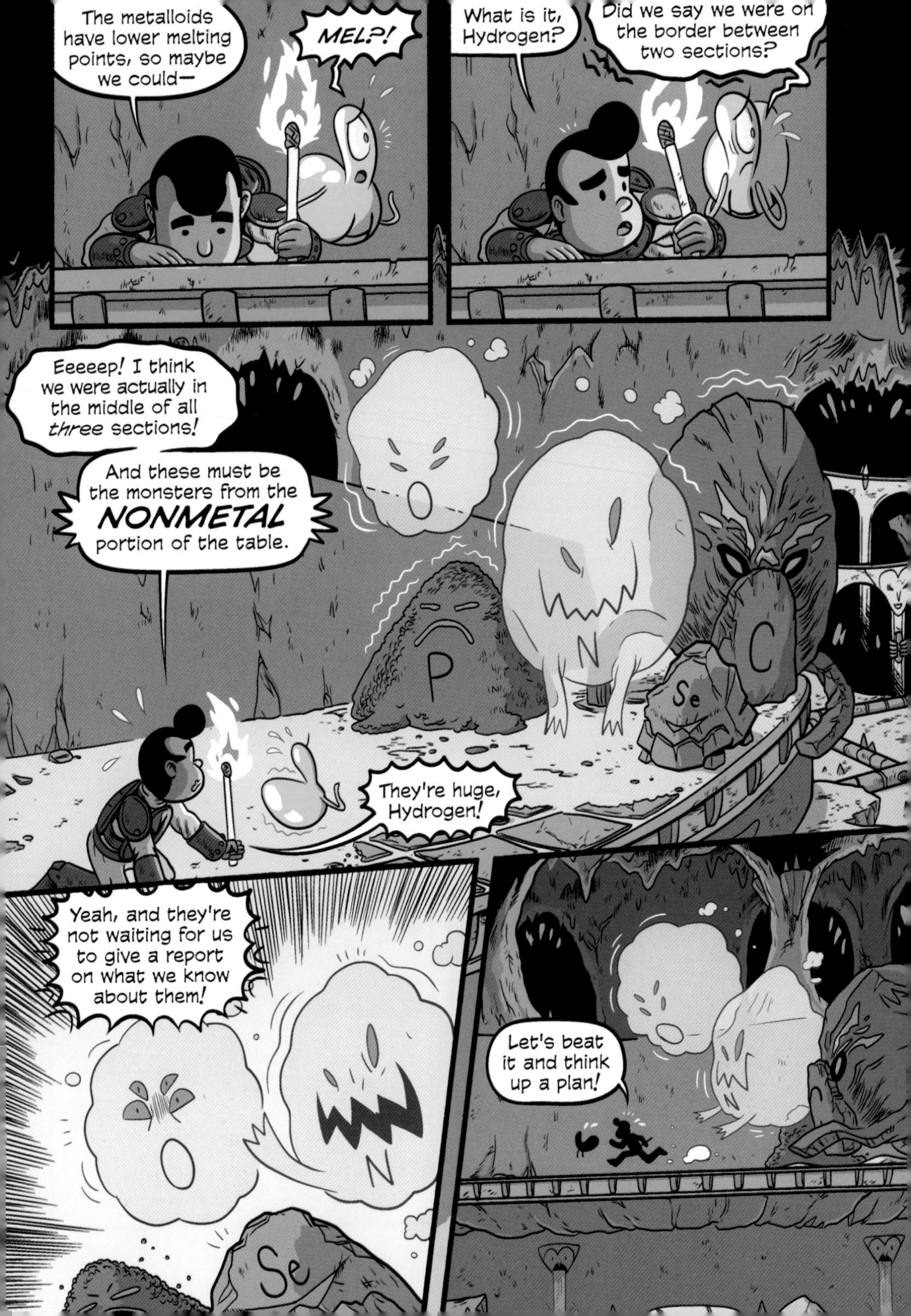

The metalloids have lower melting points, so maybe we could—
MEL?!
What is it, Hydrogen?
Did we say we were on the border between two sections?
Eeeeep! I think we were actually in the middle of all *three* sections!
And these must be the monsters from the **NONMETAL** portion of the table.
P
N
C
Se
They're huge, Hydrogen!
Yeah, and they're not waiting for us to give a report on what we know about them!
N
Se
Let's beat it and think up a plan!
N

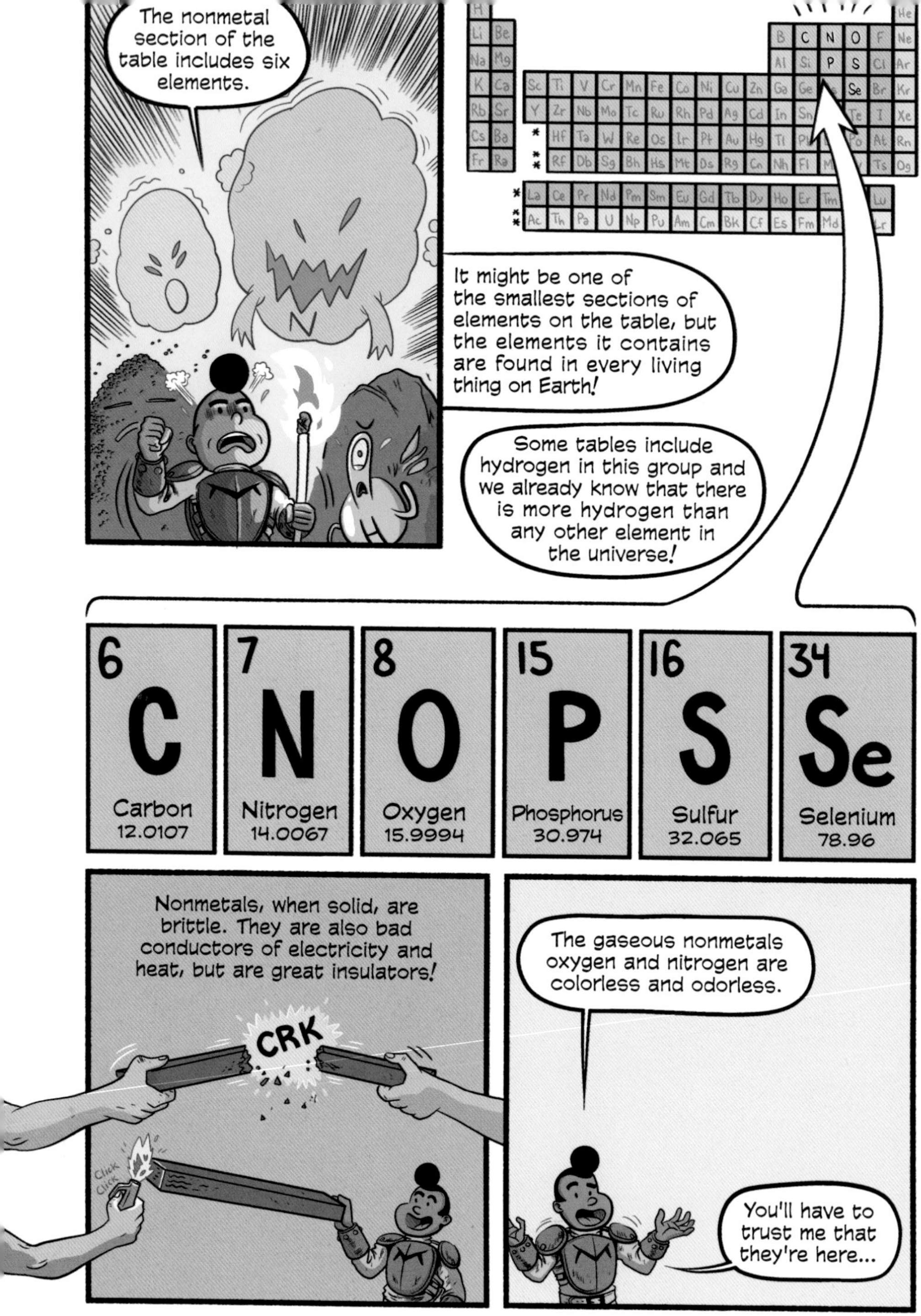
The nonmetal section of the table includes six elements.
It might be one of the smallest sections of elements on the table, but the elements it contains are found in every living thing on Earth!
Some tables include hydrogen in this group and we already know that there is more hydrogen than any other element in the universe!
6 C Carbon 12.0107
7 N Nitrogen 14.0067
8 O Oxygen 15.9994
15 P Phosphorus 30.974
16 S Sulfur 32.065
34 Se Selenium 78.96
Nonmetals, when solid, are brittle. They are also bad conductors of electricity and heat, but are great insulators!
CRK
Click Click
The gaseous nonmetals oxygen and nitrogen are colorless and odorless.
You'll have to trust me that they're here...

Nonmetals are EVERYWHERE. Take a look around the room. The chance that you will NOT be looking at something that contains a nonmetal is slim.

And that includes us! Out of all the elements that make up humans, nonmetals are the most abundant.

Oxygen - 65%
Carbon - 18.5%
Hydrogen - 9.5%
Nitrogen - 3.2%
Calcium - 1.5%
Phosphorus - 1%
Potassium - 0.4%
Sulfur - 0.3%
Sodium - 0.2%
Chlorine - 0.2%
All others - ~0.2%

Many of the substances we eat (fats, sugars, fiber) contain nonmetals like oxygen, hydrogen, nitrogen, phosphorus, sulfur, and carbon.

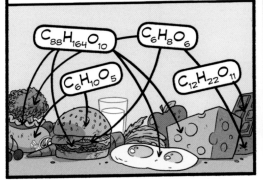

$C_{88}H_{164}O_{10}$ $C_6H_8O_6$

$C_6H_{10}O_5$ $C_{12}H_{22}O_{11}$

Speaking of carbon, no other element has more compounds than carbon. More than *nine million* compounds with carbon are known. Carbon makes up the bulk of living matter on Earth!

I'm EVERYWHERE!

Pure, solid carbon takes on different forms. Depending on how the atoms arrange themselves, you can have different solids with different properties. These different forms are called *allotropes*!

The three most common allotropes of carbon are:

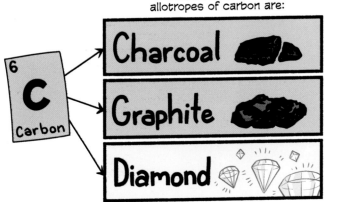

6
C
Carbon

Charcoal

Graphite

Diamond

Carbon isn't only an element that is sitting in the earth waiting for us to dig it up, either. Carbon is exchanged through humans, plants, rain, the ocean, and volcanic eruptions in a cycle called the Carbon Cycle.

All of the nonmetals have interesting qualities, uses, and histories! Sulfur stinks in the presence of hydrogen, and is used in gunpowder.

BANG

Phosphorus was discovered in 1669 by the alchemist Hennig Brand, who isolated it while boiling down his urine.

You know, for science!

Nitrogen, a gas, is normally unreactive in its natural group of two atoms. But nitrogen in nitroglycerin is much less stable, and when the bonds between nitrogen and oxygen are broken, it releases an explosive amount of energy.

Kaboom!

All of the nonmetals are important, but we'd be nowhere without oxygen! It is the third most abundant element IN THE UNIVERSE and the most abundant element in Earth's crust!

In groups of three atoms, oxygen forms ozone molecules, which protect Earth from dangerous solar radiation!

We need oxygen to fuel our bodies! Take a deep breath!

21% of that breath was oxygen!

The nonmetals are amazing, and I'm happy to sometimes be lumped in with them—

Ozone

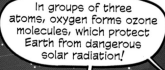

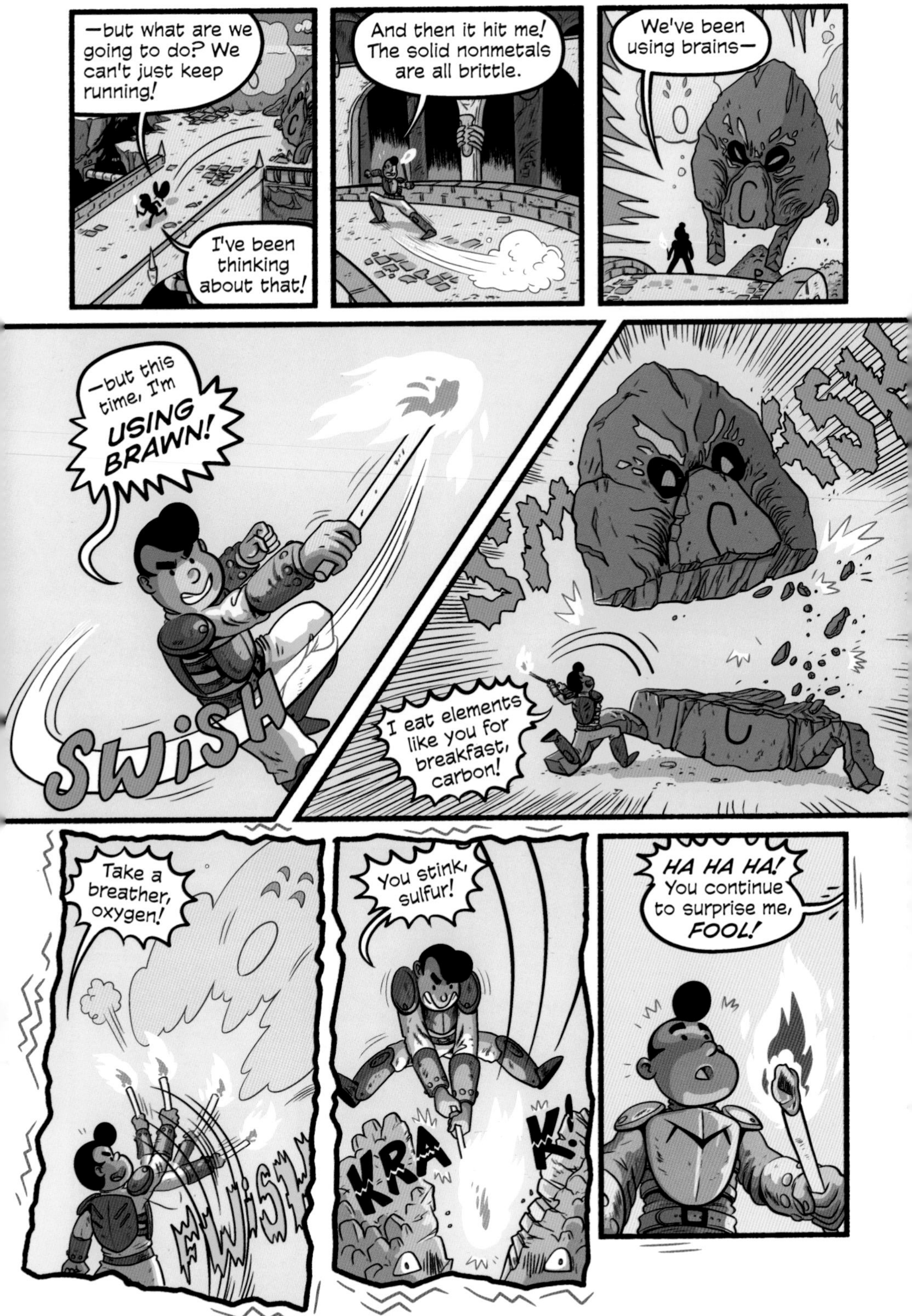

—but what are we going to do? We can't just keep running!
I've been thinking about that!
And then it hit me! The solid nonmetals are all brittle.
We've been using brains—
—but this time, I'm USING BRAWN!
SWISH
SWISH
I eat elements like you for breakfast, carbon!
Take a breather, oxygen!
SWISH
You stink, sulfur!
KRAK!
HA HA HA! You continue to surprise me, FOOL!

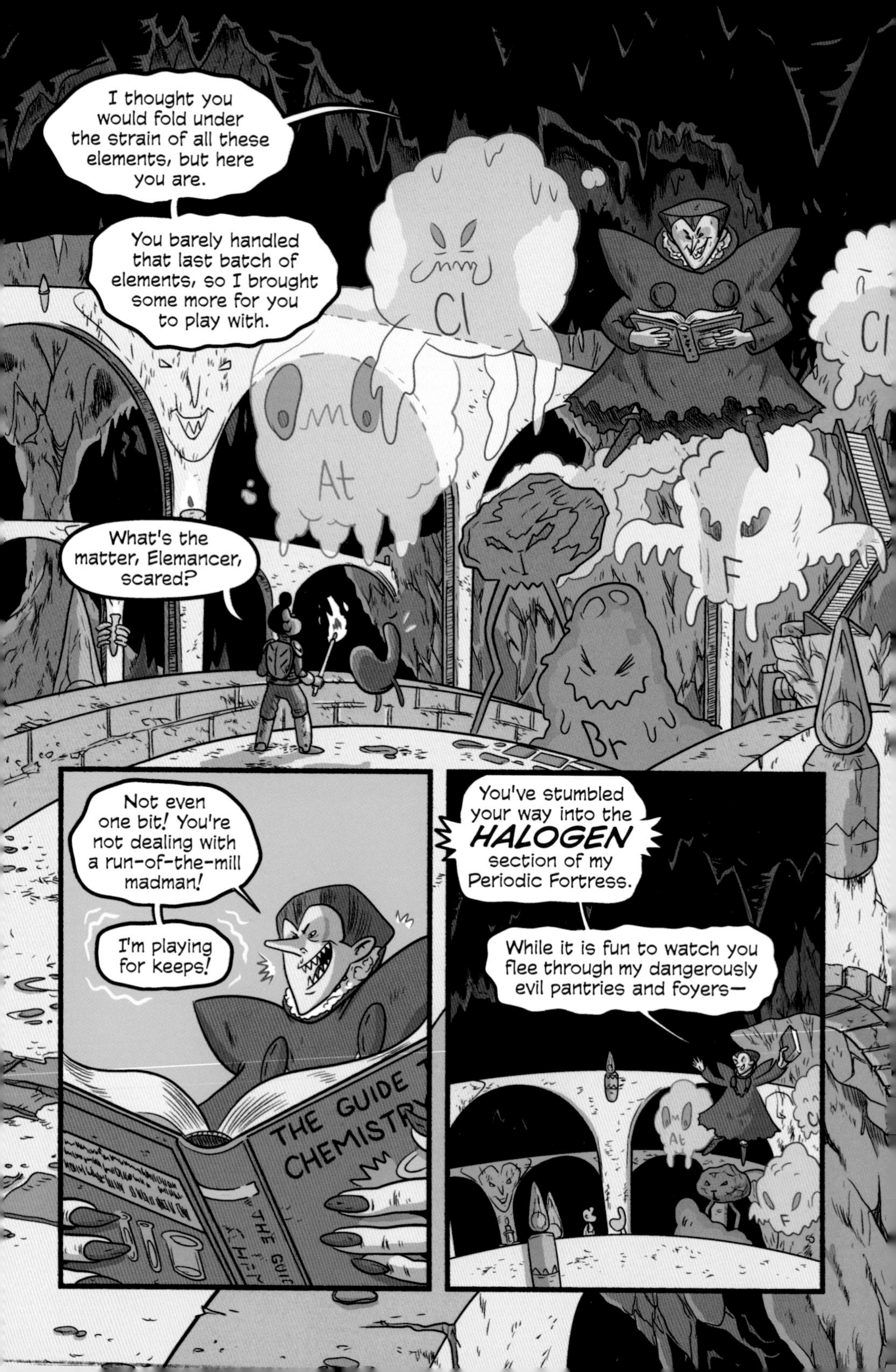

I thought you would fold under the strain of all these elements, but here you are.
You barely handled that last batch of elements, so I brought some more for you to play with.
Cl
At
F
Br
Cl
What's the matter, Elemancer, scared?
Not even one bit! You're not dealing with a run-of-the-mill madman!
I'm playing for keeps!
THE GUIDE T CHEMISTRY
You've stumbled your way into the HALOGEN section of my Periodic Fortress.
While it is fun to watch you flee through my dangerously evil pantries and foyers—
At
F

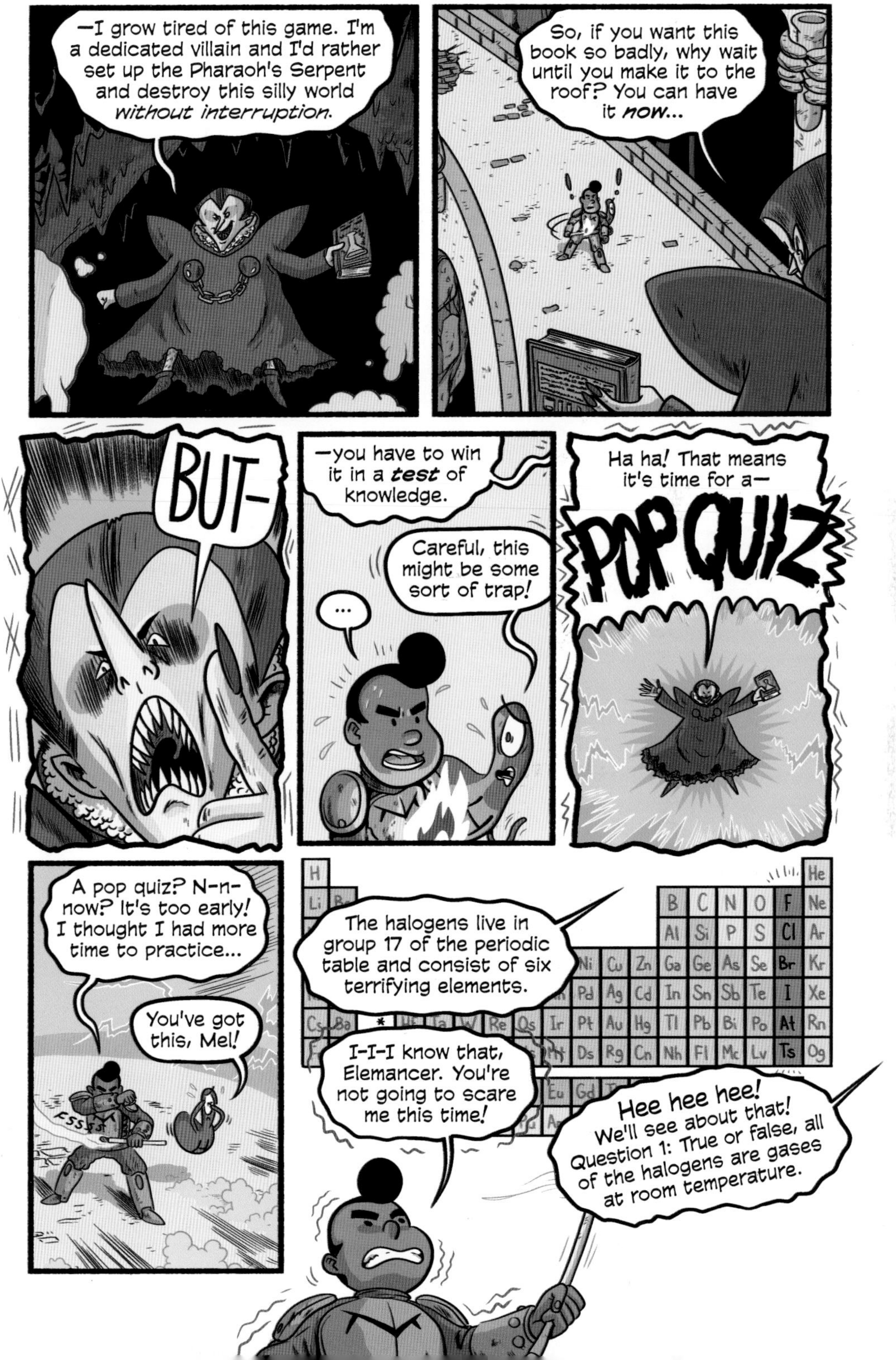
—I grow tired of this game. I'm a dedicated villain and I'd rather set up the Pharaoh's Serpent and destroy this silly world *without interruption*.
So, if you want this book so badly, why wait until you make it to the roof? You can have it ***now...***
BUT—
—you have to win it in a ***test*** of knowledge.
Careful, this might be some sort of trap!
...
Ha ha! That means it's time for a—
POP QUIZ
A pop quiz? N-n-now? It's too early! I thought I had more time to practice...
You've got this, Mel!
FSSSS
The halogens live in group 17 of the periodic table and consist of six terrifying elements.
I-I-I know that, Elemancer. You're not going to scare me this time!
Hee hee hee! We'll see about that! Question 1: True or false, all of the halogens are gases at room temperature.

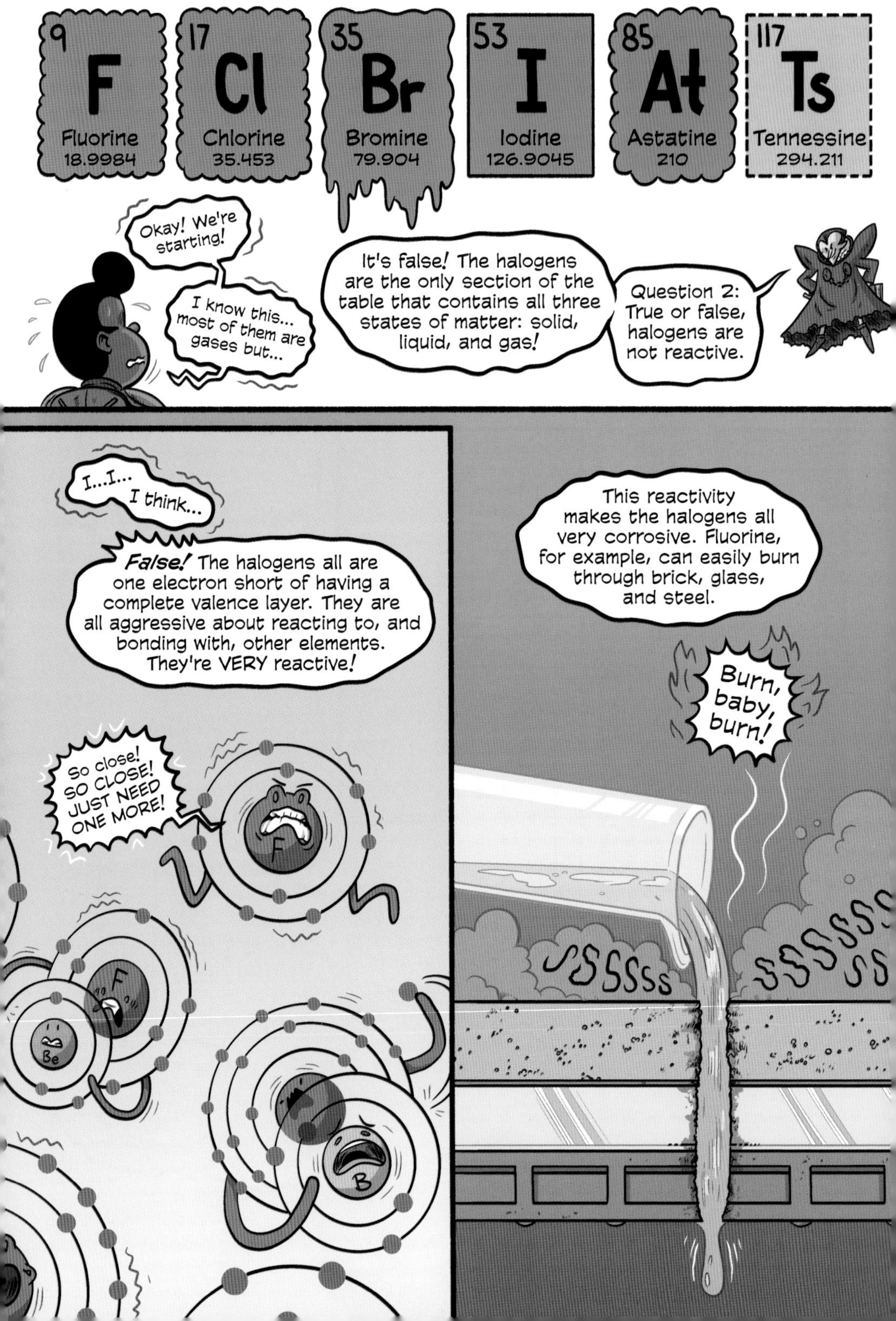
9 F Fluorine 18.9984
17 Cl Chlorine 35.453
35 Br Bromine 79.904
53 I Iodine 126.9045
85 At Astatine 210
117 Ts Tennessine 294.211
Question 2: True or false, halogens are not reactive.
It's false! The halogens are the only section of the table that contains all three states of matter: solid, liquid, and gas!
Okay! We're starting!
I know this... most of them are gases but...
I...I... I think...
False! The halogens all are one electron short of having a complete valence layer. They are all aggressive about reacting to, and bonding with, other elements. They're VERY reactive!
So close! SO CLOSE! JUST NEED ONE MORE!
F
F
Be
B
This reactivity makes the halogens all very corrosive. Fluorine, for example, can easily burn through brick, glass, and steel.
Burn, baby, burn!
SSSSSs
SSSSSS

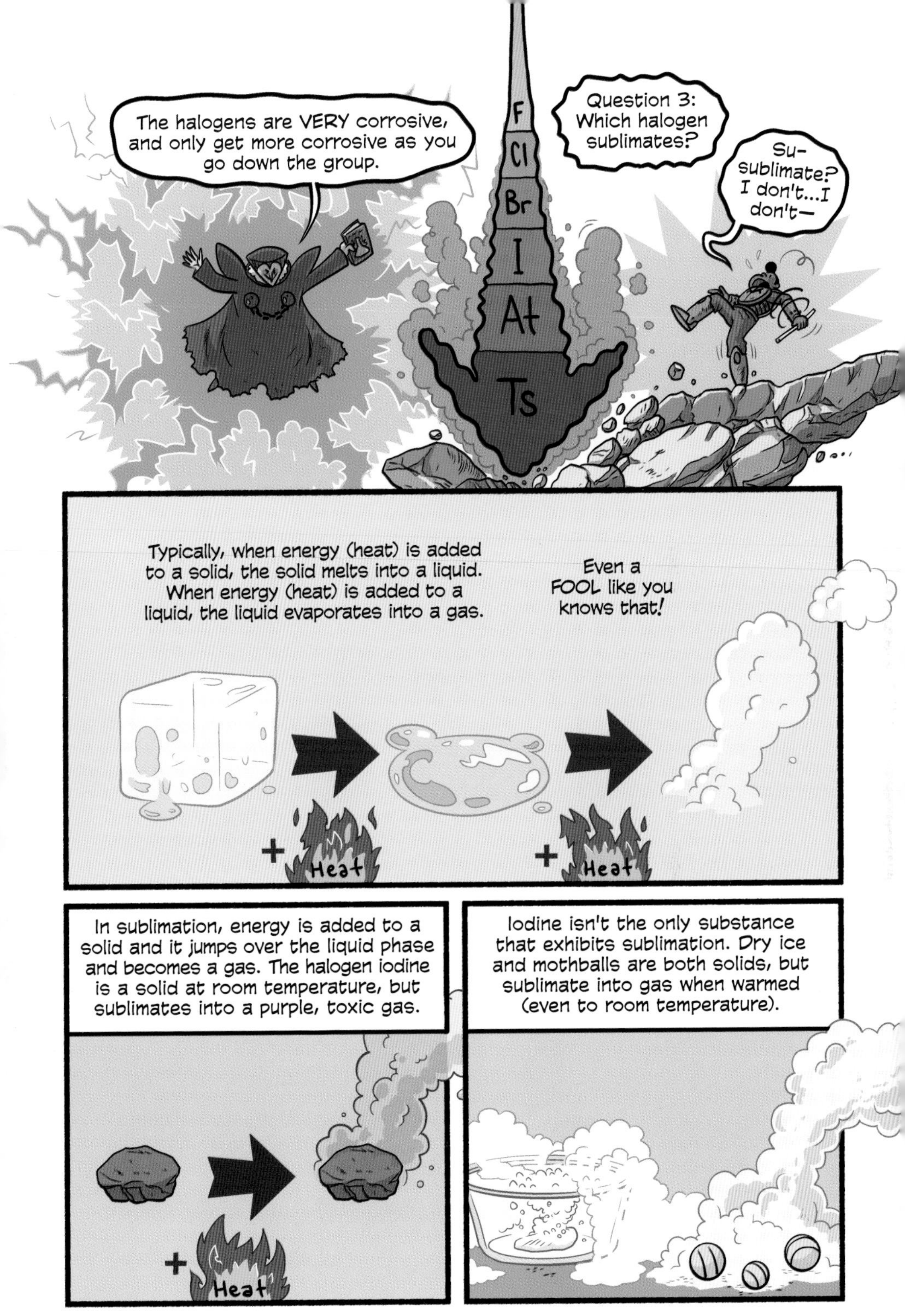
The halogens are VERY corrosive, and only get more corrosive as you go down the group.
F
Cl
Br
I
At
Ts
Question 3: Which halogen sublimates?
Su-sublimate? I don't...I don't—
Typically, when energy (heat) is added to a solid, the solid melts into a liquid. When energy (heat) is added to a liquid, the liquid evaporates into a gas.
Even a FOOL like you knows that!
+ Heat
+ Heat
In sublimation, energy is added to a solid and it jumps over the liquid phase and becomes a gas. The halogen iodine is a solid at room temperature, but sublimates into a purple, toxic gas.
+ Heat
Iodine isn't the only substance that exhibits sublimation. Dry ice and mothballs are both solids, but sublimate into gas when warmed (even to room temperature).

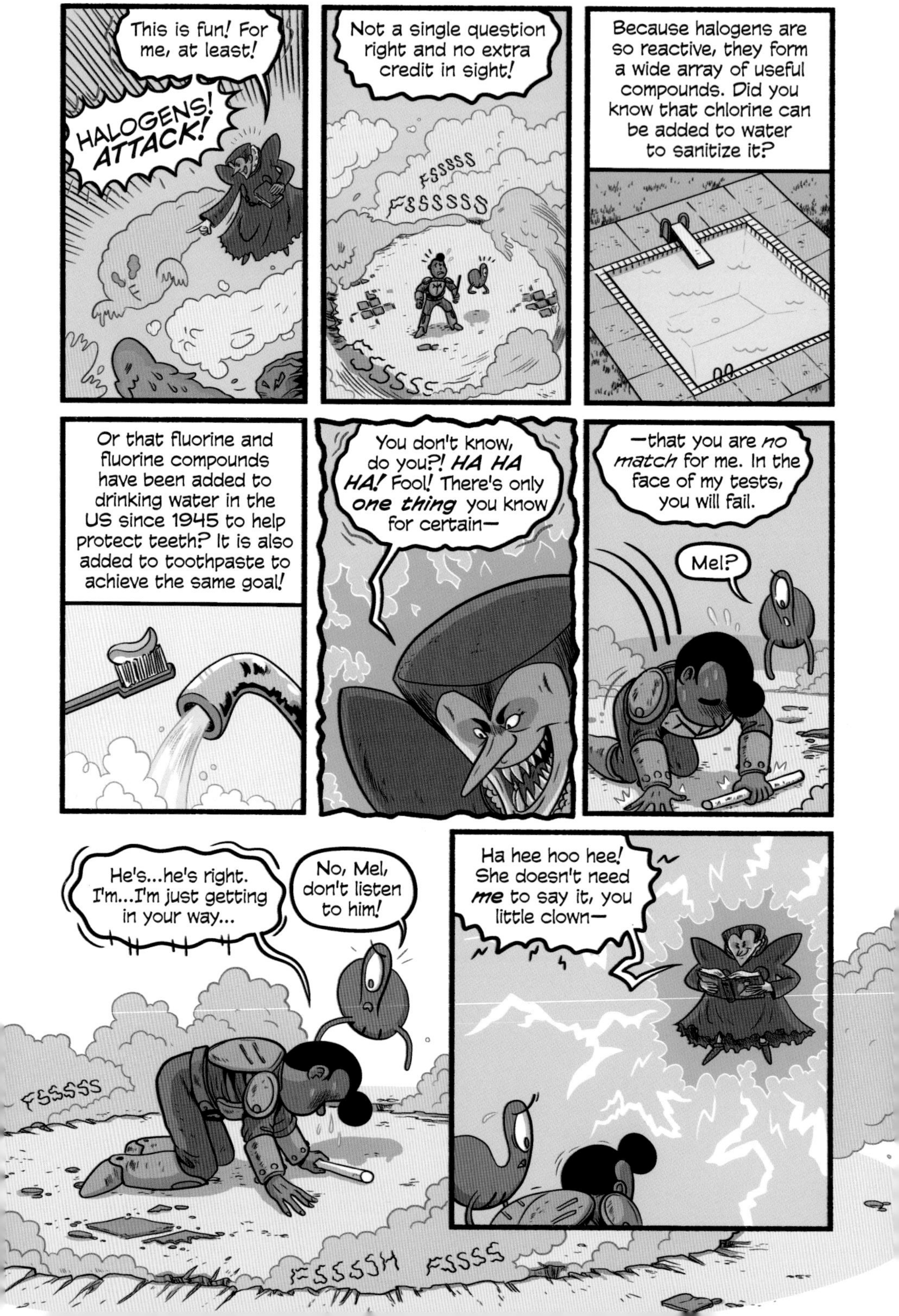
This is fun! For me, at least!
HALOGENS! ATTACK!
Not a single question right and no extra credit in sight!
FSSSSS
FSSSSSS
SSSSS
Because halogens are so reactive, they form a wide array of useful compounds. Did you know that chlorine can be added to water to sanitize it?
Or that fluorine and fluorine compounds have been added to drinking water in the US since 1945 to help protect teeth? It is also added to toothpaste to achieve the same goal!
You don't know, do you?! HA HA HA! Fool! There's only one thing you know for certain—
—that you are no match for me. In the face of my tests, you will fail.
Mel?
He's...he's right. I'm...I'm just getting in your way...
No, Mel, don't listen to him!
Ha hee hoo hee! She doesn't need me to say it, you little clown—
FSSSSS
FSSSSH FSSSS

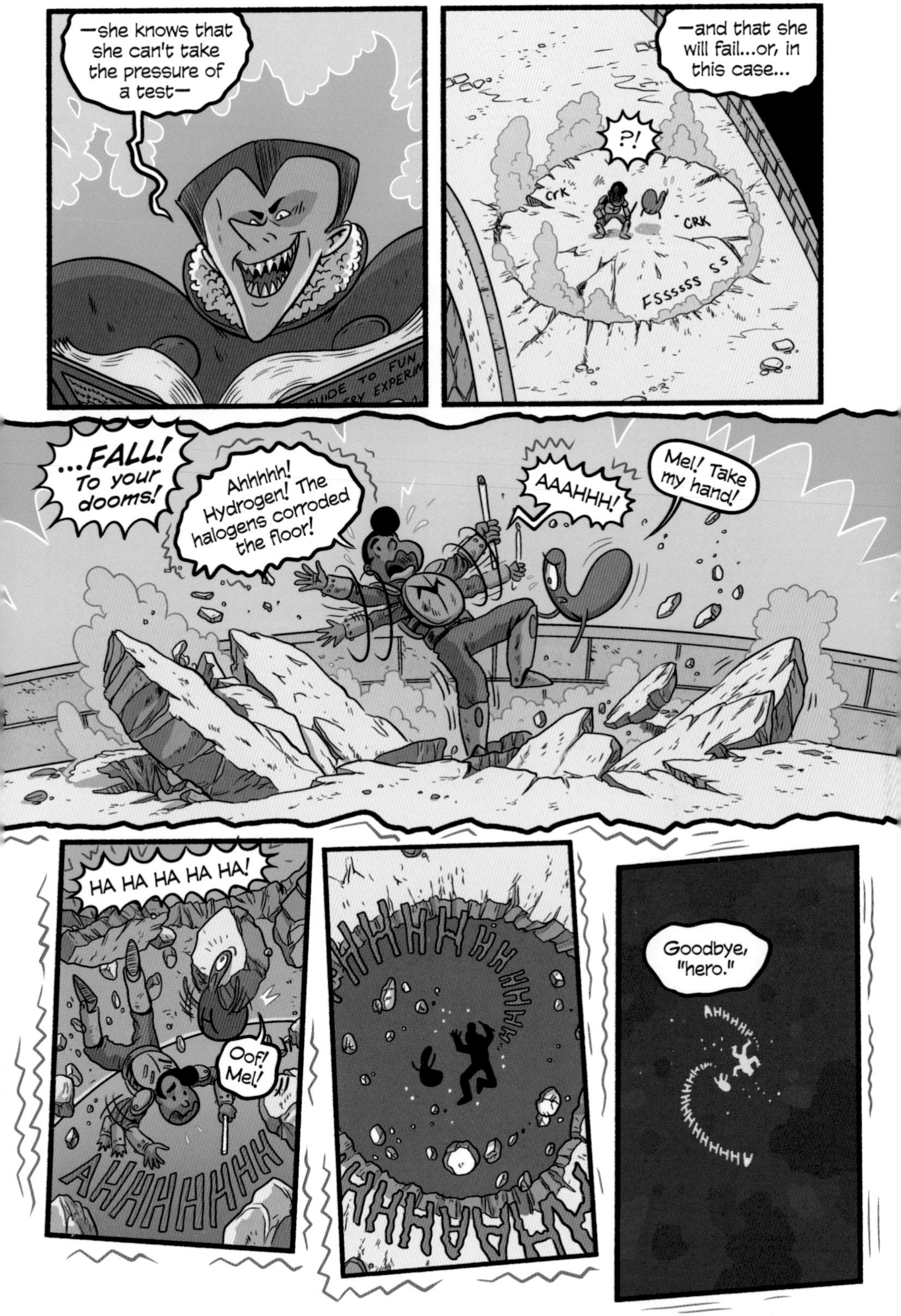
—she knows that she can't take the pressure of a test—
—and that she will fail...or, in this case...
?!
CRK
CRK
FSSSSSS SS
...FALL! To your dooms!
Ahhhhh! Hydrogen! The halogens corroded the floor!
AAAHHH!
Mel! Take my hand!
HA HA HA HA HA!
Oof! Mel!
Goodbye, "hero."

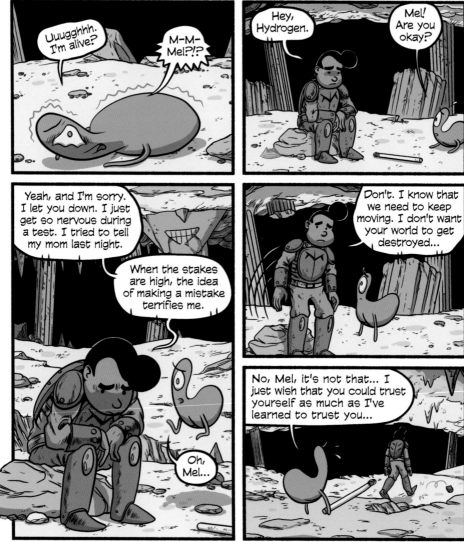

Uuugghhh. I'm alive?

M-M-Mel?!?

Hey, Hydrogen.

Mel! Are you okay?

Yeah, and I'm sorry. I let you down. I just get so nervous during a test. I tried to tell my mom last night.

When the stakes are high, the idea of making a mistake terrifies me.

Oh, Mel...

Don't. I know that we need to keep moving. I don't want your world to get destroyed...

No, Mel, it's not that... I just wish that you could trust yourself as much as I've learned to trust you...

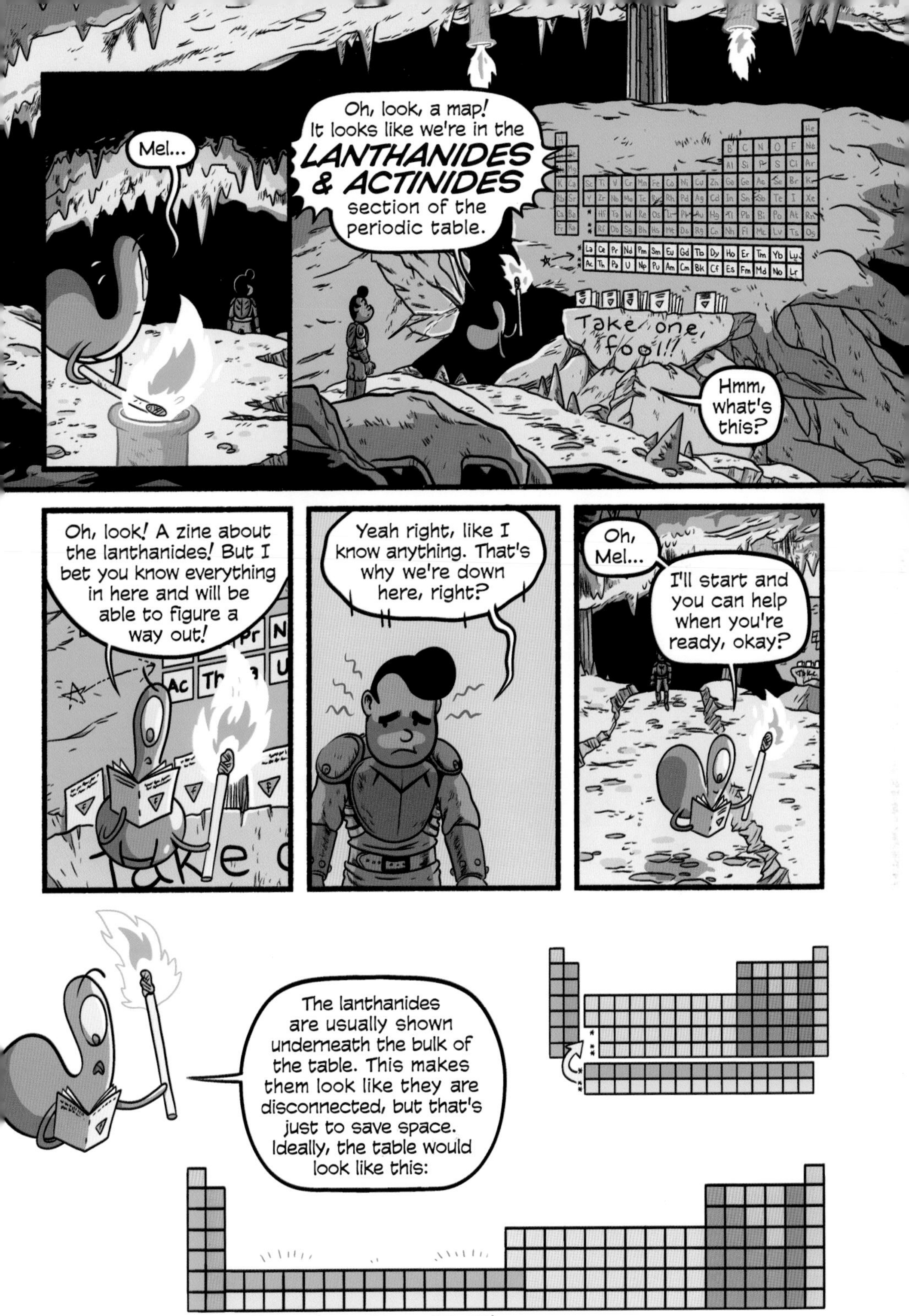
Mel...
Oh, look, a map! It looks like we're in the LANTHANIDES & ACTINIDES section of the periodic table.
Take one, fool!!
Hmm, what's this?
Oh, look! A zine about the lanthanides! But I bet you know everything in here and will be able to figure a way out!
Yeah right, like I know anything. That's why we're down here, right?
Oh, Mel...
I'll start and you can help when you're ready, okay?
The lanthanides are usually shown underneath the bulk of the table. This makes them look like they are disconnected, but that's just to save space. Ideally, the table would look like this:

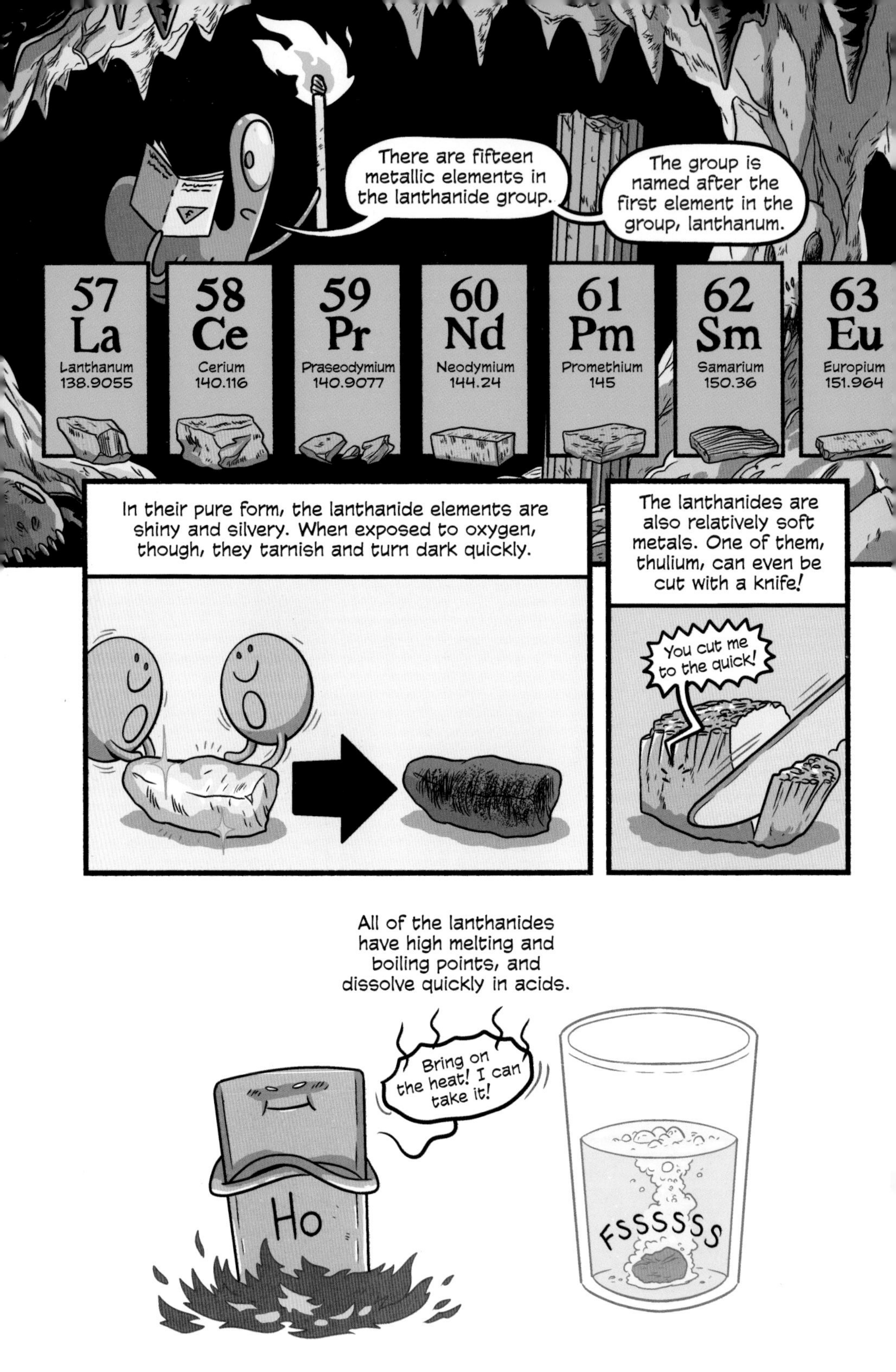
There are fifteen metallic elements in the lanthanide group.
The group is named after the first element in the group, lanthanum.
57 La Lanthanum 138.9055
58 Ce Cerium 140.116
59 Pr Praseodymium 140.9077
60 Nd Neodymium 144.24
61 Pm Promethium 145
62 Sm Samarium 150.36
63 Eu Europium 151.964
In their pure form, the lanthanide elements are shiny and silvery. When exposed to oxygen, though, they tarnish and turn dark quickly.
The lanthanides are also relatively soft metals. One of them, thulium, can even be cut with a knife!
You cut me to the quick!
All of the lanthanides have high melting and boiling points, and dissolve quickly in acids.
Bring on the heat! I can take it!
Ho
FSSSSSS

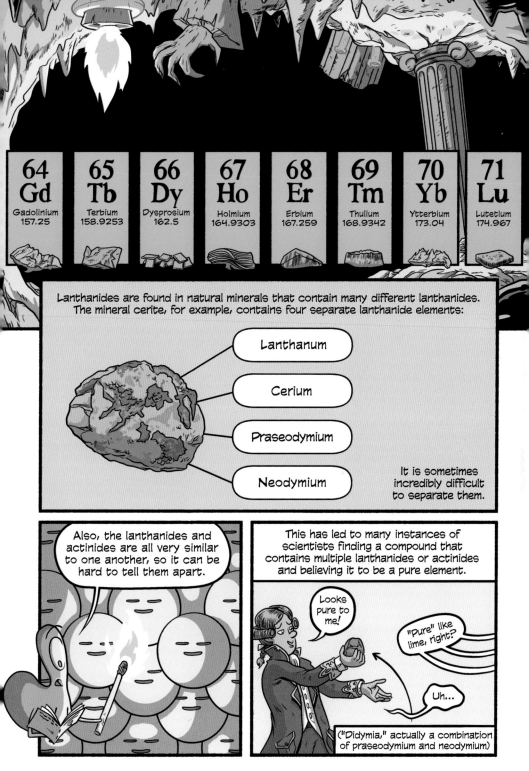

64 Gd Gadolinium 157.25

65 Tb Terbium 158.9253

66 Dy Dysprosium 162.5

67 Ho Holmium 164.9303

68 Er Erbium 167.259

69 Tm Thulium 168.9342

70 Yb Ytterbium 173.04

71 Lu Lutetium 174.967

Lanthanides are found in natural minerals that contain many different lanthanides. The mineral cerite, for example, contains four separate lanthanide elements:

- Lanthanum
- Cerium
- Praseodymium
- Neodymium

It is sometimes incredibly difficult to separate them.

Also, the lanthanides and actinides are all very similar to one another, so it can be hard to tell them apart.

This has led to many instances of scientists finding a compound that contains multiple lanthanides or actinides and believing it to be a pure element.

Looks pure to me!

"Pure" like lime, right?

Uh...

("Didymia," actually a combination of praseodymium and neodymium)

New techniques, like *spectrometry*, were developed to separate and distinguish the lanthanides and actinides from each other.

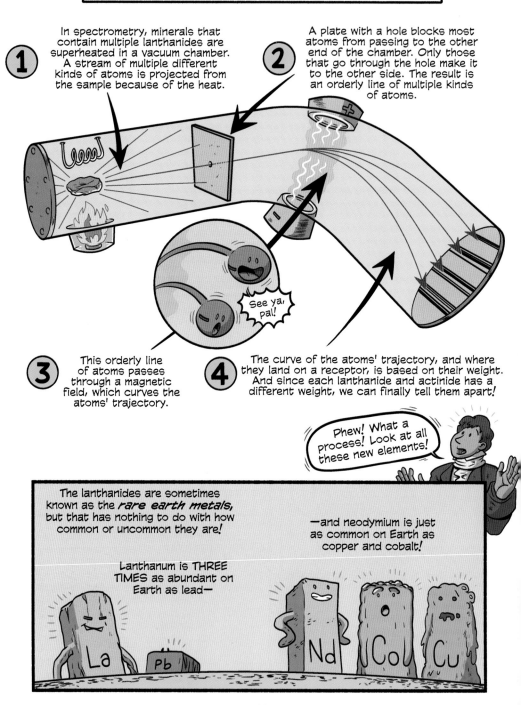

1 In spectrometry, minerals that contain multiple lanthanides are superheated in a vacuum chamber. A stream of multiple different kinds of atoms is projected from the sample because of the heat.

2 A plate with a hole blocks most atoms from passing to the other end of the chamber. Only those that go through the hole make it to the other side. The result is an orderly line of multiple kinds of atoms.

See ya, pal!

3 This orderly line of atoms passes through a magnetic field, which curves the atoms' trajectory.

4 The curve of the atoms' trajectory, and where they land on a receptor, is based on their weight. And since each lanthanide and actinide has a different weight, we can finally tell them apart!

Phew! What a process! Look at all these new elements!

The lanthanides are sometimes known as the *rare earth metals*, but that has nothing to do with how common or uncommon they are!

—and neodymium is just as common on Earth as copper and cobalt!

Lanthanum is THREE TIMES as abundant on Earth as lead—

La

Pb

Nd

Co

Cu

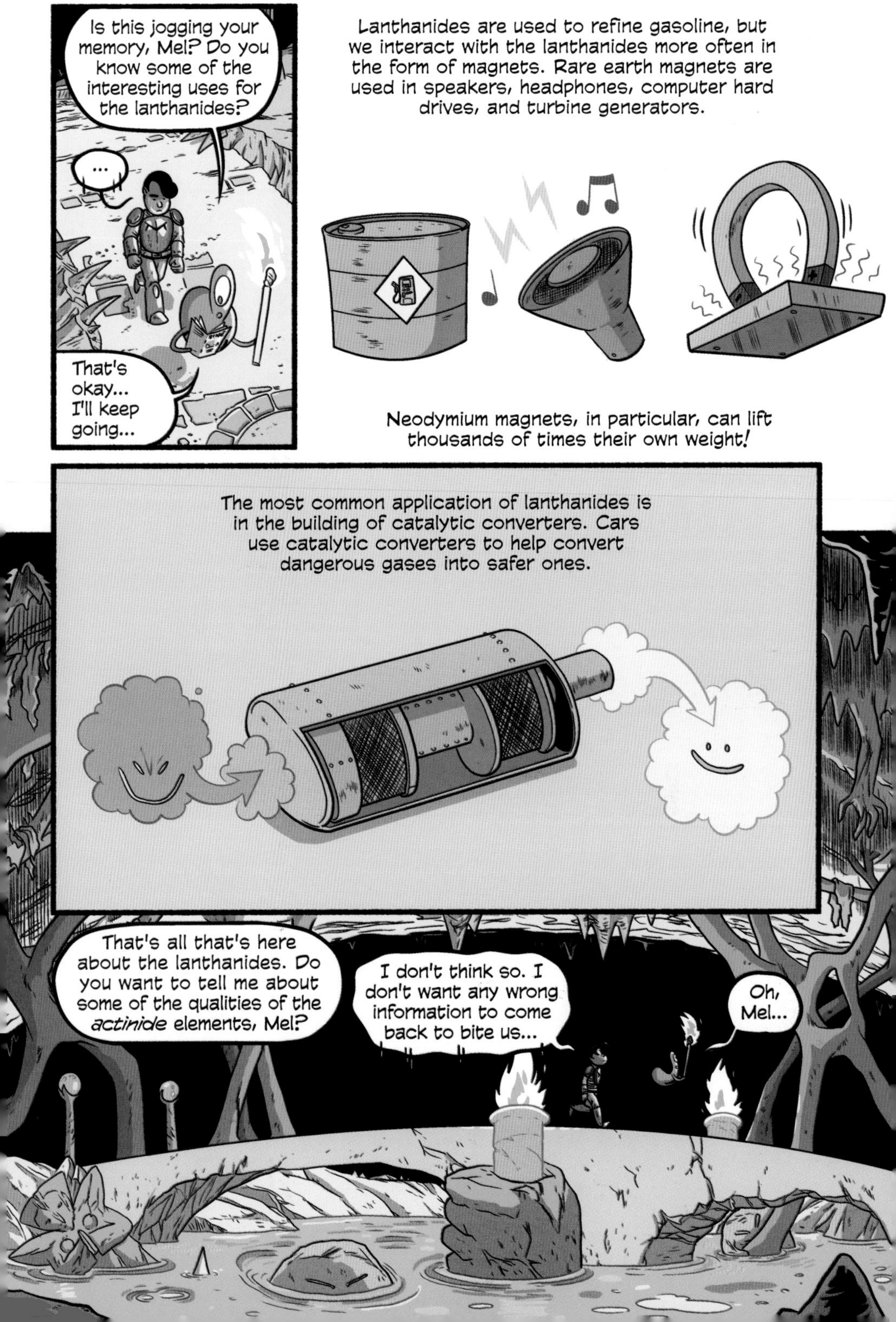

Is this jogging your memory, Mel? Do you know some of the interesting uses for the lanthanides?
...
That's okay... I'll keep going...
Lanthanides are used to refine gasoline, but we interact with the lanthanides more often in the form of magnets. Rare earth magnets are used in speakers, headphones, computer hard drives, and turbine generators.
Neodymium magnets, in particular, can lift thousands of times their own weight!
The most common application of lanthanides is in the building of catalytic converters. Cars use catalytic converters to help convert dangerous gases into safer ones.
That's all that's here about the lanthanides. Do you want to tell me about some of the qualities of the *actinide* elements, Mel?
I don't think so. I don't want any wrong information to come back to bite us...
Oh, Mel...

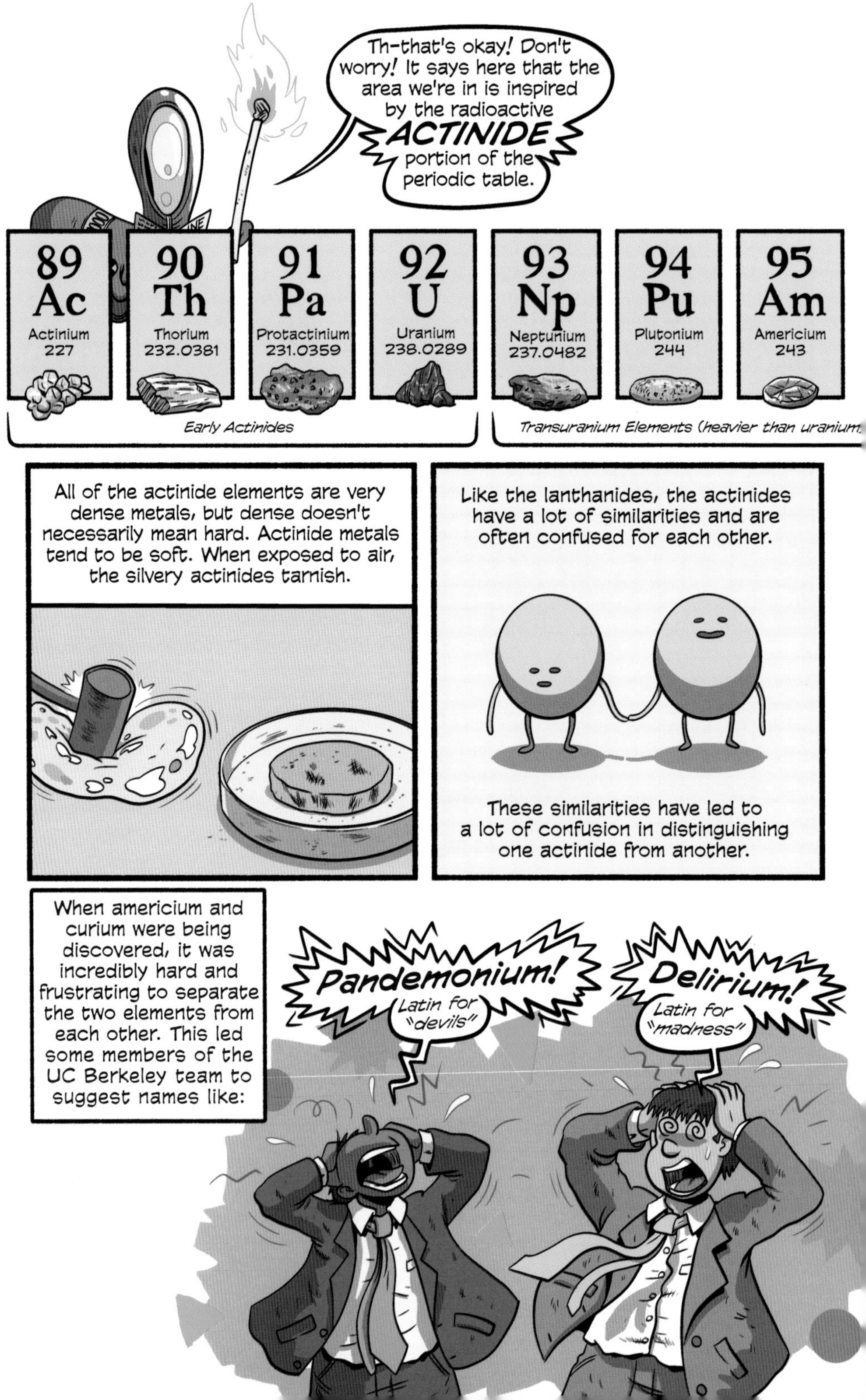

Th-that's okay! Don't worry! It says here that the area we're in is inspired by the radioactive ACTINIDE portion of the periodic table.
89 Ac Actinium 227
90 Th Thorium 232.0381
91 Pa Protactinium 231.0359
92 U Uranium 238.0289
93 Np Neptunium 237.0482
94 Pu Plutonium 244
95 Am Americium 243
Early Actinides
Transuranium Elements (heavier than uranium
All of the actinide elements are very dense metals, but dense doesn't necessarily mean hard. Actinide metals tend to be soft. When exposed to air, the silvery actinides tarnish.
Like the lanthanides, the actinides have a lot of similarities and are often confused for each other.
These similarities have led to a lot of confusion in distinguishing one actinide from another.
When americium and curium were being discovered, it was incredibly hard and frustrating to separate the two elements from each other. This led some members of the UC Berkeley team to suggest names like:
Pandemonium!
Latin for "devils"
Delirium!
Latin for "madness"

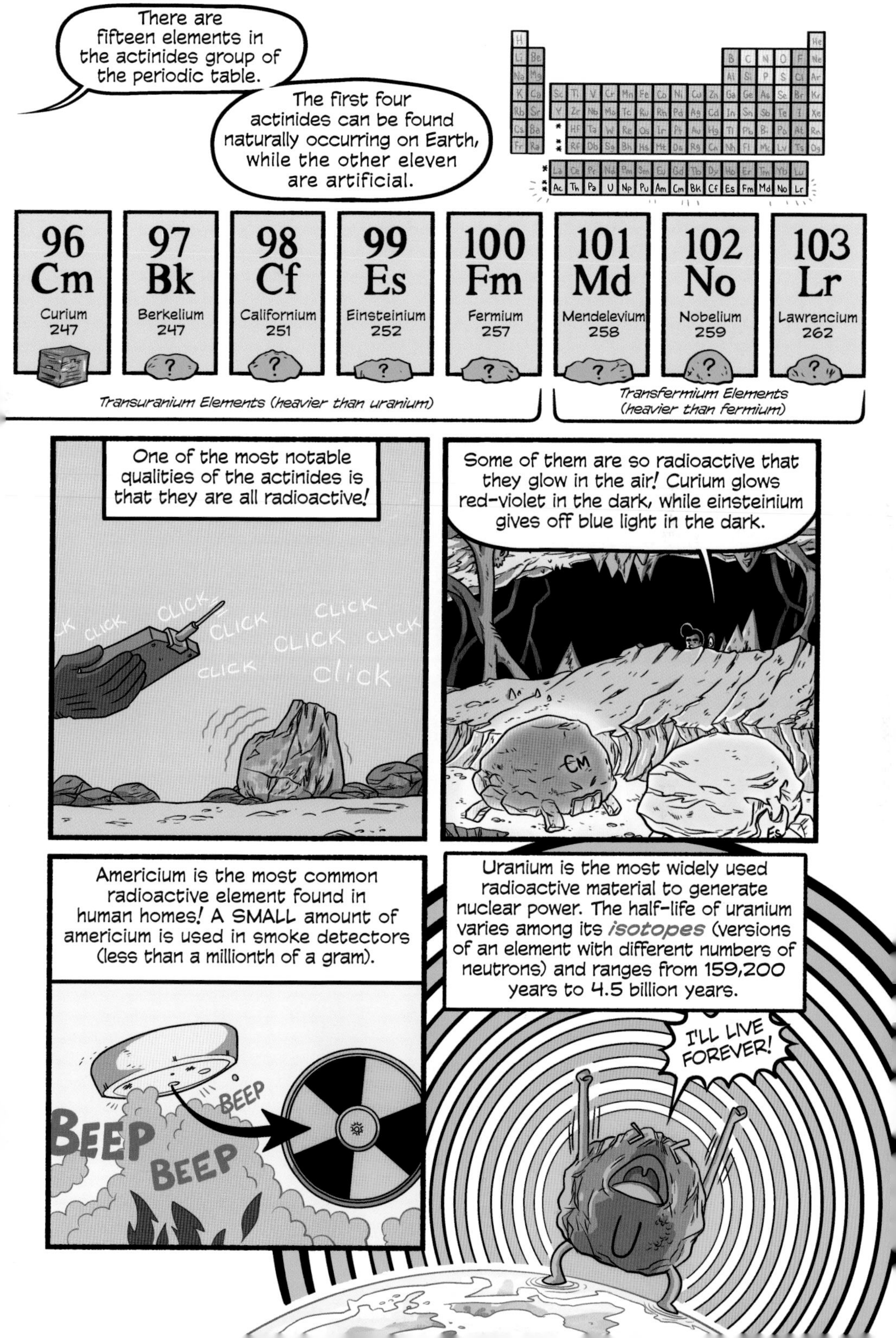
There are fifteen elements in the actinides group of the periodic table.
The first four actinides can be found naturally occurring on Earth, while the other eleven are artificial.
Ac Th Pa U Np Pu Am Cm Bk Cf Es Fm Md No Lr
96 Cm Curium 247
97 Bk Berkelium 247
98 Cf Californium 251
99 Es Einsteinium 252
100 Fm Fermium 257
101 Md Mendelevium 258
102 No Nobelium 259
103 Lr Lawrencium 262
Transuranium Elements (heavier than uranium)
Transfermium Elements (heavier than fermium)
One of the most notable qualities of the actinides is that they are all radioactive!
CLICK CLICK CLICK CLICK CLICK CLICK CLICK click
Some of them are so radioactive that they glow in the air! Curium glows red-violet in the dark, while einsteinium gives off blue light in the dark.
CM
Es
Americium is the most common radioactive element found in human homes! A SMALL amount of americium is used in smoke detectors (less than a millionth of a gram).
BEEP BEEP BEEP
Uranium is the most widely used radioactive material to generate nuclear power. The half-life of uranium varies among its *isotopes* (versions of an element with different numbers of neutrons) and ranges from 159,200 years to 4.5 billion years.
I'LL LIVE FOREVER!

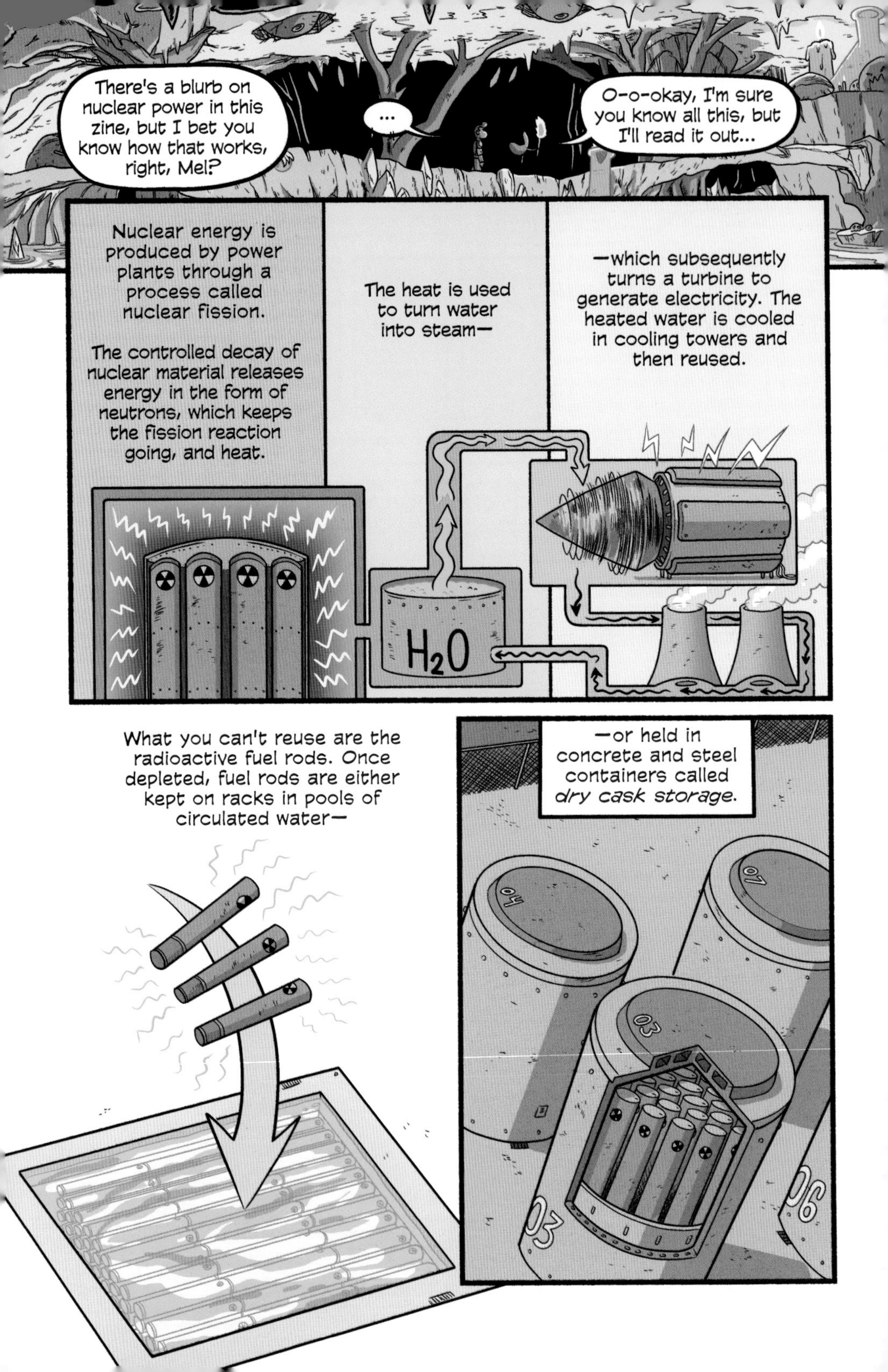
There's a blurb on nuclear power in this zine, but I bet you know how that works, right, Mel?
...
O-o-okay, I'm sure you know all this, but I'll read it out...
Nuclear energy is produced by power plants through a process called nuclear fission.
The controlled decay of nuclear material releases energy in the form of neutrons, which keeps the fission reaction going, and heat.
The heat is used to turn water into steam—
—which subsequently turns a turbine to generate electricity. The heated water is cooled in cooling towers and then reused.
H_2O
What you can't reuse are the radioactive fuel rods. Once depleted, fuel rods are either kept on racks in pools of circulated water—
—or held in concrete and steel containers called *dry cask storage*.
04
07
03
03
06

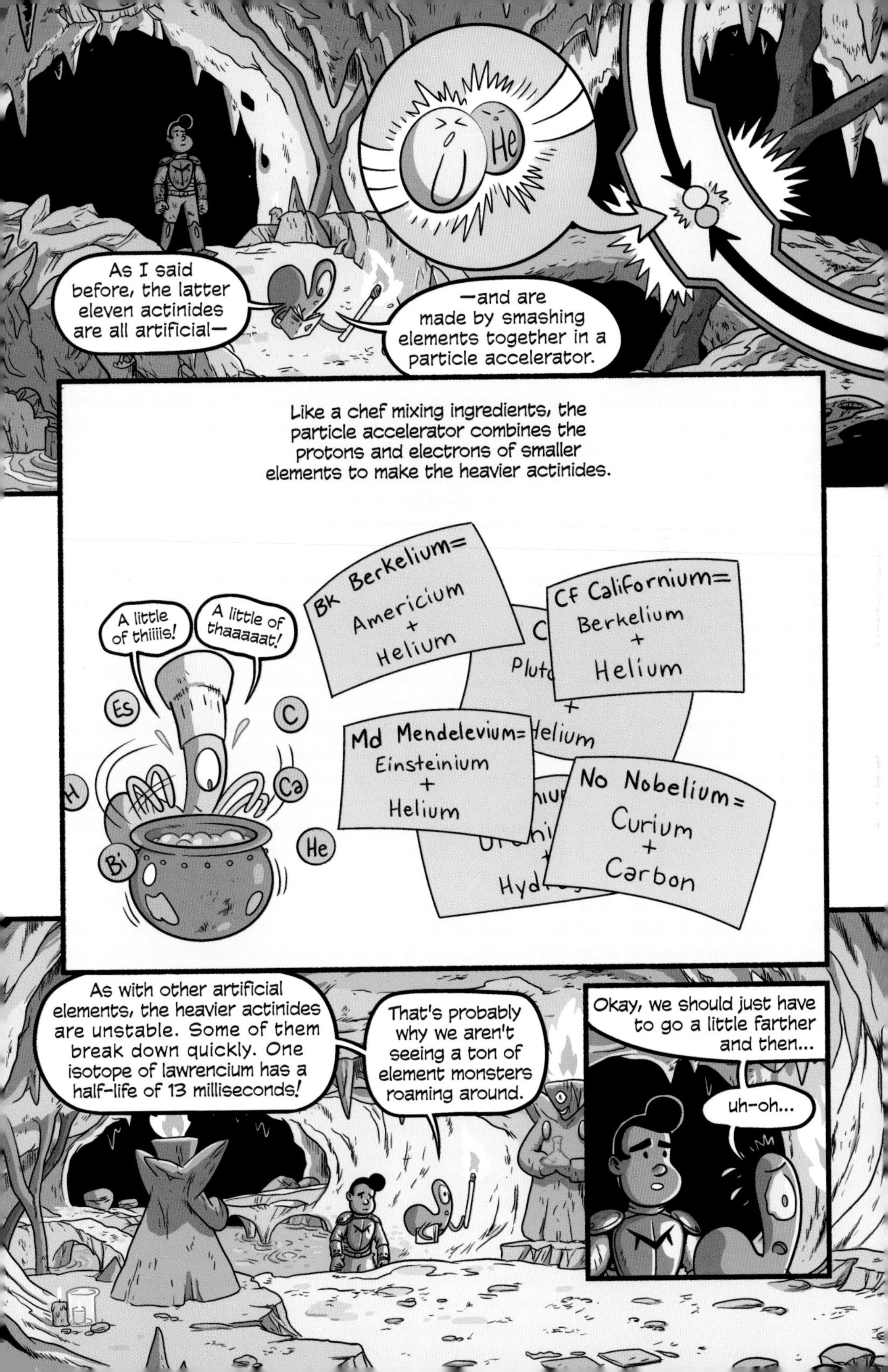

He
As I said before, the latter eleven actinides are all artificial—
—and are made by smashing elements together in a particle accelerator.
Like a chef mixing ingredients, the particle accelerator combines the protons and electrons of smaller elements to make the heavier actinides.
A little of thiiiis!
A little of thaaaaat!
Es
C
Ca
He
Bi
Bk Berkelium= Americium + Helium
Cf Californium= Berkelium + Helium
Md Mendelevium= Einsteinium + Helium
No Nobelium= Curium + Carbon
As with other artificial elements, the heavier actinides are unstable. Some of them break down quickly. One isotope of lawrencium has a half-life of 13 milliseconds!
That's probably why we aren't seeing a ton of element monsters roaming around.
Okay, we should just have to go a little farther and then...
uh-oh...

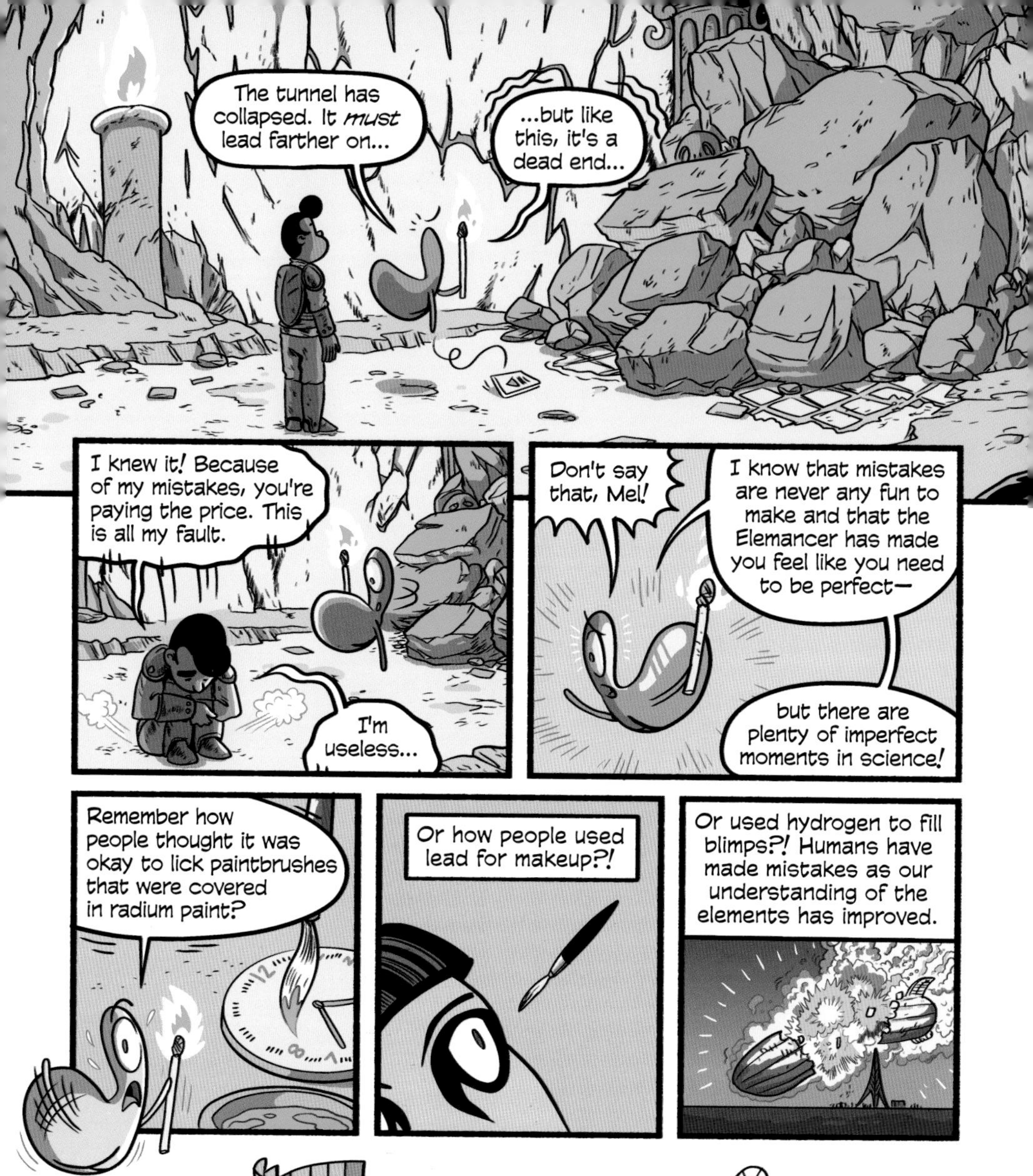
The tunnel has collapsed. It *must* lead farther on...
...but like this, it's a dead end...
I knew it! Because of my mistakes, you're paying the price. This is all my fault.
I'm useless...
Don't say that, Mel!
I know that mistakes are never any fun to make and that the Elemancer has made you feel like you need to be perfect—
but there are plenty of imperfect moments in science!
Remember how people thought it was okay to lick paintbrushes that were covered in radium paint?
Or how people used lead for makeup?!
Or used hydrogen to fill blimps?! Humans have made mistakes as our understanding of the elements has improved.

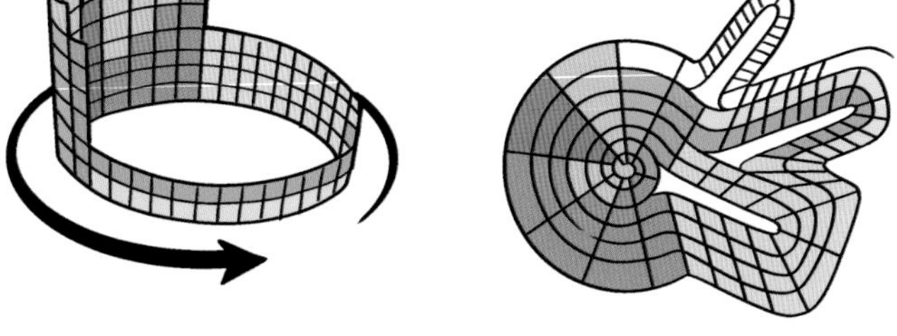

Even the periodic table of elements isn't perfect. Having a table that loops like a cylinder or connects in a circle would better illustrate the repeating, periodic nature of the elements' traits.

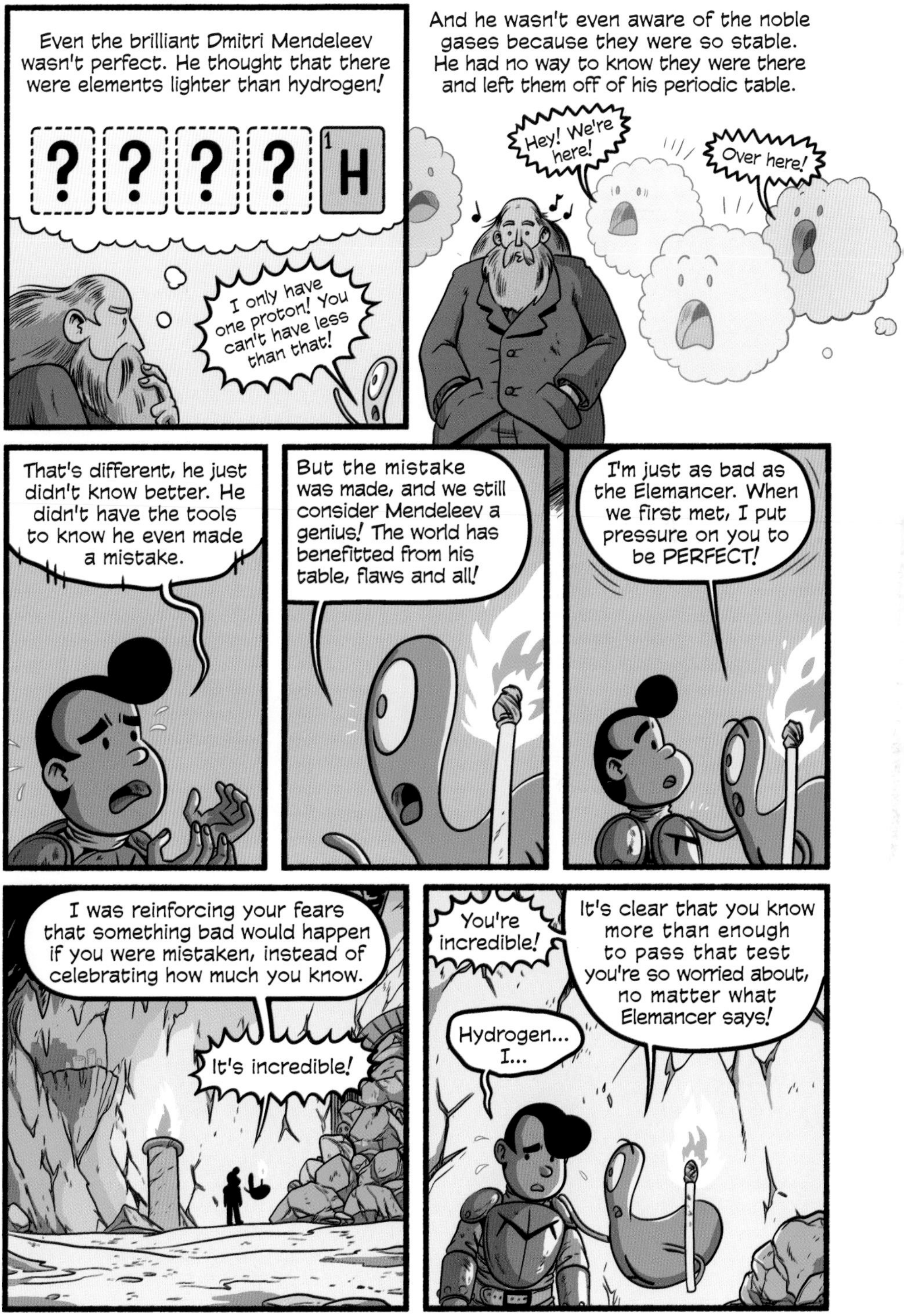

Even the brilliant Dmitri Mendeleev wasn't perfect. He thought that there were elements lighter than hydrogen!
? ? ? ? 1 H
I only have one proton! You can't have less than that!
And he wasn't even aware of the noble gases because they were so stable. He had no way to know they were there and left them off of his periodic table.
Hey! We're here!
Over here!
That's different, he just didn't know better. He didn't have the tools to know he even made a mistake.
But the mistake was made, and we still consider Mendeleev a genius! The world has benefitted from his table, flaws and all!
I'm just as bad as the Elemancer. When we first met, I put pressure on you to be PERFECT!
I was reinforcing your fears that something bad would happen if you were mistaken, instead of celebrating how much you know.
It's incredible!
You're incredible!
It's clear that you know more than enough to pass that test you're so worried about, no matter what Elemancer says!
Hydrogen... I...

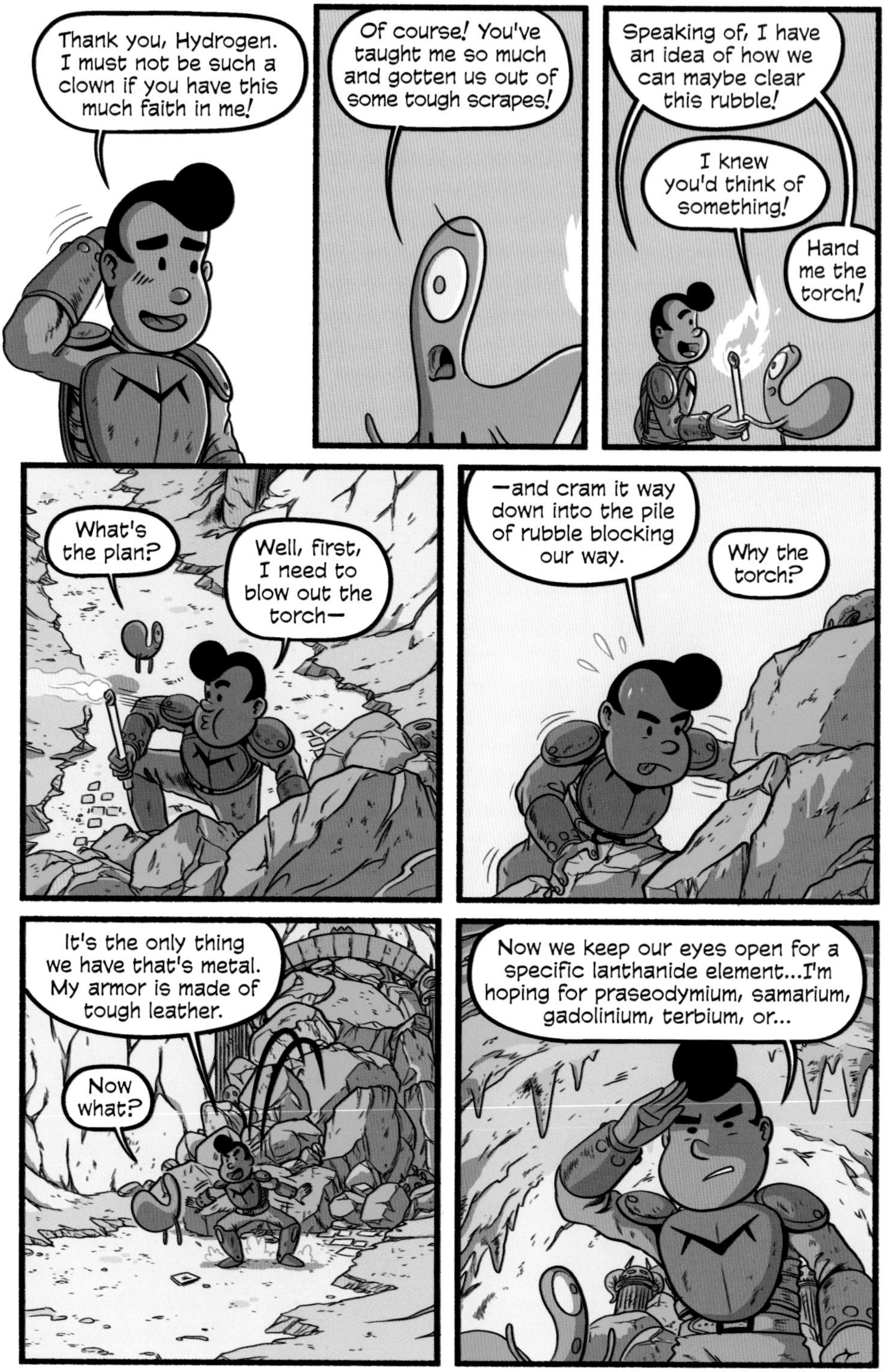
Thank you, Hydrogen. I must not be such a clown if you have this much faith in me!
Of course! You've taught me so much and gotten us out of some tough scrapes!
Speaking of, I have an idea of how we can maybe clear this rubble!
I knew you'd think of something!
Hand me the torch!
What's the plan?
Well, first, I need to blow out the torch—
—and cram it way down into the pile of rubble blocking our way.
Why the torch?
It's the only thing we have that's metal. My armor is made of tough leather.
Now what?
Now we keep our eyes open for a specific lanthanide element...I'm hoping for praseodymium, samarium, gadolinium, terbium, or...

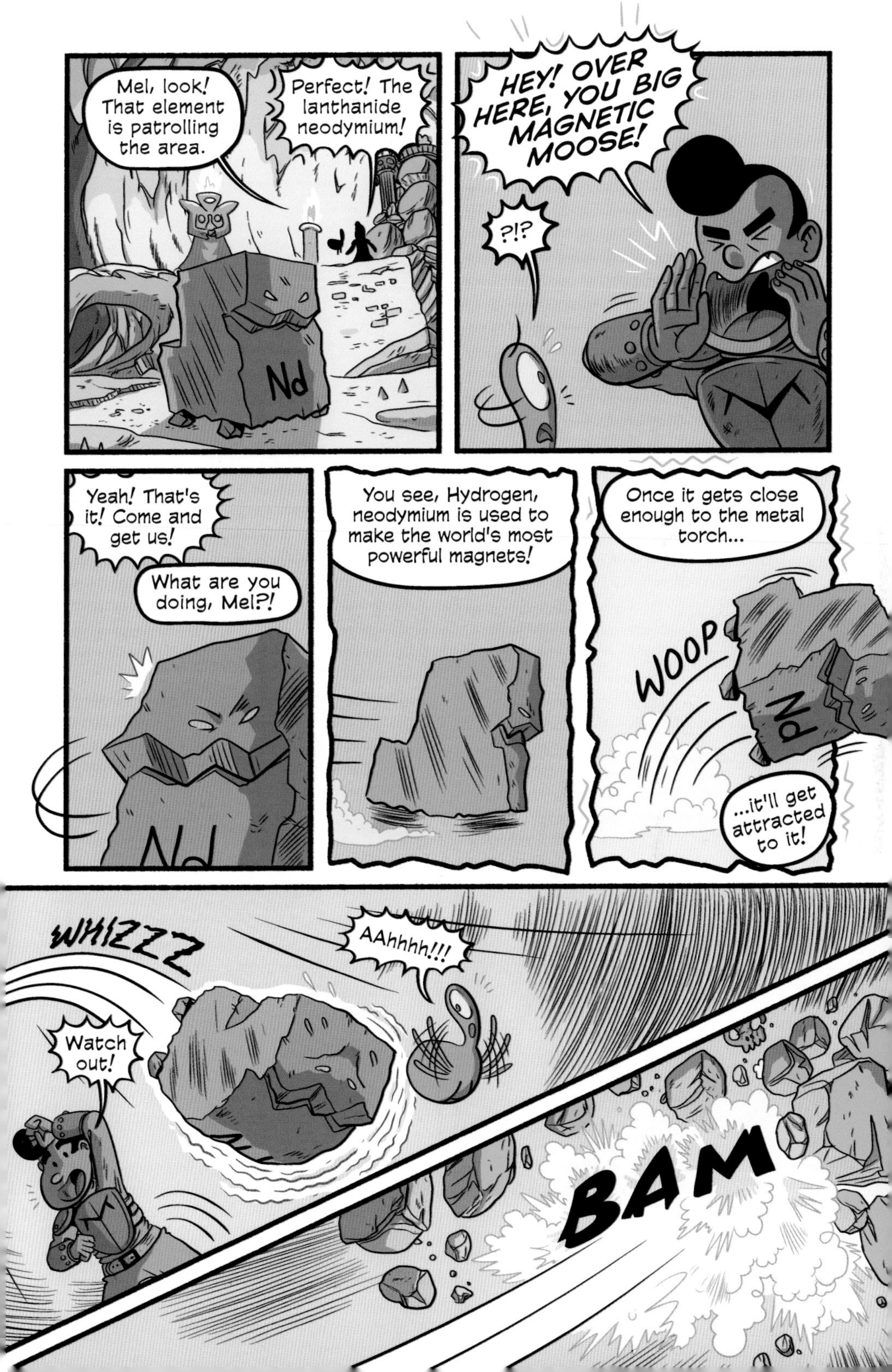
Mel, look! That element is patrolling the area.
Perfect! The lanthanide neodymium!
Nd
HEY! OVER HERE, YOU BIG MAGNETIC MOOSE!
?!?
Yeah! That's it! Come and get us!
What are you doing, Mel?!
Nd
You see, Hydrogen, neodymium is used to make the world's most powerful magnets!
Once it gets close enough to the metal torch...
WOOP
Nd
...it'll get attracted to it!
WHIZZZ
AAhhhh!!!
Watch out!
BAM

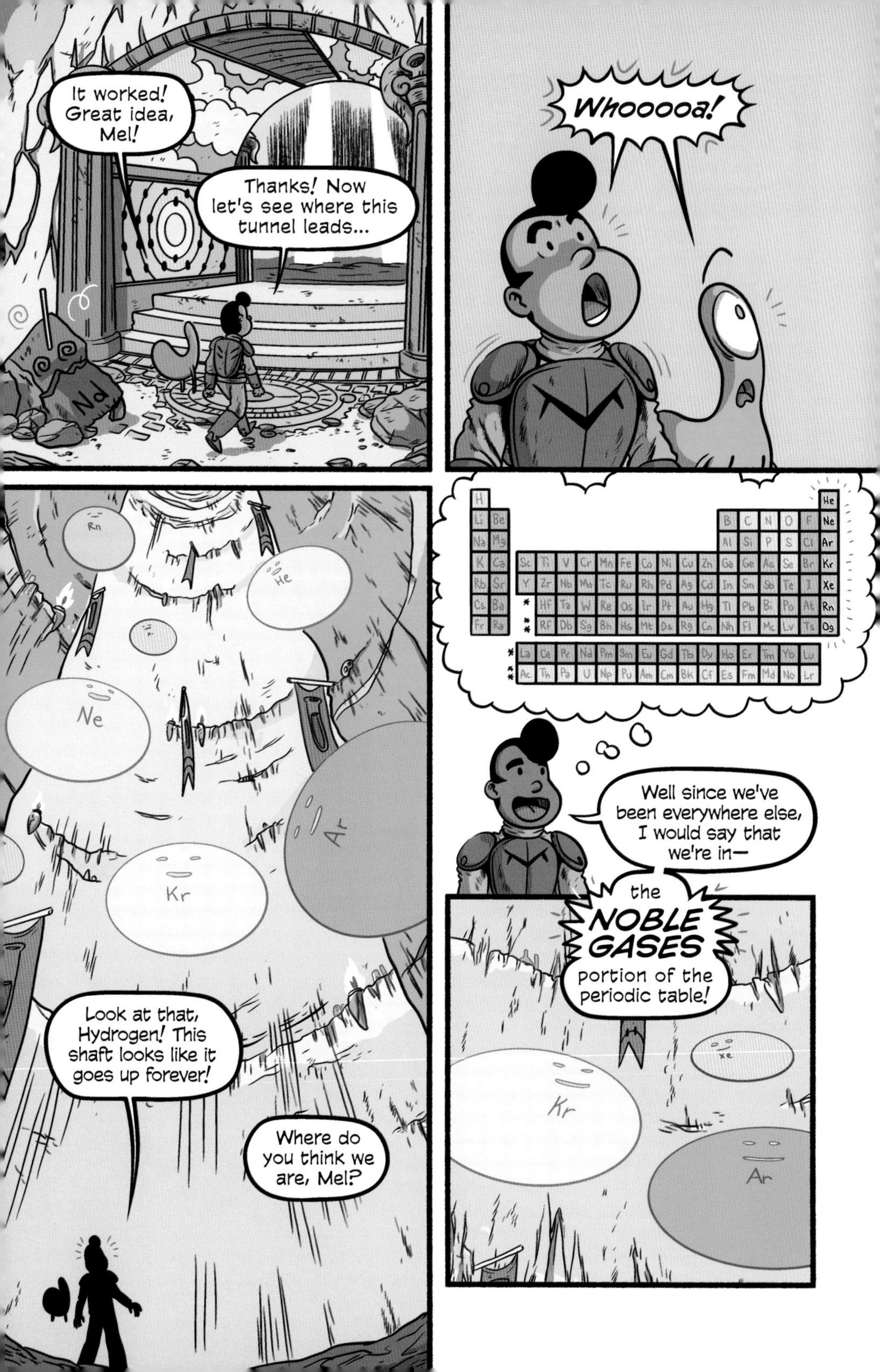

It worked! Great idea, Mel!
Thanks! Now let's see where this tunnel leads...
Nd
Whoooooa!
Rn
He
Ne
Kr
Ar
Look at that, Hydrogen! This shaft looks like it goes up forever!
Where do you think we are, Mel?
H He
Li Be B C N O F Ne
Na Mg Al Si P S Cl Ar
K Ca Sc Ti V Cr Mn Fe Co Ni Cu Zn Ga Ge As Se Br Kr
Rb Sr Y Zr Nb Mo Tc Ru Rh Pd Ag Cd In Sn Sb Te I Xe
Cs Ba * Hf Ta W Re Os Ir Pt Au Hg Tl Pb Bi Po At Rn
Fr Ra ** Rf Db Sg Bh Hs Mt Ds Rg Cn Nh Fl Mc Lv Ts Og
* La Ce Pr Nd Pm Sm Eu Gd Tb Dy Ho Er Tm Yb Lu
** Ac Th Pa U Np Pu Am Cm Bk Cf Es Fm Md No Lr
Well since we've been everywhere else, I would say that we're in—
the NOBLE GASES portion of the periodic table!
Xe
Kr
Ar

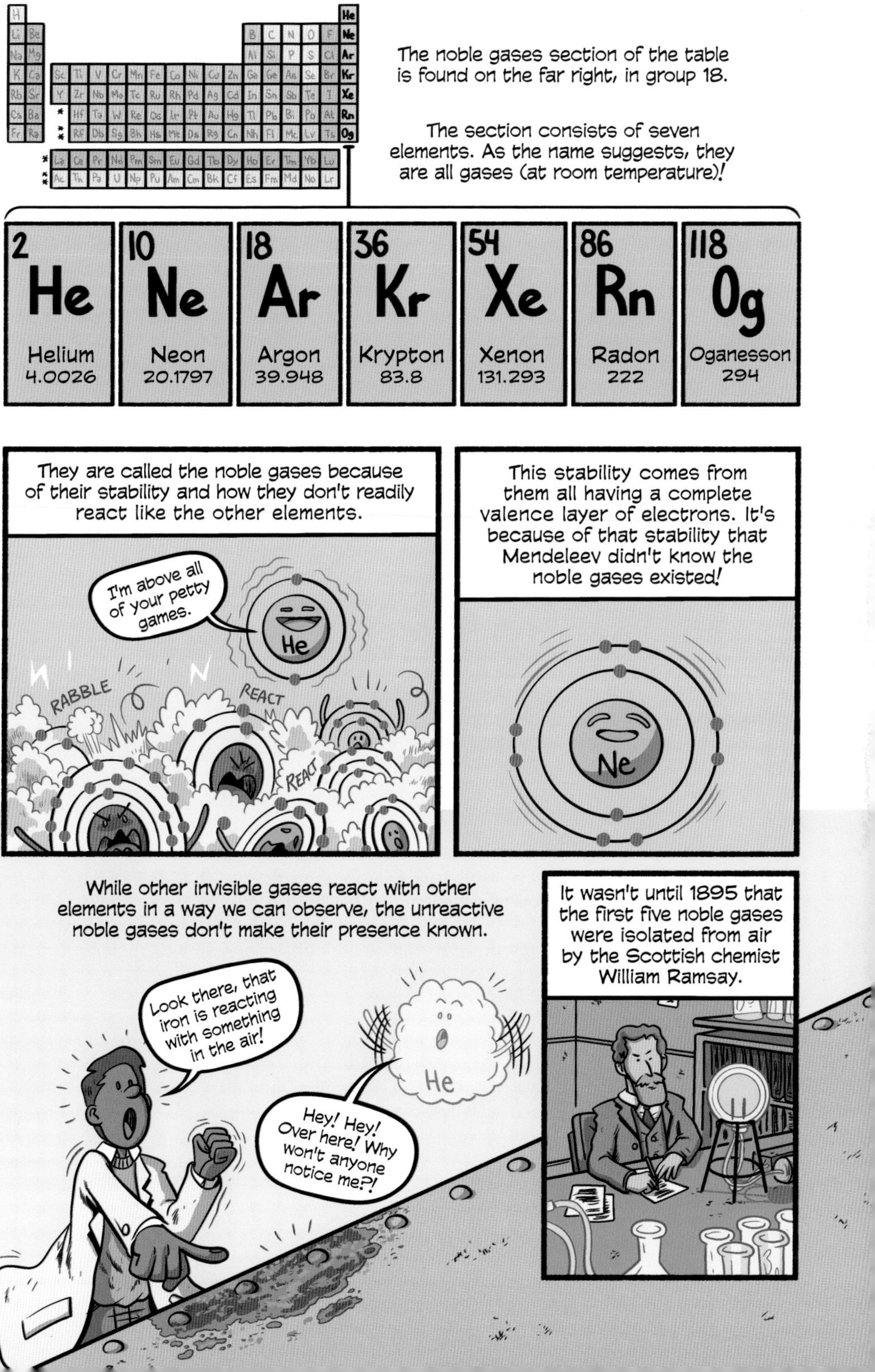

The noble gases section of the table is found on the far right, in group 18.
The section consists of seven elements. As the name suggests, they are all gases (at room temperature)!
2 He Helium 4.0026
10 Ne Neon 20.1797
18 Ar Argon 39.948
36 Kr Krypton 83.8
54 Xe Xenon 131.293
86 Rn Radon 222
118 Og Oganesson 294
They are called the noble gases because of their stability and how they don't readily react like the other elements.
I'm above all of your petty games.
He
RABBLE
REACT
REACT
This stability comes from them all having a complete valence layer of electrons. It's because of that stability that Mendeleev didn't know the noble gases existed!
Ne
While other invisible gases react with other elements in a way we can observe, the unreactive noble gases don't make their presence known.
Look there, that iron is reacting with something in the air!
He
Hey! Hey! Over here! Why won't anyone notice me?!
It wasn't until 1895 that the first five noble gases were isolated from air by the Scottish chemist William Ramsay.

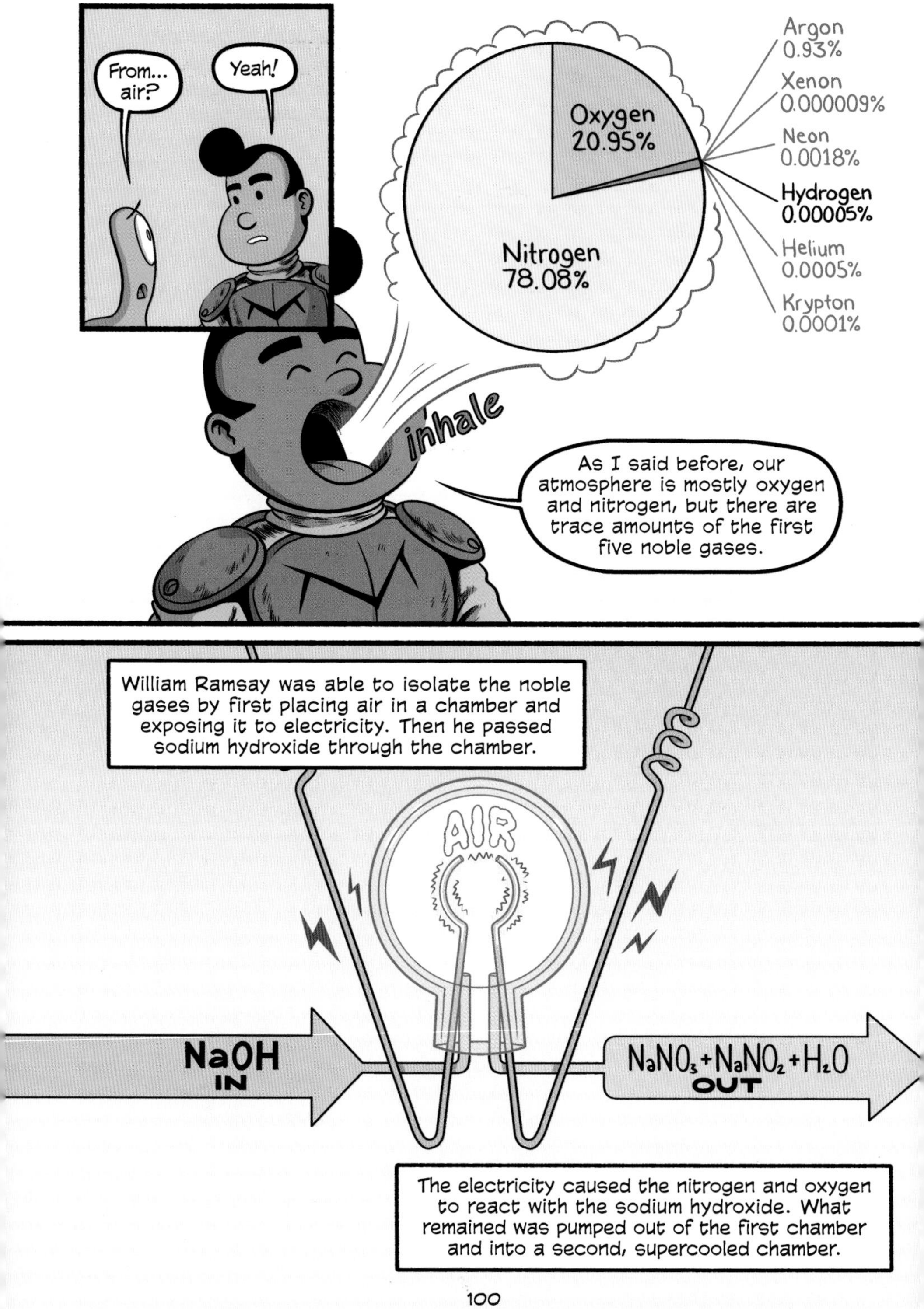
From... air?
Yeah!
Oxygen 20.95%
Nitrogen 78.08%
Argon 0.93%
Xenon 0.000009%
Neon 0.0018%
Hydrogen 0.00005%
Helium 0.0005%
Krypton 0.0001%
inhale
As I said before, our atmosphere is mostly oxygen and nitrogen, but there are trace amounts of the first five noble gases.
William Ramsay was able to isolate the noble gases by first placing air in a chamber and exposing it to electricity. Then he passed sodium hydroxide through the chamber.
AIR
NaOH IN
NaNO3 + NaNO2 + H2O OUT
The electricity caused the nitrogen and oxygen to react with the sodium hydroxide. What remained was pumped out of the first chamber and into a second, supercooled chamber.

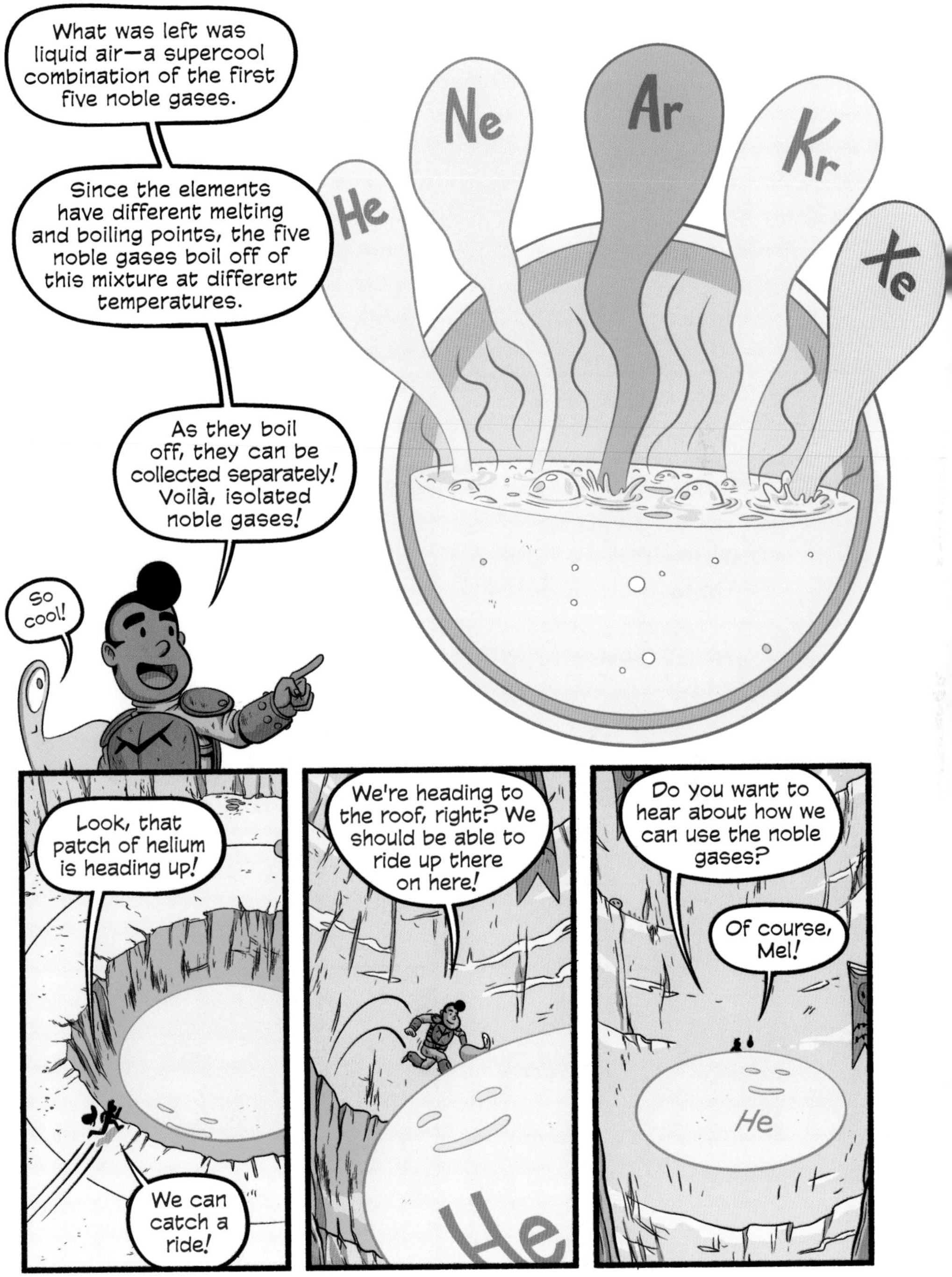
What was left was liquid air—a supercool combination of the first five noble gases.
Since the elements have different melting and boiling points, the five noble gases boil off of this mixture at different temperatures.
As they boil off, they can be collected separately! Voilà, isolated noble gases!
He
Ne
Ar
Kr
Xe
So cool!
Look, that patch of helium is heading up!
We can catch a ride!
We're heading to the roof, right? We should be able to ride up there on here!
He
Do you want to hear about how we can use the noble gases?
Of course, Mel!
He

Helium is used to make balloons and blimps float because it has a lower atomic mass than nitrogen or oxygen.

It would take a *lot* of helium to lift a person.

He

If you weighed 100 pounds, you would need at least 33,000 helium balloons to float!

Argon is used in steelmaking to purify metal, and to create an *inert atmosphere*, where oxygen must be omitted to stop metals from combusting, like in welding—

—or where oxygen must be omitted to preserve an object (like storing historic documents).

Xenon gas can be used as an antiseptic! Light given off by electrically excited xenon can purify the air and xenon lasers can kill bacteria!

Ahhhh! What a world!

What a world!

Neon glows when electrified. The color can be changed by mixing different elements with the neon, giving us a range of colorful lights to make attention-grabbing signs!

OPEN

PLAY

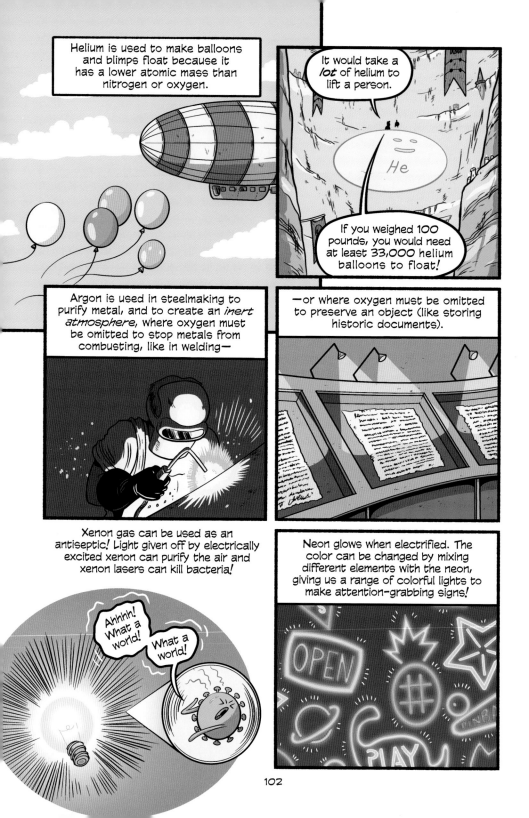

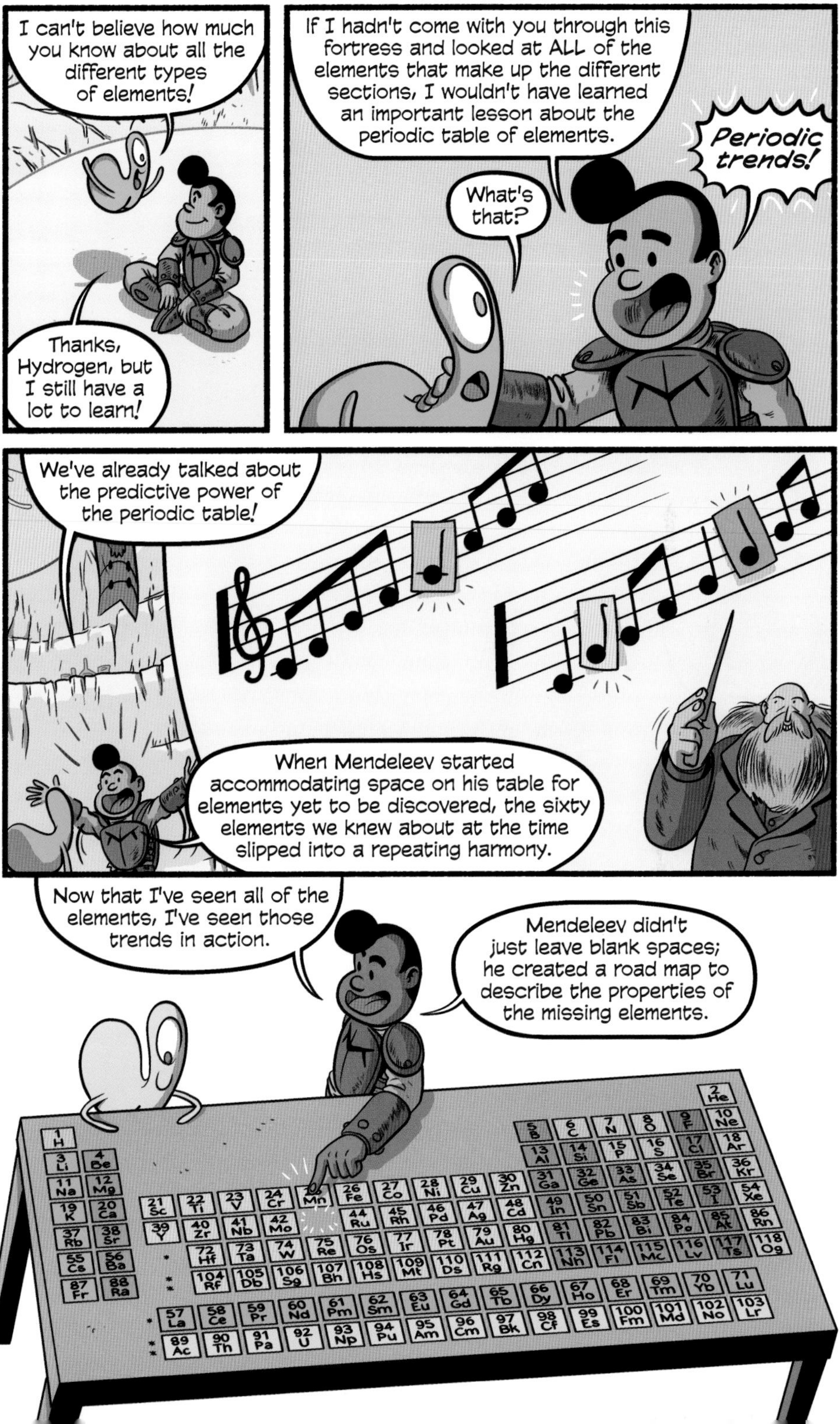

I can't believe how much you know about all the different types of elements!
Thanks, Hydrogen, but I still have a lot to learn!
If I hadn't come with you through this fortress and looked at ALL of the elements that make up the different sections, I wouldn't have learned an important lesson about the periodic table of elements.
What's that?
Periodic trends!
We've already talked about the predictive power of the periodic table!
When Mendeleev started accommodating space on his table for elements yet to be discovered, the sixty elements we knew about at the time slipped into a repeating harmony.
Now that I've seen all of the elements, I've seen those trends in action.
Mendeleev didn't just leave blank spaces; he created a road map to describe the properties of the missing elements.

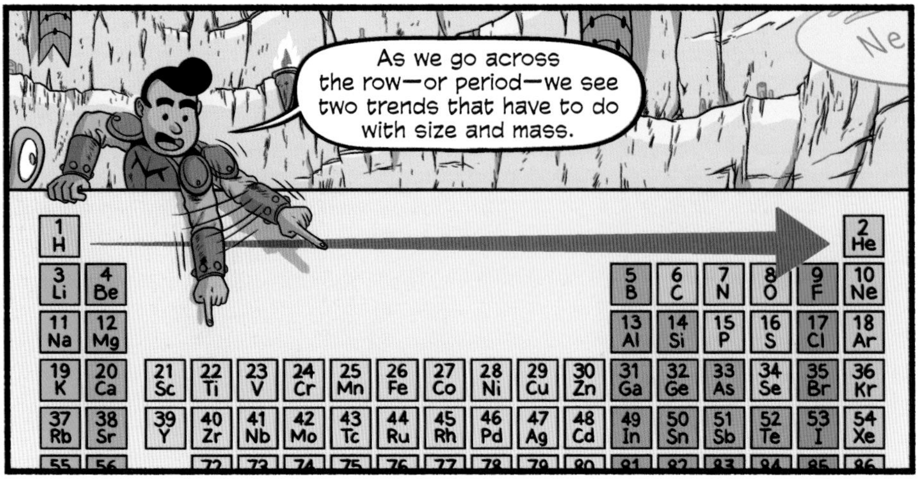
As we go across the row—or period—we see two trends that have to do with size and mass.
Ne
1 H
2 He
3 Li 4 Be
5 B 6 C 7 N 8 O 9 F 10 Ne
11 Na 12 Mg
13 Al 14 Si 15 P 16 S 17 Cl 18 Ar
19 K 20 Ca 21 Sc 22 Ti 23 V 24 Cr 25 Mn 26 Fe 27 Co 28 Ni 29 Cu 30 Zn 31 Ga 32 Ge 33 As 34 Se 35 Br 36 Kr
37 Rb 38 Sr 39 Y 40 Zr 41 Nb 42 Mo 43 Tc 44 Ru 45 Rh 46 Pd 47 Ag 48 Cd 49 In 50 Sn 51 Sb 52 Te 53 I 54 Xe

From left to right, the elements generally have more mass. The atomic number of the element increases. That means more protons and electrons. More particles, more mass!

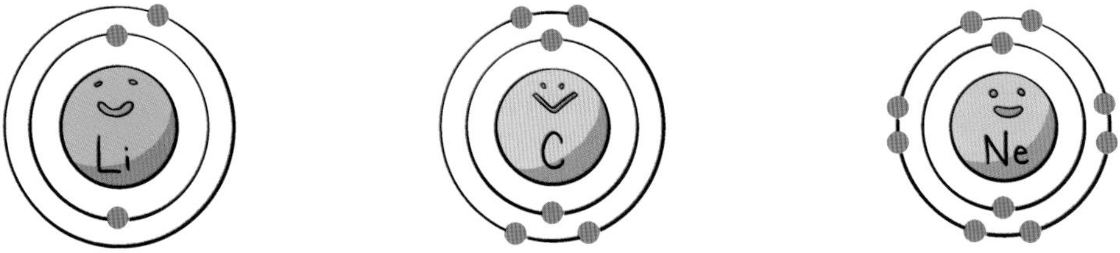
Li
C
Ne

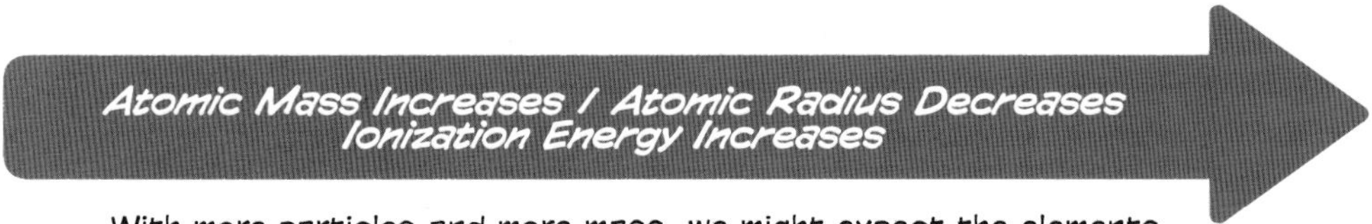
Atomic Mass Increases / Atomic Radius Decreases
Ionization Energy Increases

With more particles and more mass, we might expect the elements to get bigger, but they actually get slightly smaller. As the atomic number increases, more electrons are added.

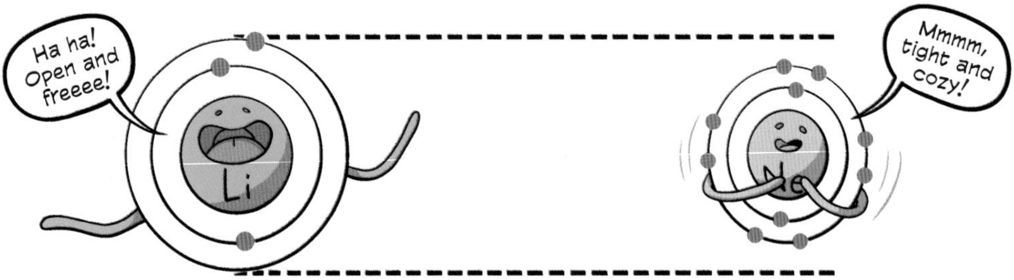
Ha ha! Open and freeee!
Li
Mmmm, tight and cozy!

As an element's atomic number (and number of protons) increases, the larger positive charge of the nucleus holds the negatively charged electrons tighter. This results in a smaller atomic radius. Because the atom has a tighter grip, the energy needed for an atom to release an electron (its ionization energy) increases as you go from left to right.

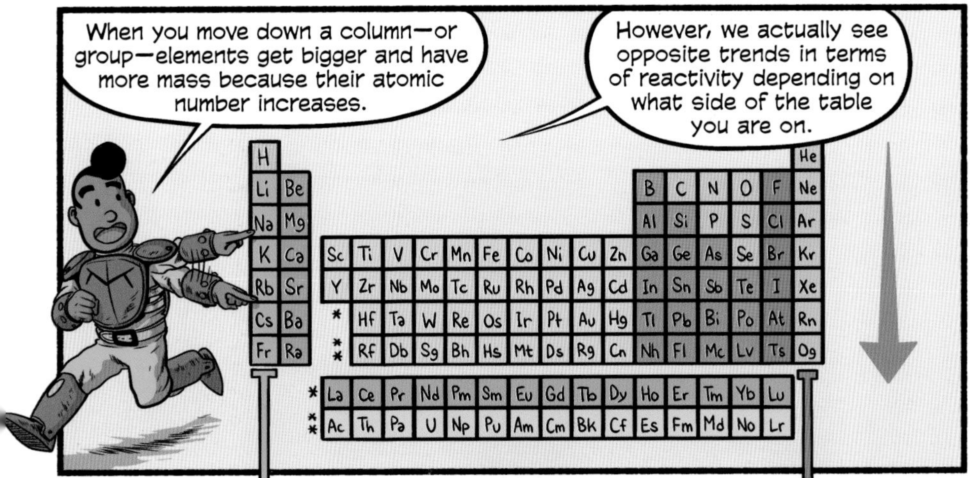
When you move down a column—or group—elements get bigger and have more mass because their atomic number increases.
However, we actually see opposite trends in terms of reactivity depending on what side of the table you are on.
H He
Li Be B C N O F Ne
Na Mg Al Si P S Cl Ar
K Ca Sc Ti V Cr Mn Fe Co Ni Cu Zn Ga Ge As Se Br Kr
Rb Sr Y Zr Nb Mo Tc Ru Rh Pd Ag Cd In Sn Sb Te I Xe
Cs Ba * Hf Ta W Re Os Ir Pt Au Hg Tl Pb Bi Po At Rn
Fr Ra ** Rf Db Sg Bh Hs Mt Ds Rg Cn Nh Fl Mc Lv Ts Og
* La Ce Pr Nd Pm Sm Eu Gd Tb Dy Ho Er Tm Yb Lu
** Ac Th Pa U Np Pu Am Cm Bk Cf Es Fm Md No Lr

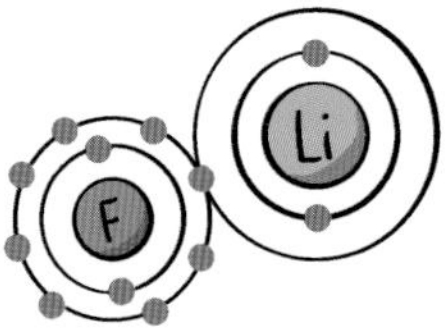
F
Li

On the left side of the table, you have elements with one or two valence electrons. They are very reactive, and get ***more*** reactive as you go down the group.

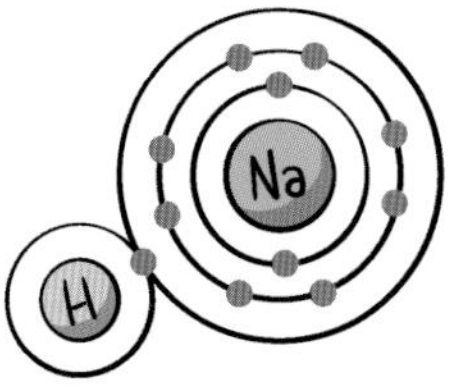
Na
H

Because the atoms get bigger as you go down the group, they have a looser grip on that spare electron and less energy is needed for that atom to release an electron. More reactive!

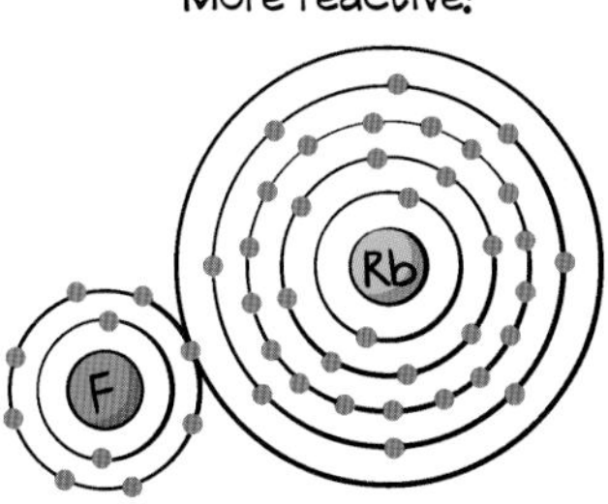
Rb
F

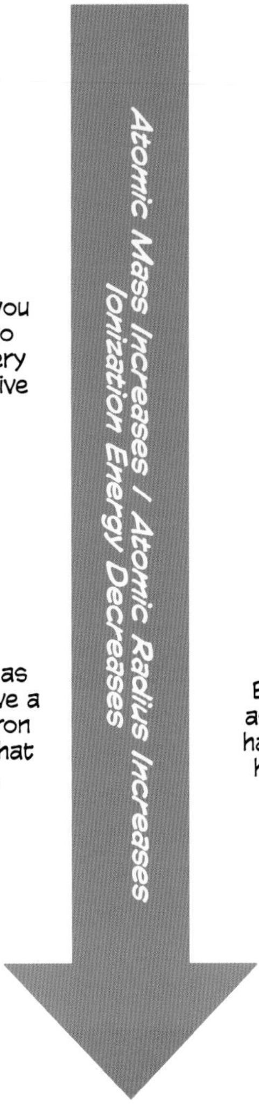
Atomic Mass Increases / Atomic Radius Increases
Ionization Energy Decreases

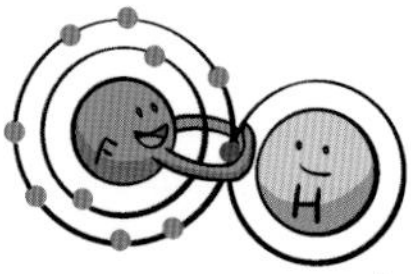
F
H

On the right side of the table, you have elements that are one or two electrons short of a complete valence layer. They are very reactive, and get ***less*** reactive as you go down the group.

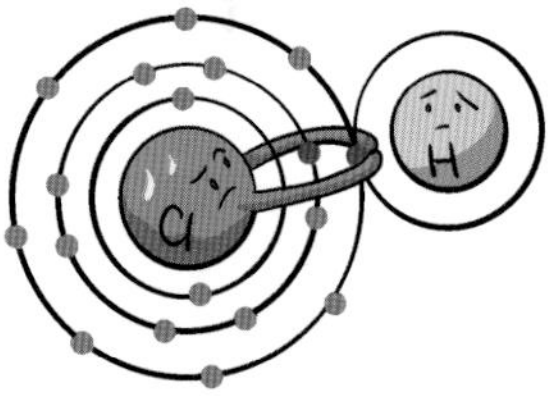
Cl
H

Because the atoms get bigger as you go down the group, they have a harder time grabbing and holding on to spare electrons. Less reactive!

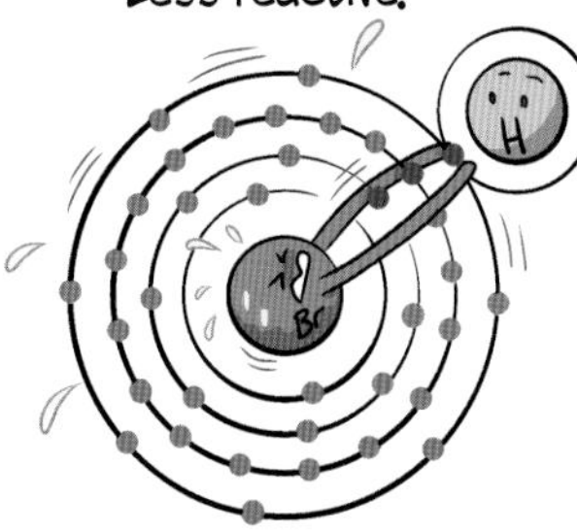
Br
H

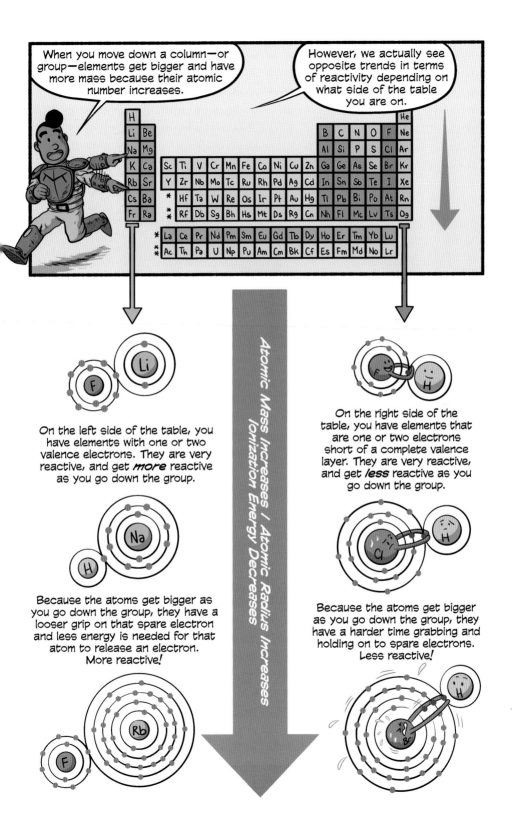

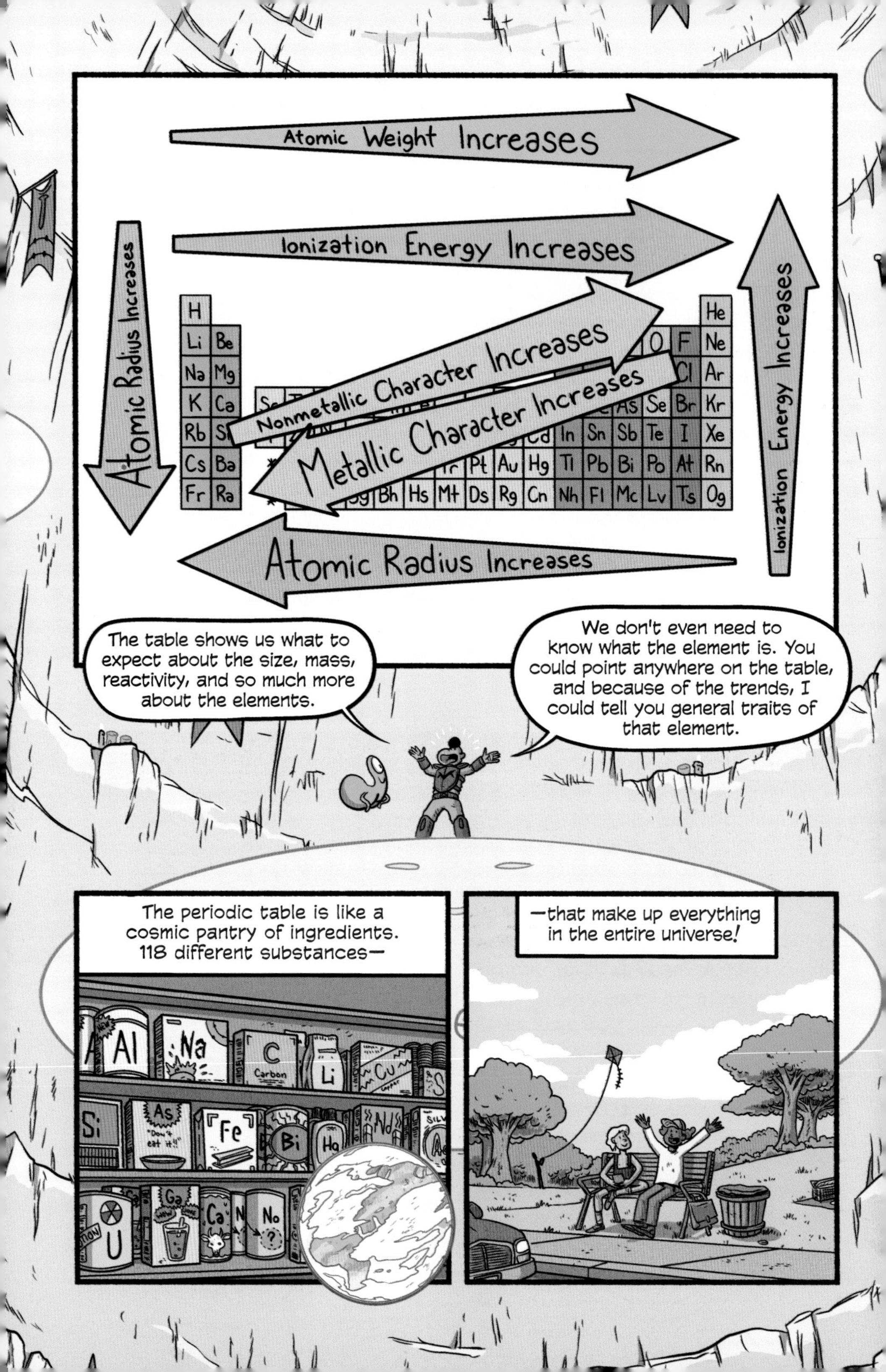
Atomic Weight Increases
Ionization Energy Increases
Atomic Radius Increases
Nonmetallic Character Increases
Metallic Character Increases
Ionization Energy Increases
Atomic Radius Increases
The table shows us what to expect about the size, mass, reactivity, and so much more about the elements.
We don't even need to know what the element is. You could point anywhere on the table, and because of the trends, I could tell you general traits of that element.
The periodic table is like a cosmic pantry of ingredients. 118 different substances—
Al
Na
C
Carbon
Li
Cu
Si
As
"Don't eat it!!"
Fe
Bi
Ga
Ca
No
U
—that make up everything in the entire universe!

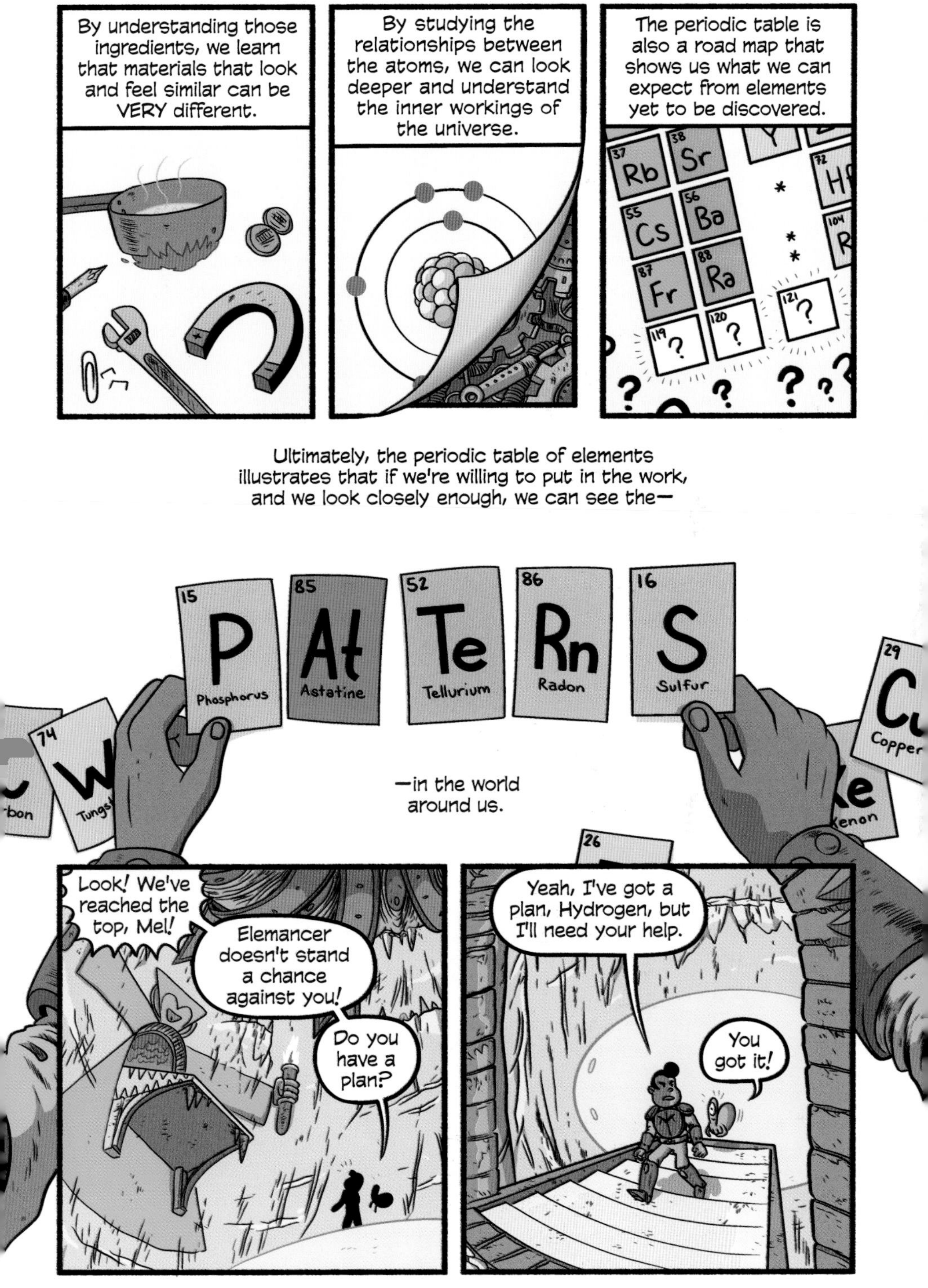

By understanding those ingredients, we learn that materials that look and feel similar can be VERY different.
By studying the relationships between the atoms, we can look deeper and understand the inner workings of the universe.
The periodic table is also a road map that shows us what we can expect from elements yet to be discovered.
37 Rb
38 Sr
55 Cs
56 Ba
87 Fr
88 Ra
119 ?
120 ?
121 ?
Ultimately, the periodic table of elements illustrates that if we're willing to put in the work, and we look closely enough, we can see the—
15 P Phosphorus
85 At Astatine
52 Te Tellurium
86 Rn Radon
16 S Sulfur
—in the world around us.
Look! We've reached the top, Mel!
Elemancer doesn't stand a chance against you!
Do you have a plan?
Yeah, I've got a plan, Hydrogen, but I'll need your help.
You got it!

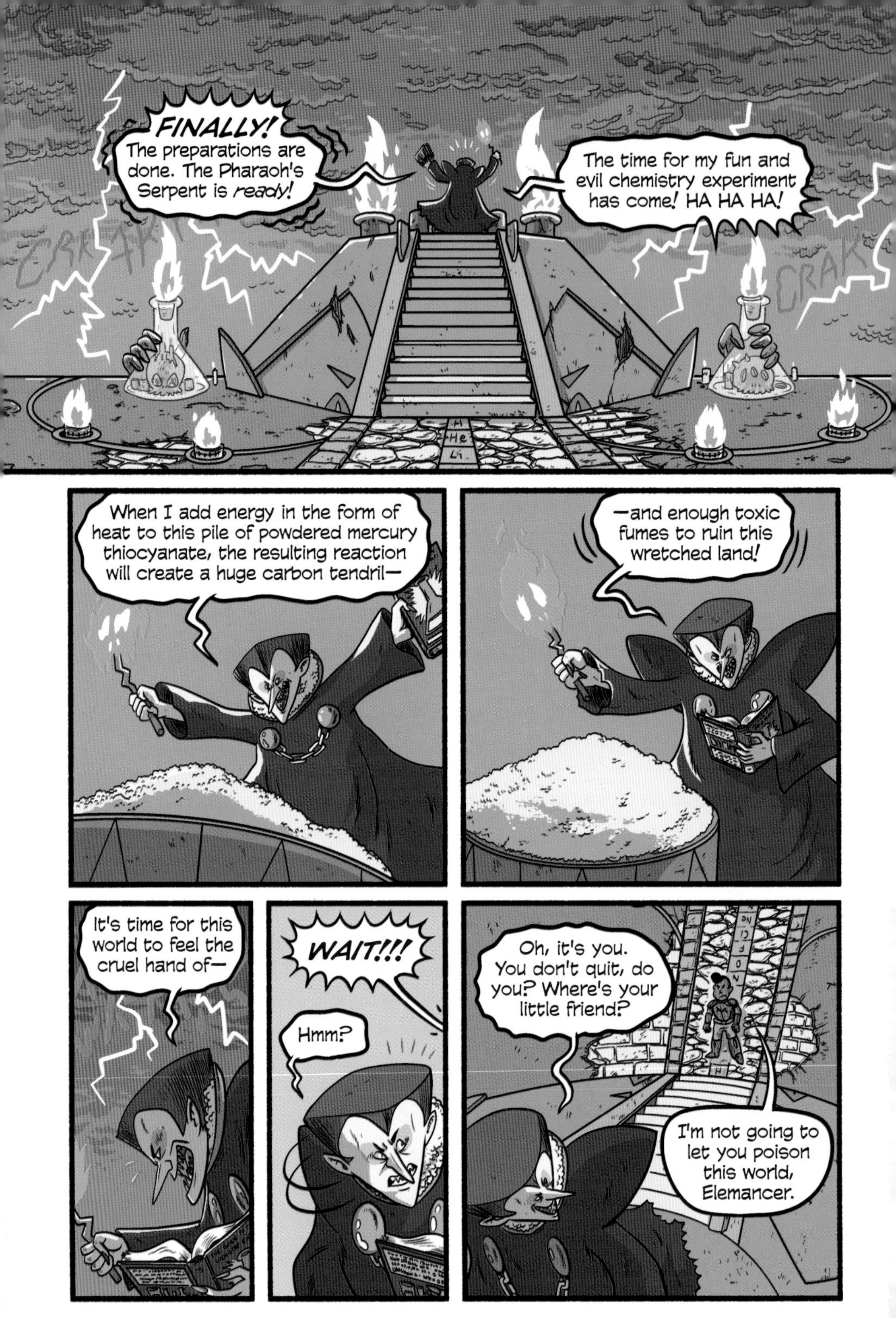
FINALLY! The preparations are done. The Pharaoh's Serpent is *ready*!
The time for my fun and evil chemistry experiment has come! HA HA HA!
When I add energy in the form of heat to this pile of powdered mercury thiocyanate, the resulting reaction will create a huge carbon tendril—
—and enough toxic fumes to ruin this wretched land!
It's time for this world to feel the cruel hand of—
WAIT!!!
Hmm?
Oh, it's you. You don't quit, do you? Where's your little friend?
I'm not going to let you poison this world, Elemancer.

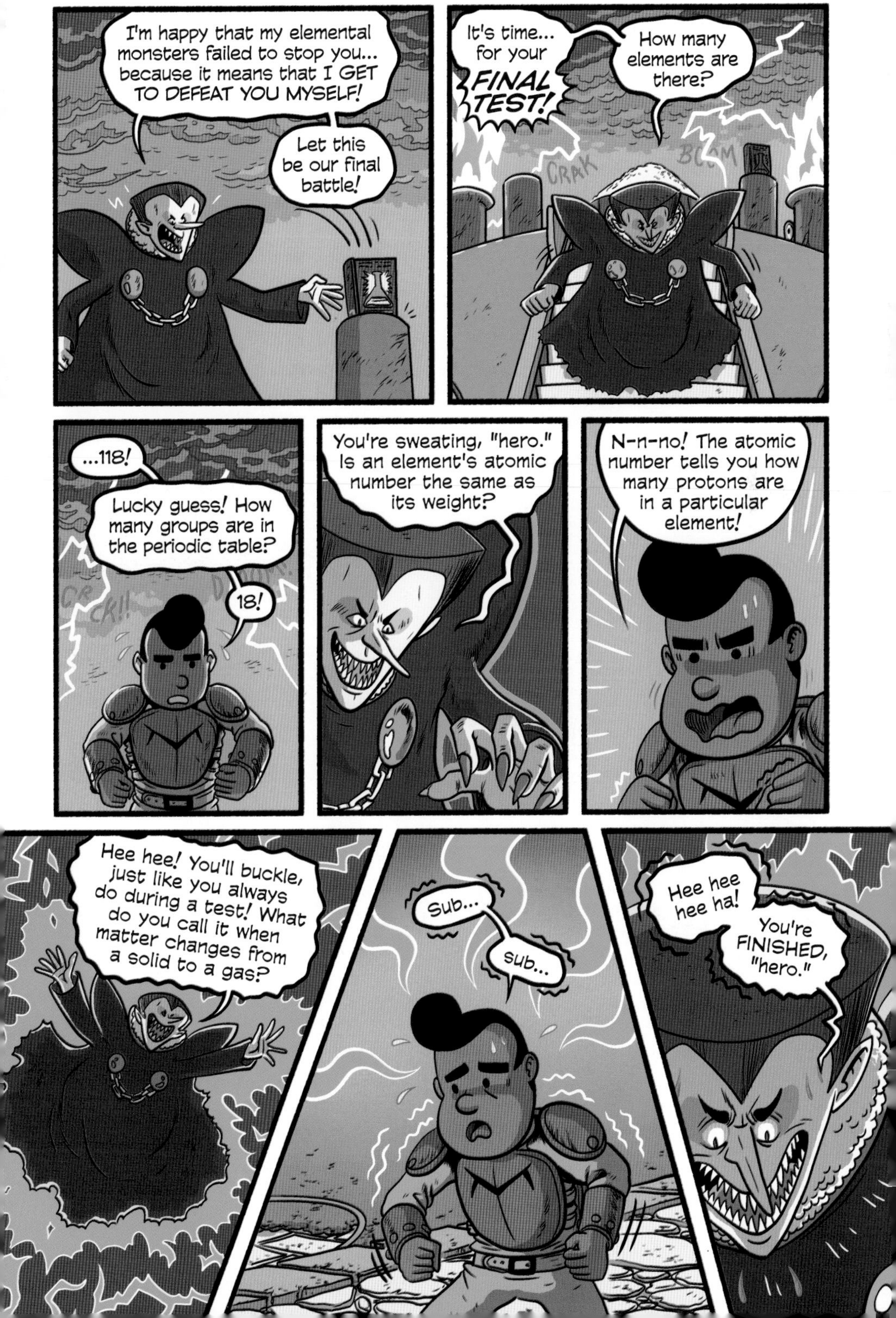
I'm happy that my elemental monsters failed to stop you... because it means that I GET TO DEFEAT YOU MYSELF!
Let this be our final battle!
It's time... for your FINAL TEST!
How many elements are there?
CRAK
BOOM
...118!
Lucky guess! How many groups are in the periodic table?
18!
You're sweating, "hero." Is an element's atomic number the same as its weight?
N-n-no! The atomic number tells you how many protons are in a particular element!
Hee hee! You'll buckle, just like you always do during a test! What do you call it when matter changes from a solid to a gas?
Sub...
sub...
Hee hee hee ha!
You're FINISHED, "hero."

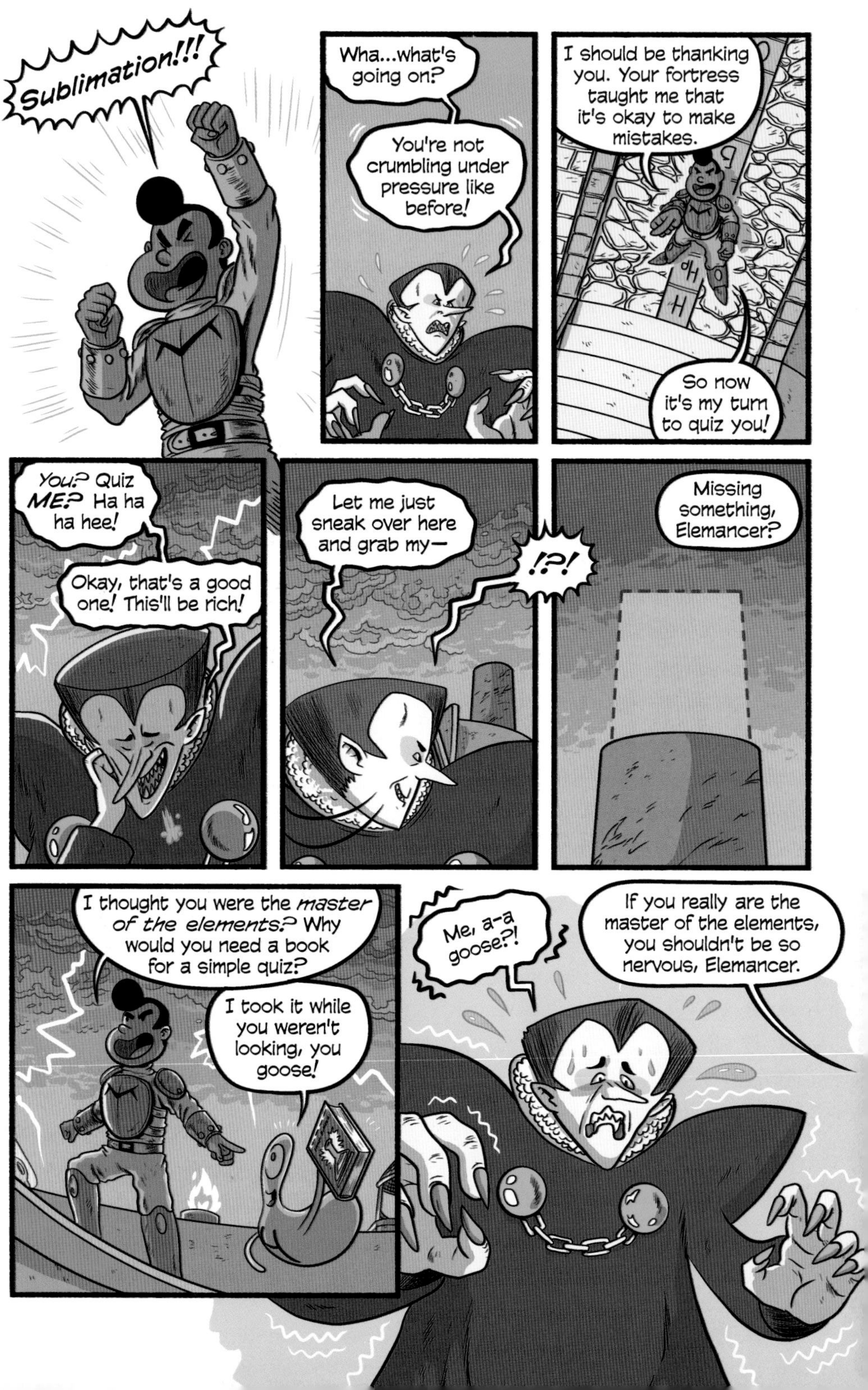
Sublimation!!!
Wha...what's going on?
You're not crumbling under pressure like before!
I should be thanking you. Your fortress taught me that it's okay to make mistakes.
So now it's my turn to quiz you!
You? Quiz ME? Ha ha ha hee!
Okay, that's a good one! This'll be rich!
Let me just sneak over here and grab my—
!?!
Missing something, Elemancer?
I thought you were the master of the elements? Why would you need a book for a simple quiz?
I took it while you weren't looking, you goose!
Me, a-a goose?!
If you really are the master of the elements, you shouldn't be so nervous, Elemancer.

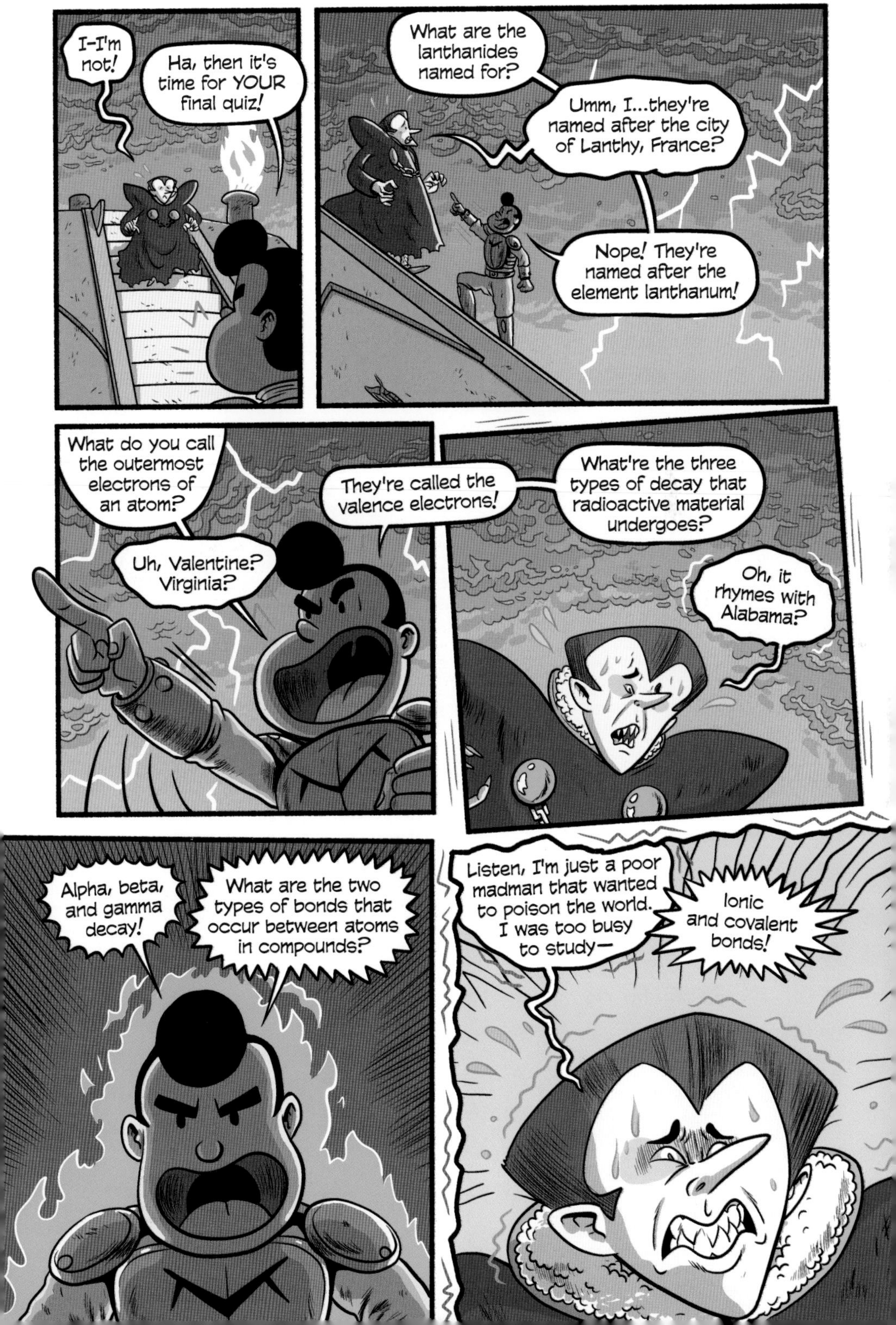

I-I'm not!
Ha, then it's time for YOUR final quiz!
What are the lanthanides named for?
Umm, I...they're named after the city of Lanthy, France?
Nope! They're named after the element lanthanum!
What do you call the outermost electrons of an atom?
Uh, Valentine? Virginia?
They're called the valence electrons!
What're the three types of decay that radioactive material undergoes?
Oh, it rhymes with Alabama?
Alpha, beta, and gamma decay!
What are the two types of bonds that occur between atoms in compounds?
Listen, I'm just a poor madman that wanted to poison the world. I was too busy to study—
Ionic and covalent bonds!

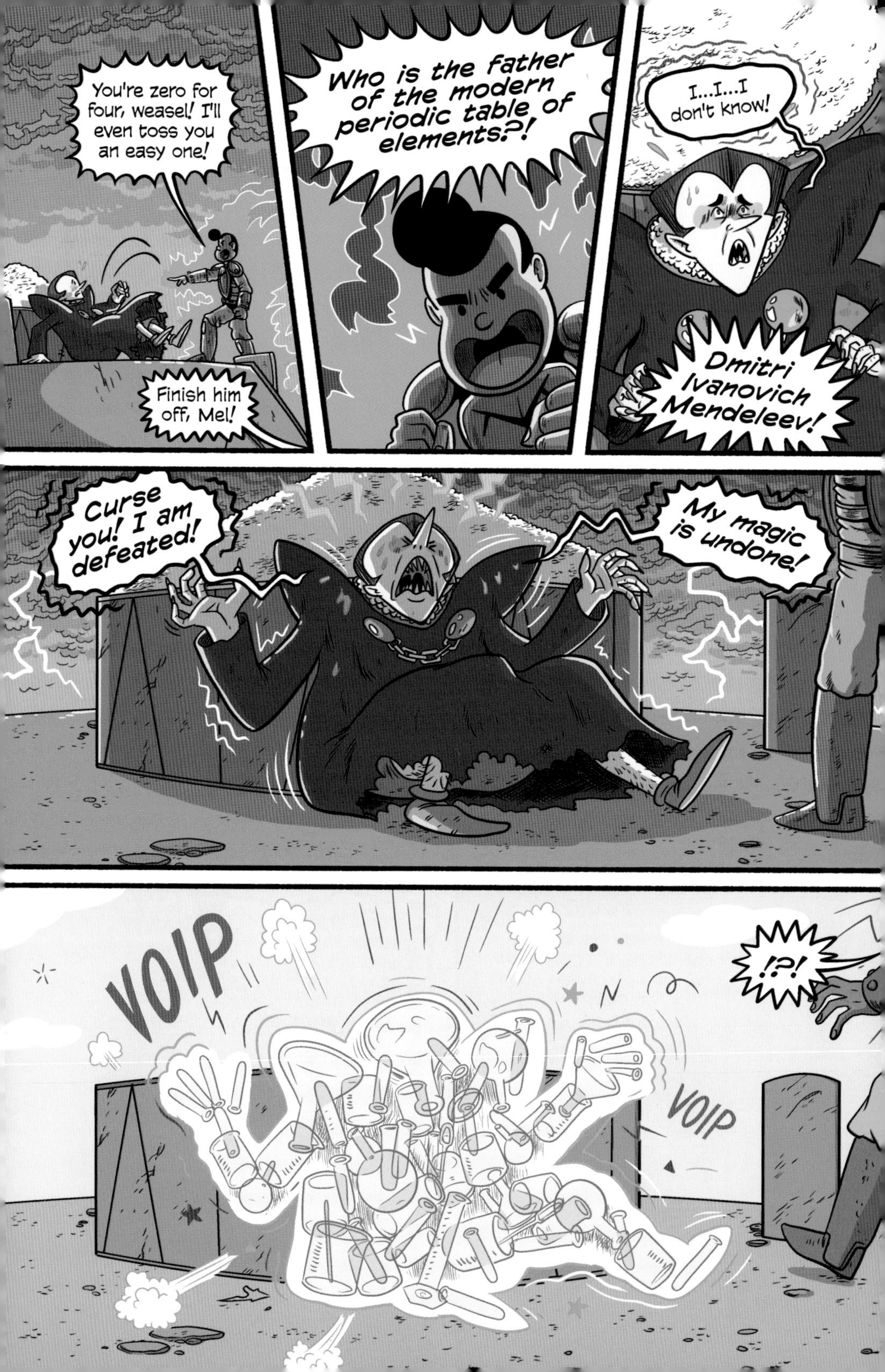
You're zero for four, weasel! I'll even toss you an easy one!
Finish him off, Mel!
Who is the father of the modern periodic table of elements?!
I...I...I don't know!
Dmitri Ivanovich Mendeleev!
Curse you! I am defeated!
My magic is undone!
VOIP
VOIP
!?!

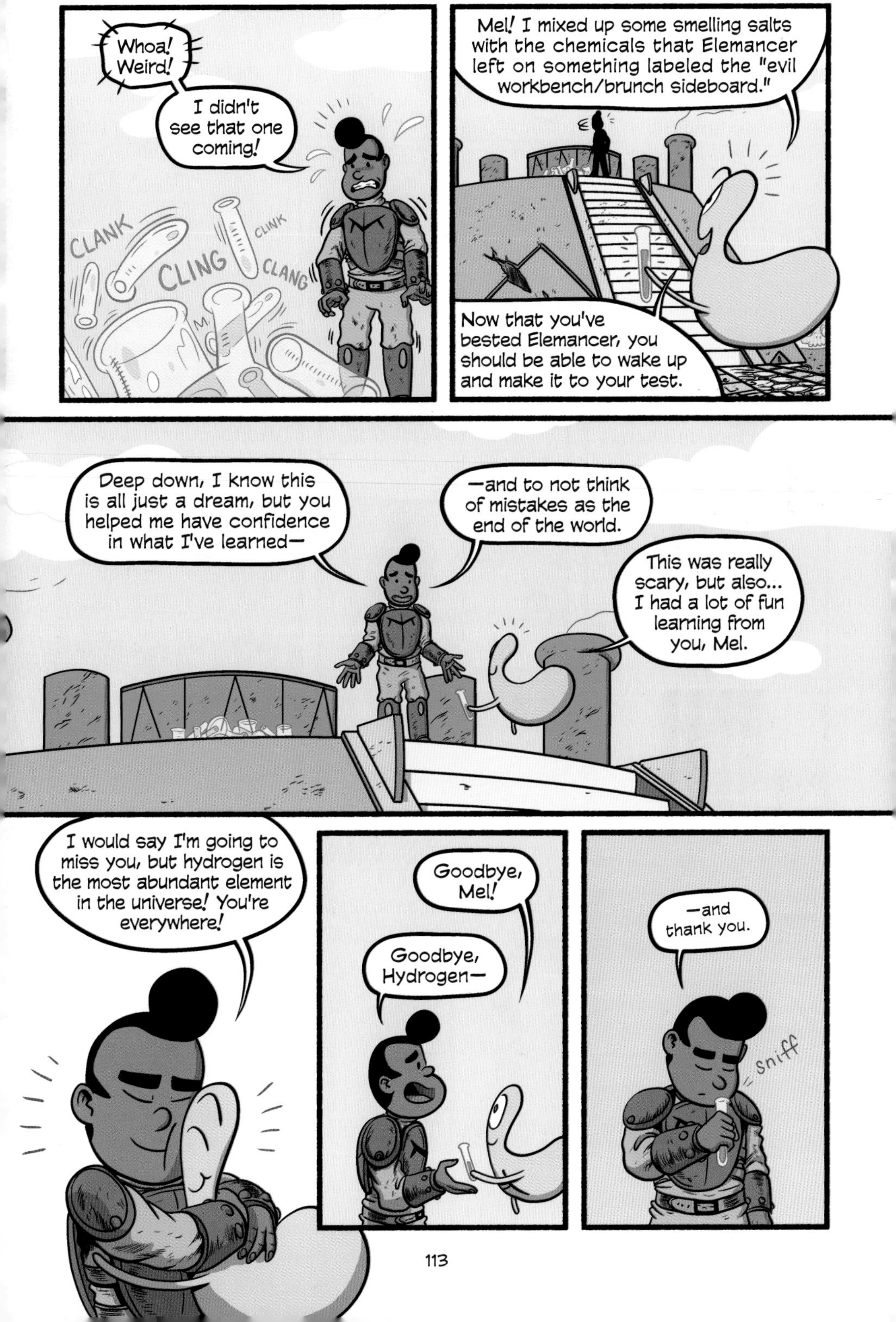
Whoa! Weird!
I didn't see that one coming!
CLANK
CLING
CLINK
CLANG
Mel! I mixed up some smelling salts with the chemicals that Elemancer left on something labeled the "evil workbench/brunch sideboard."
Now that you've bested Elemancer, you should be able to wake up and make it to your test.
Deep down, I know this is all just a dream, but you helped me have confidence in what I've learned—
—and to not think of mistakes as the end of the world.
This was really scary, but also... I had a lot of fun learning from you, Mel.
I would say I'm going to miss you, but hydrogen is the most abundant element in the universe! You're everywhere!
Goodbye, Mel!
Goodbye, Hydrogen—
—and thank you.
sniff

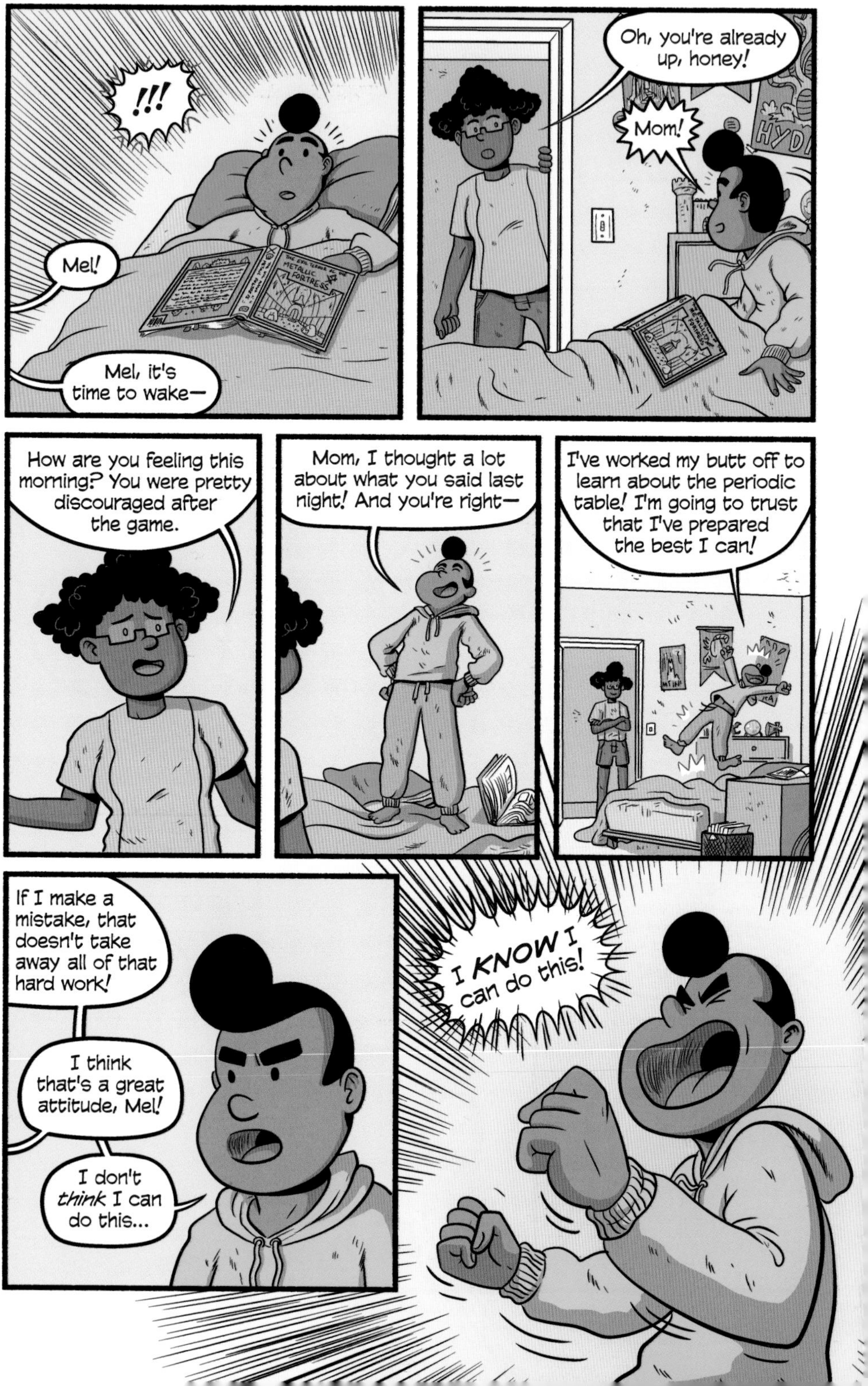
!!!
Mel!
Mel, it's time to wake—
Oh, you're already up, honey!
Mom!
How are you feeling this morning? You were pretty discouraged after the game.
Mom, I thought a lot about what you said last night! And you're right—
I've worked my butt off to learn about the periodic table! I'm going to trust that I've prepared the best I can!
If I make a mistake, that doesn't take away all of that hard work!
I think that's a great attitude, Mel!
I don't *think* I can do this...
I **KNOW** I can do this!

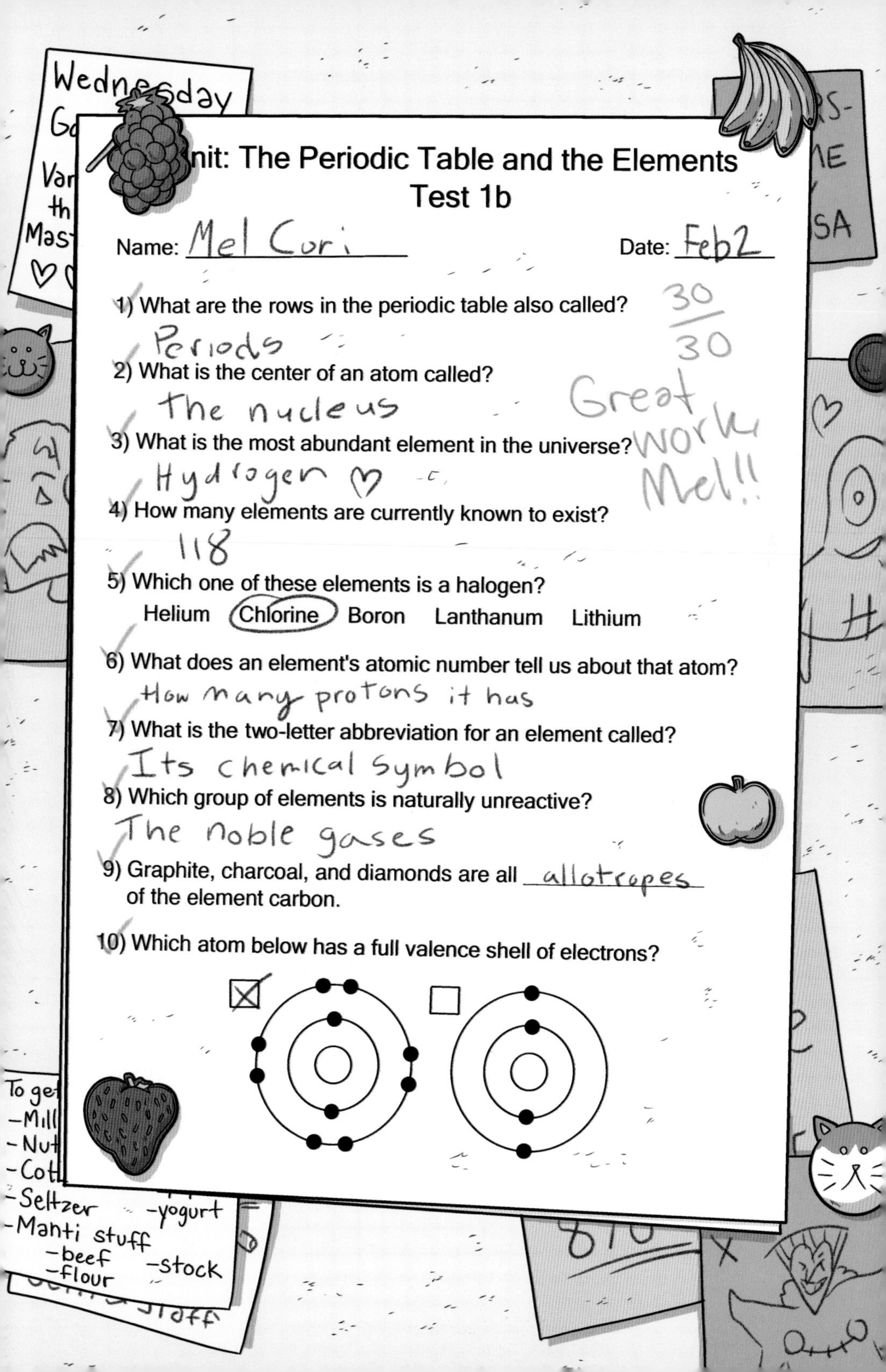
Unit: The Periodic Table and the Elements
Test 1b
Name: Mel Cori
Date: Feb2
30/30
Great work Mel!!
1) What are the rows in the periodic table also called?
Periods
2) What is the center of an atom called?
the nucleus
3) What is the most abundant element in the universe?
Hydrogen
4) How many elements are currently known to exist?
118
5) Which one of these elements is a halogen?
Helium Chlorine Boron Lanthanum Lithium
6) What does an element's atomic number tell us about that atom?
How many protons it has
7) What is the two-letter abbreviation for an element called?
Its chemical symbol
8) Which group of elements is naturally unreactive?
The noble gases
9) Graphite, charcoal, and diamonds are all allotropes of the element carbon.
10) Which atom below has a full valence shell of electrons?
Wednesday
-Seltzer -yogurt
-Manti stuff
-beef -stock
-flour

PERIODIC TABLE OF ELEMENTS

Period ↓ / Group →	1	2	3	4	5	6	7	8	9	10	11	12	13	14	15	16	17	18
1	1 H																	2 He
2	3 Li	4 Be											5 B	6 C	7 N	8 O	9 F	10 Ne
3	11 Na	12 Mg											13 Al	14 Si	15 P	16 S	17 Cl	18 Ar
4	19 K	20 Ca	21 Sc	22 Ti	23 V	24 Cr	25 Mn	26 Fe	27 Co	28 Ni	29 Cu	30 Zn	31 Ga	32 Ge	33 As	34 Se	35 Br	36 Kr
5	37 Rb	38 Sr	39 Y	40 Zr	41 Nb	42 Mo	43 Tc	44 Ru	45 Rh	46 Pd	47 Ag	48 Cd	49 In	50 Sn	51 Sb	52 Te	53 I	54 Xe
6	55 Cs	56 Ba	*	72 Hf	73 Ta	74 W	75 Re	76 Os	77 Ir	78 Pt	79 Au	80 Hg	81 Tl	82 Pb	83 Bi	84 Po	85 At	86 Rn
7	87 Fr	88 Ra	**	104 Rf	105 Db	106 Sg	107 Bh	108 Hs	109 Mt	110 Ds	111 Rg	112 Cn	113 Nh	114 Fl	115 Mc	116 Lv	117 Ts	118 Og

*	57 La	58 Ce	59 Pr	60 Nd	61 Pm	62 Sm	63 Eu	64 Gd	65 Tb	66 Dy	67 Ho	68 Er	69 Tm	70 Yb	71 Lu
**	89 Ac	90 Th	91 Pa	92 U	93 Np	94 Pu	95 Am	96 Cm	97 Bk	98 Cf	99 Es	100 Fm	101 Md	102 No	103 Lr

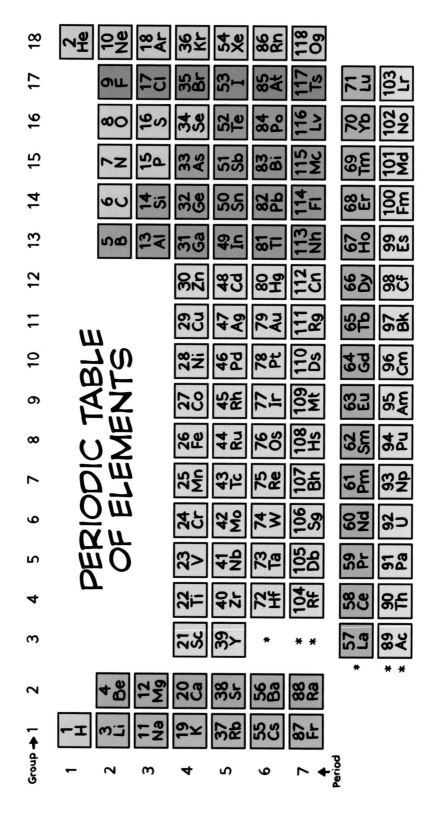

METRIC MEASUREMENT CONVERSIONS

METRIC		IMPERIAL (US)
1 millimeter (mm)	≈	0.039 inches (in)
1 centimeter (cm)	≈	0.39 inches (in)
1 meter (m)	≈	3.28 feet (ft)
1 kilometer (km)	≈	0.62 miles (mi)
1 km per hour (kph)	≈	0.62 miles per hour (mph)
1 gram (g)	≈	0.002 pounds (lb)
1 kilogram (kg)	≈	2.20 pounds (lb)
1 liter (l)	≈	0.035 cubic feet (ft³)
1 cubic meter (m³)	≈	35.31 cubic feet (ft³)
1 cubic kilometer (km³)	≈	0.24 cubic miles (mi³)
0° Celsius (C)	≈	32° Fahrenheit (F)
100° Celsius (C)	≈	212° Fahrenheit (F)
1000° Celsius (C)	≈	1832° Fahrenheit (F)
2000° Celsius (C)	≈	3664° Fahrenheit (F)

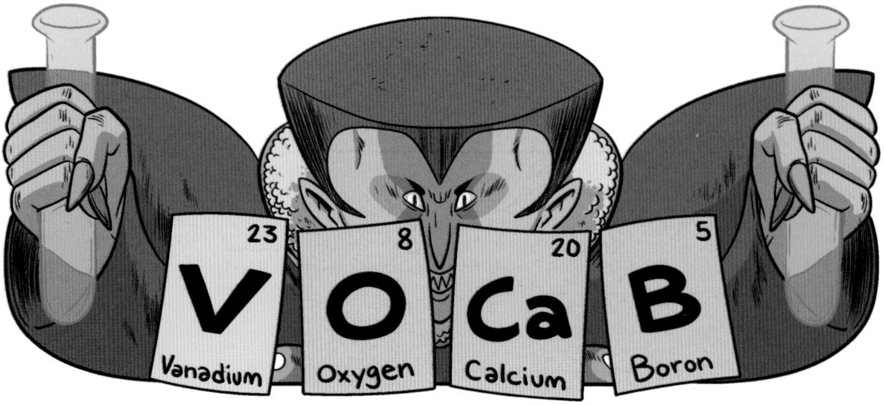
23
V
Vanadium
8
O
Oxygen
20
Ca
Calcium
5
B
Boron

Allotrope
A different form of a chemical element that exists at the same temperature. For example, charcoal, graphite, and diamonds are all allotropes of carbon.

Alloy
A metallic compound that contains two or more metallic elements. Bronze, brass, and stainless steel are all examples of alloys.

Atom
A tiny unit of stuff that's made of smaller particles: protons, electrons, and neutrons. The number of small particles determines an atom's element.

Atomic mass
The average mass of the protons, neutrons, and electrons in an element. Atomic mass is measured in incredibly small units called atomic mass units (amu).

Atomic number
The number of protons in the nucleus of an atom of an element. Elements are laid out on the periodic table of elements in order of increasing atomic number.

Chemical symbol
A shorthand representation for an element that consists of one or two letters (C = carbon, Na = sodium, etc.). It is used to help write out chemical formulas. The first letter of a chemical symbol is always uppercase, and the second letter (if present) is always lowercase.

Conductor
A substance that has the ability to transmit heat, electricity, and/or sound. Metal heats up when exposed to fire because it is conductive. Electricians use rubber gloves to protect themselves from electrical shock because rubber is not conductive.

Ductile
A quality of metal that describes its ability to be drawn out (like into a wire).

Electron
A negatively charged particle in an atom. Electrons are found outside of the nucleus of an atom and are involved with how the elements bond and react to each other. In an atom, there is one electron for every proton.

Element
A substance made of one particular type of atom. Helium, carbon, and gold are all examples of elements. The 118 elements, and maybe some that haven't been discovered yet, make up everything in the universe.

Groups
The vertical columns of the periodic table of elements. Elements that are in the same group tend to share traits.

Isotope
A different version of an element. Isotopes of an element will have the same number of electrons and protons, but may vary in the number of neutrons they have as well as in weight and half-lives.

Malleable
A metal that is malleable has the ability to be shaped or bent.

Mole
A unit of measurement used to express vast numbers of very small particles like atoms, molecules, or electrons. It is defined as exactly $6.02214076 \times 10^{23}$ (or 602,214,076,000,000,000,000,000) particles.

Molecule
An electrically neutral group of two or more atoms held together by chemical bonds. Molecules can contain one element (like oxygen, O_2) or different elements (like water, H_2O).

Neutron
A particle that is neutral (has no electrical charge) and is found in the nucleus of an atom. It weighs the same as a proton, but less than an electron.

Nucleus
The center of an atom. It is positively charged and comprised of neutrons and protons.

Particle accelerator
A scientific instrument that can speed up particles for various tests, or bombard particles into one another. While early particle accelerators were handheld and didn't pack quite a punch, modern accelerators are HUGE. The Large Hadron Collider is 27 km around!

Periodic table of elements
A tool to organize and understand the elements that make up the world around us. The periodic table arranges elements according to atomic number, and provides insights into trends and similarities among the elements.

Periods
The horizontal rows of the periodic table of elements.

Proton
A positively charged particle that is found in the nucleus of an atom. In an atom, there is one proton for every electron. The number of protons in an element majorly governs its identity. If the number of protons in an atom changes (due to radiation, bombardment, etc.), the identity and qualities of that atom will also change.

Valence layer
The outermost layer of electrons in an element. The electrons in this layer are known as the valence electrons. An element's reactivity with other elements is partially determined by the number of electrons in this layer.

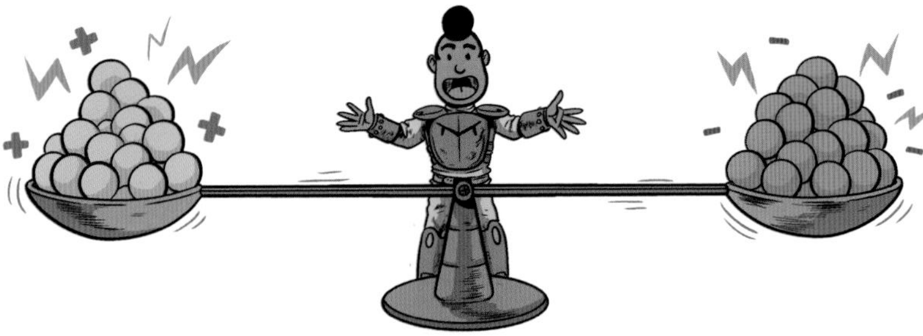

Thanks

Thank you to my friends and family for supporting me mentally and emotionally. Special thanks to Chris Green, Kayla Greet, Josh Rosen, Laura Terry, Maris Wicks, and Sophie Yanow for being digital coworkers and providing me with good advice and positivity!

Thank you to Ayanna Jones and Dr. Scott McN. Sieburth for their invaluable feedback on the science of this book, and to Ayanna Jones for her incredible introduction.

Thank you to the whole team at First Second, especially Robyn Chapman and Sunny Lee, for helping me make such a fun book!

Thank you to my agent, Stephen Barr, for his support and for being an all-around great guy!

Big thanks to Tim Stout for his amazing editorial guidance; this book is so much better for his storytelling expertise.

And biggest thanks to my wife, Tess, for her constant love, support, laughter, and hugs.

Bibliography

Jackson, Tom. *The Elements Book: A Visual Encyclopedia of the Periodic Table*. New York, NY: DK Publishing, 2017.

James, Tim. *Elemental: How the Periodic Table Can Now Explain (Nearly) Everything*. New York, NY: Abrams Press, 2019.

Kean, Sam. *The Disappearing Spoon: And Other True Tales of Madness, Love, and the History of the World from the Periodic Table of the Elements*. New York, NY: Back Bay Books, 2011.

Still, Ben. *The Secret Life of the Periodic Table: Unlocking the Mysteries of All 118 Elements*. Buffalo, NY: Firefly Books, 2016.

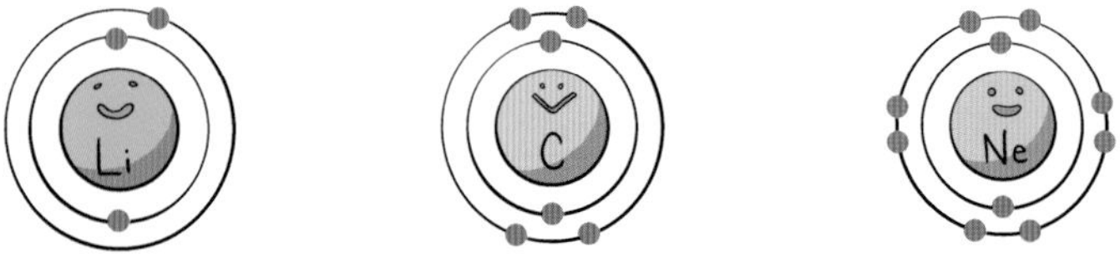

Li
C
Ne